POETS AND CRITICS

Poets
and
Critics

Essays from CANADIAN LITERATURE 1966–1974

Edited by
George Woodcock

Toronto OXFORD UNIVERSITY PRESS 1974

PUBLICATION OF THIS BOOK WAS ASSISTED BY
THE CANADA COUNCIL

ISBN 0-19-540224-3

1 2 3 - 6 5 4

Printed in Canada by
Web Offset Publications Limited

Contents

Introduction

The seventeen essays on eighteen modern Canadian poets which comprise this volume have appeared in *Canadian Literature* over the past eight years, which is a little more than half the journal's lifetime, and they extend—at least in poetry—the earlier anthology from *Canadian Literature, A Choice of Critics*, which was published in 1966. That only essays on poetry have been chosen on this occasion is partly because a collection of *all* the more significant essays from the 1966-74 period of the journal, extending into all the fields of literature, would have resulted in a volume far too unwieldy in size; it also reflects a feeling that over the past decade, in spite of an extraordinary upsurge in dramatic writing and the publication of a great deal of highly interesting fiction, poetry has remained the most active, the most productive, and the most innovative field of writing in Canada.

The publication of verse in recent years has increased so rapidly that this volume cannot claim in any sense to be a survey of Canadian poetry in the modern era, which for us begins roughly at the start of the 1930s, a generation after its onset in Europe and the United States. During one period of twelve years, as I discovered when I recently wrote the chapter on Canadian poetry from 1960 to 1972 for the second edition of the *Literary History of Canada*, over 1,200 volumes of verse—large and small—were published by some 600 poets in English alone in this country; and that figure does not include those who had merely published occasional poems in the rapidly proliferating literary magazines. Obviously the eighteen poets discussed here cannot be counted as representative of this small army of verse writers and speakers, to assess whose true significance one would have to explore in depth the contemporary literary ambiance with its itinerant reading poets and its small presses and smaller ephemeral magazines. Indeed, the eighteen poets do not even include all the major poetic figures of our time and country; A. J. M. Smith, for example, is absent as a poet though not as a critic, and absent also are Raymond Souster and Alden Nowlan.

The explanation for these gaps is that in this selection we have been concerned as much with the critics as with the poets, or perhaps rather we have been concerned to find those happy conjunctions when a poet meets the right critic. One might easily have doubled the size of this volume with essays on other poets who have as good a claim to attention as those here included; the result would have been a more complete but in some ways a more diffuse book, and the claim to include all major poets would have been a manifestation of critical authority which I had no desire to perpetrate. Rather than saying: 'These are all of our major poets', it seemed better and more honest to say: 'These are *among* our major poets, and we present the essays on them because they are examples of good critics writing on good poets.' In this way two forms of creativity are brought together.

There are some interesting links and parallels between the development of Canadian poetry and that of Canadian criticism. One of the important facts about this volume, at least to me as its editor, is that—without giving thought to anything else than the quality of criticism—I found myself picking a surprisingly large number of essays by critics who were themselves practising poets. In the final selection, ten of the seventeen essays turned out to have been written by poets observing other poets—and by poets in this context I mean those who have taken their craft seriously enough to publish more than one volume of verse. And in this selection, we have by no means exhausted the list of good poet-critics writing in Canada today: D. G. Jones, Eli Mandel, and Louis Dudek, to give only three examples, are absent.

The close link between poetry and criticism in Canada is all the more significant in view of the fact that there is not a similar link between criticism and fiction writing. Except for Margaret Atwood, who is also and perhaps primarily a poet, none of our important novelists has performed very impressively as a critic. The non-fiction complement to fiction seems to be reportive journalism, at which writers like Mordecai Richler, Brian Moore, Hugh MacLennan, and Jack Ludwig—and Margaret Laurence as well, if one extends reportage to include good travel writing—have been very successful without showing any real aptitude for criticism.

The link between poetry and criticism is a historic one. There have, of course, always been poets, like Birney and Layton in our time and place, who have reacted in a romantic manner against criticism and raged against those who are mythically supposed to have been the killers of Keats and other frail versifiers. But if we look back down the list of memorable critics, an astonishing number have also been outstanding poets, from Dryden, through Coleridge and Arnold, through Baudelaire and Mallarmé, down in our own day to Eliot and Pound, to Read and Empson.

Those very names dispel the thought, which nowadays might very well spring to one's mind, that poets tend to be critics as well because they are more likely than novelists to be academics. The earlier poet-critics were not academics, and the link between poetry and criticism sprang mainly from a tendency among poets in period of great creativity— whether for themselves or in the general world of poetry—to work intensely on both the intellectual and the intuitive levels. Poetry is a craft which demands more intense and meticulous intellectual disciplines than fiction, and it does so by very reason of the irrationality of its sources.

One observes that the times when poet-critics make an important appearance in the world of letters are usually times when literatures are taking form or undergoing profound changes which amount to a kind of cultural rebirth. Dryden and Coleridge lived and worked at times when the language was being put to new and wider uses. The key roles of Baudelaire and Mallarmé in the renovation of poetry, of Eliot and Pound in the modern movements in England and the United States, are too familiar to need exposition; we are feeling their effects even today.

In the case of Canada the situation is equally clear. We are still in an age which for any people is one of its most vital phases; that in which our classic writers are—most of them—still living. In this respect we are rather like the United States about forty years ago. As critics we have lived beside the archetypes of our own tradition. Our criticism began to take shape, as a mature examination of poetry first and of other forms later, at a time—the end of the 1920s—when our first definably Canadian writing began to appear. The poet A. J. M. Smith was one of the first vital voices, and I have always been pleased that—after a long silence as a critic— he returned to this activity in 1959 in the first issue of *Canadian Literature* and has since contributed many fine pieces, of which in the present collection two are included.

Smith was a pioneer at a time when native criticism was not much appreciated because few regarded our literature as sufficiently important to need it, and some of his greatest critical insights went into the series of anthologies that helped to shape our view of Canadian poetry. It was not, in fact, until the 1950s that the need for a Canadian criticism that would chart the progress of the literary movement and would seriously examine the works of Canadian writers was recognized. And then—the continued life and success of *Canadian Literature* is evidence of it—the criticism appeared, and the best of it was criticism that used the faculties needed in poetry, but in changed proportions, for while in poetry it is the intelligence that shapes the gifts of intuition, in criticism it is intuition that illuminates the action of intelligence.

Where poets are critics, criticism can never be a mere academic exercise or a routine of higher journalism. It will carry its own creative element and, in ways that are often arcane, help to shape the literature it examines and of which, by virtue of its imaginativeness, it is part. And poet-critics, by their very presence, raise the sensitivity level of criticism as a whole, so that the presence of many poets in Canadian universities has undoubtedly influenced academic criticism, to the extent that here we have not been subjected to the pedantic excesses that flourished in the United States at the height of the New Criticism. Our best academic critics, like Milton Wilson and other contributors to this volume, have learnt the uses of the imagination in interpretation as well as in creation.

George Woodcock

E. J. Pratt
Apostle of Corporate Man

Frank Davey

The vision of E. J. Pratt has provided the major area for dispute among critics. Early commentators, such as John Sutherland,[1] Desmond Pacey,[2] and Northrop Frye,[3] saw Pratt as a Christian humanist; to Vincent Sharman in 1964 he seems to have been an atheist;[4] and to Peter Buitenhuis, editor of the recent *Selected Poems,* both of these views represent misreadings of Pratt's work. 1 Buitenhuis's opinion Pratt is a man drawn 'toward relativism and agnosticism'.[5] In the general stressing of Pratt's religious views, the importance of Frye's observation that Pratt is a 'spokesman rather than a critic of public opinion and generally accepted social reactions'[6] has been largely overlooked. It was reiterated by Fred Cogswell in 1964, but not as pointing the direction to the key aspects of Pratt's world-view. 'The conception of heroism in Pratt is of the kind that belongs to our age, to an industrial democracy,' said Frye.[7] Continued Cogswell, 'he [Pratt] is the poet . . . of mass action over individual action.'[8]

Stated briefly, the problems which have so far engaged Pratt critics are two: the first, what is his poetry about, and the second, what world-view does this poetry project? The convolutions of some of the early critics, notably John Sutherland, to get the 'right' answer to the first question have been adequately exposed and documented by Earle Birney.[9] But even Peter Buitenhuis shies from the obvious answers that Pratt's subject matter may be no more than the stories he tells and that his vision may be no more than the values which his protagonists embody. A careful reading of Pratt's work, in fact, suggests very strongly that Pratt was much more straightforward as an artist than most of his sophisticated critics care to admit. He seems to have been seldom concerned with such profound questions as are easily raised by too analytical an approach to his work. Is a whale ('The Cachalot') more to be admired than Pratt's brave fellow Newfoundlanders who die pursuing it? Is 'the great Panjandrum' ('The Truant') also the god that awaits Pratt's mother behind *The Iron Door*? Can the ship *Titanic* be an instance of *hubris* when the locomotive, 'The 6000', is not? Are the priest of the *Roosevelt* and the saintly Brébeuf both 'truants'? Can the K-148 ('The Submarine') be eulogized for its 'mechanic power' while German armoured vehicles are declared 'crueller than the hordes of Tamburlaine'?[10]

Although these and other ambiguities in Pratt's work can be resolved if considered as peripheral to one simple and pervasive idea in Pratt, his critics have been thrown by them into confusion. Not only are such ambiguities responsible for the Christian humanist-atheist-agnostic controversy, but for his 'Tyrannosaurus Rex' ('The Great Feud') being Christ to Sutherland and 'mere instinctive physical courage' to Desmond Pacey, for his cachalot being 'heroic energy'[11] to Pacey but thoroughly a whale to Earle Birney,[12] and for *The Iron Door* being pessimistic to Vincent Sharman[13] but optimistic to Peter Buitenhuis.[14] And while Frye can call Pratt a defender of 'generally accepted social reactions',[15] Pacey can state, 'Pratt obviously believes that all worthwhile human achievement rests not on conformity but on non-conformity.'[16] No wonder Pacey is led to declare, 'I suspect that a good deal of the ambiguity in Pratt is not deliberate but involuntary, and that there is not only confusion among critics but also confusion in the poet.'[17]

Once one gets past the confusions of the critics, from John Sutherland's fantastic system-building to Vincent Sharman's humorously perverse interpretation of *Brébeuf and his Brethren*,[18] and begins an open-minded reading of Pratt's poems, one can see that Pacey was indeed correct in terming these poems 'deceptively simple'.[19] But, unfortunately for Mr Pacey and his brethren, this simplicity is deceptive not in masking something more complex but merely in being, disappointingly no more than itself. Pratt's shark ('The Shark') is only a shark, admirable for its latent and impersonal power. Pratt's cachalot is an aggressive and virile whale, stunning in its inherited energy and strength, but referential to no symbolic meaning outside itself. His Brébeuf is not remarkable either as a Christian or as a Christ-figure, but as an instance of the power to be gained by an individual through allegiance to the ideals of a group. The Jesuits are more impressive to Pratt as power-figures than are the Indians because the odds are higher against them and thus more demanding of power. Similarly, in *Dunkirk* the strength of the British infantry is more admirable than that of the German Panzers, and in *Behind the Log* the strength of the beleagured convoy is more admirable than that of the relatively secure U-boats.

Power, then, is one of the keys to Pratt's uncomplicated vision. He is fascinated by power much the way men have been fascinated by powerful automobiles and tempted to identify vicariously with them. Further, Pratt displays our culture's love of the underdog, believing along with this culture that the underdog somehow marshals more impressive power in either victory or defeat than any favourite can. Thus Pratt's sympathy for the dying cachalot, for the tortured Brébeuf and Lalement, for the battered sailors of the *Roosevelt* and the *Antinoë*, for the *Orillia* in *Behind the Log*, for the harassed John A. Macdonald in *Towards the Last Spike*, for 'the truant', or again for the British rear-guard at Dunkirk. And thus also Pratt's scorn for the crew and passengers of the *Titanic*, who would, had they managed themselves properly, have had all in their favour, and conversely his reverent awe for that 'grey shape with the palaeolithic face'.

Pratt's vision, unlike Brébeuf's is unashamedly worldly. The power he respects and eulogizes is nearly always power wielded or shared in the here and now by inhabitants of this world. Divine power is contrastingly unimpressive to Pratt. He has only the vaguest sense of what stretches beyond 'the iron door'; he sees the power of the *Roosevelt*'s priest as overshadowed by that of her sailors, the power of 'the great Panjandrum' as totally overshadowed by that of the audacious and worldly 'truant'. Only in the very moving opening pages of *Brébeuf and his Brethren* does the Protestant Pratt exhibit any sensitivity to the mysteries of the divine, and here only because his common-sense attitudes have been forced to yield to the artistic necessity of identifying with the Catholic hero.

Werner Sombart[20] and R. H. Tawney[21] have convincingly documented how modern capitalism had its birth in medieval scholasticism and Protestant secularization of the scholastic method. Tawney in particular has demonstrated how Protestantism in Western culture has been the prerequisite for a common-sense handling of reality, a respect for worldly power, and a high valuation of the ability to manipulate material objects. It is this complex of characteristics that we see in the attitudes of E. J. Pratt: a respect for raw material power ('The Shark', 'The Submarine', 'The 6000'), a complete and disciplined attention to things of this world (*Behind the Log, Towards the Last Spike*), and, except briefly in *Brébeuf*, a blind eye for mystery and eternity. From the Renaissance through the eighteenth century such a world-view energized the mercantilist sensibility so well recorded by Defoe. In the nineteenth century it allied itself with Spencer's distortions of Darwinian theory and secured prolonged life for *laissez-faire* economics. In the twentieth century it seeks yet more worldly power for the 'truant' human race through the mechanical excesses of corporate enterprise. As Marshall McLuhan reported in *The Mechanical Bride*:

> The puritan both retained the scholastic method in theology and gave it expression in the precision and austerity of his secular existence. So that it is scarcely fantastic to say that a great modern business is a secular adaptation of the most striking features of medieval scholastic culture. Confronted with the clockwork precision of scholastic method, Lewis Mumford could think only of the mechanical parallel of a smoothly working textile plant. The object of this systematic process is now production and finance rather than God.[22]

And with corporate enterprise we have entered deeply into the world of E. J. Pratt. What are the gods of this world but organization, planning, efficiency, regimentation, discipline, and order? To Pratt, nature has this order and efficiency. This is implicit in the fish analogy of 'The Submarine', in his account of the architecture of the cachalot, in the 'metallic teeth' of 'The Shark', in the very waves which 'crashed down in volleys flush against the hull' of the *Roosevelt*; it is, in fact, inscribed deep within the iceberg's 'palaeolithic face'. Men, in Pratt's view, acquire such order and efficiency not as individuals but as members of corporate groups. This, as we shall see, is the message of *The Titanic, Brébeuf and his Brethren, Towards the Last Spike*, and many other of the poet's works.

Pratt seems to have the distinction among modern poets of being an enemy of individual action. One of the few characters in Pratt who acts not as an agent of society or member of a social order is the seaman Uno Wertanen of the *Roosevelt*. This momentary action, however, is both unwitting and unwanted.

> The crew could see him grab and plunge and cling,
> Using his legs as a rudder so to swing
> Her head around to the wreck and with sheer
> Abandon of his youth to try to steer
> His open, wilful, single-handed craft . . .

Markedly isolated, even exiled, by storm and accident from his social group, Wertanen drowns. Other individualists in Pratt are the seal-hunters of *The Eagle* who are cut off from their social order by a blizzard which catches them out upon the ice. Here, deprived of the structure and power of society, the individual human being is incapable of surviving.

> . . . like sheep we huddled and broke
> Here one would fall as hunger took hold
> Of his step; here one would sleep as the cold
> Crept into his blood, and another would kneel
> Athwart the body of some dead seal,
> And with knife and nails would tear it apart
> To flesh his teeth in its frozen heart,
> And another dreamed that the storm was past
> And raved of his bunk and brandy and food, . . .
> ('The Ice Floes')

The most blatant individualist in all of Pratt's work is 'The Brawler in Who's Who'. Acknowledged for individual heroism by 'two DSO's', the brawler has come to this achievement through murdering his infant brother and his mother, through making 'a Bedlam' of his schools, and through fighting in war like the Tyrannosaurus Rex of 'The Great Feud'. In this poem Pratt clearly links individual heroism both with seriously anti-social behaviour and with diminished chances for survival. The brawler, who has dissociated himself from the protection of the social order, dies in the middle of life, murdered.

In contrast to the people above, individual men in Pratt who act as loyal members of a group acquire the possibility not only of survival but also of participating in great and laudable deeds. To the modern reader, schooled to resent oppression of the individual by 'bureaucracies' or 'establishments' of any sort,

Pratt's quotation from the seamen's contract at the opening of *The Roosevelt and the Antinoë* is mildly humorous.

> ... they, the crew,
> Should pledge themselves to conduct, *faithful, true*,
> *And orderly, in honest, sober manner;*
> *At all times in their duties diligent;*
> *To the master's lawful word obedient,*
> *In everything relating to the vessel—*
> *Safety of passengers, cargo, and store,*
> *Whether on board, in boats, or on the shore.*

Yet to Pratt this passage underlines a frame of mind essential to the heroism which is later to be displayed by the crew. In this poem even the radio stations have an almost sentimentalized social responsibility.

> Thousands of dials in studio and station
> Were 'off the air' by an ungrudged consent—
> That the six-hundred-metre wave might keep
> Upon the sea that night its high command.

Throughout Pratt's work there is a pervasive theme of collective action, of strength gained by identification with a group or cause. In 'The Great Feud' disaster befalls the land dwellers when they ignore the ape's command,

> But as their allies, ye shall spend,
> In one grand consummating blow
> Of death against the common foe,
> Your strength to a triumphant end,

and fall into lethal internecine struggle. This calamity is precipitated by another of Pratt's unfortunate individualists, Tyrannosaurus Rex, whose folly is that he will affiliate with neither side but instead battles both groups on his own. In 'The Cachalot' all of the individuals involved in the final struggle can identify with an order larger than themselves. The whalers form a traditional sea-going social unit, and the cachalot, Pratt is eager to tell us, can trace back his ancestry 'a thousand years'. The whale's particular greatness is informed by ancestors that had followed Lief Ericsson, Marco Polo, Columbus, da Gama, 'Cortez, Cavendish, and Drake', that had sunk a Dutch battleship in the English Channel and a British one at Trafalgar. *Dunkirk* is similarly a poem not about individuals, but also about a social group, a nation, extending both in numbers like the whaler's crew and in history like the cachalot's ancestors.

> Milleniums it had taken to make their stock.
> Piltdown hung on the frontals of their fathers.
> They had lain as sacrifices
> Upon the mortuary slabs of Stonehenge . . .
> They had signed up with Frobisher,
> Had stifled cries in the cockpits of Trafalgar.
> They had emptied their veins into the Marne.

In *Behind the Log* and *Towards the Last Spike* Pratt's emphasis on the collective nature of the great successes of man is already well known, being noted by both Frye[23] and Buitenhuis.[24] From the Commodore's warning that in the convoy 'there is but little room / For rugged individualists' to the poet's observation that the battle was fought by 'men with surnames blotted by their jobs / into a scrawl of anonymity', *Behind the Log* is a story of ships rather than of men, of corporate heroism rather than of individual bravery. The Commodore himself does little more than co-operate in the general flow of events. In *Towards the Last Spike* Pratt celebrates another instance of collective action. Here, in a superficial reading, either Macdonald or Van Horne can appear as a hero. Yet once again Pratt makes the network of interaction and interdependency abundantly clear. Van Horne supports Macdonald, and Macdonald reciprocates. Both men are further supported by Tupper, Stephen, and Smith, and all five are in turn reliant on the loyalty, sweat, and ingenuity of the thousands of workers who, in dedication to their task,

> lost their identity; as groups,
> As gangs, they massed, divided, subdivided,
> Like numerals only . . .

Even *Brébeuf and his Brethren* loses much of the complexity which has puzzled critics from John Sutherland to Vincent Sharman when it is regarded as merely another Prattian eulogy of the power gained by men when they unite hierarchically in a common belief to a common purpose. The Christianity and the

Catholicism of Brébeuf and the other priests are essentially peripheral to the central meaning of the poem. These are merely parts of the vision which binds the participants to their tasks, and, as such, are parallel to the goal of the sea-to-sea railway in *Towards the Last Spike* or the goal of convoy survival in *Behind the Log*. Thus both Sharman's questioning of Pratt's attitude to Christianity in the poem and Sutherland's desire to show the poem as optimistically Christian are relatively unimportant. What is important in considering *Brébeuf and his Brethren* is the fact that Pratt admires any kind of heroic collective action against long odds, whether it be against the sea, the Nazis, the mountains, or the heathen—or even, as in 'The Truant', against 'the great Panjandrum' himself.

Throughout *Brébeuf and his Brethren* what seems most striking to Pratt is that Brébeuf does not act as an individual. He is before all else a member of a corporate body, the Jesuit order, and as such is informed by 'the winds of God' which are blowing into the hearts of many men at this time across Europe. Further, he is directly informed by divine presence, a 'Real Presence'—by his vision of 'a bleeding form / Falling beneath the instrument of death'. Thus he is more than the agent of a holy order; he is the agent of divine will as well. Knowing that he may face martyrdom in the New World, Brébeuf studies the temptations that such a fate can offer. What is the chief temptation?—that of 'the brawler', individual glory. Here Brébeuf learns the lesson of Eliot's Becket, that martyrdom must not be sought for its own sake but only encountered through performing 'the will of God'.

The theme of 'French imperialism in North America' noted by Buitenhuis[25] seems to be present in the poem only to heighten the impression that Brébeuf is no more than a participant in a complex of events much larger than himself. Note how his name here is only one on a list of makers in a great enterprise.

> New France restored! Champlain, Masse, Brébeuf
> Were in Quebec, hopes riding high as ever.
> Davost and Daniel soon arrived to join
> The expedition west. Midsummer tide,
> The busiest the Colony had ever known,
> Was over: forty-three canoes to meet
> The hazards of return; . . .

And as Brébeuf is carried by these events, he is admired by Pratt largely because he is worthy of them, because he is loyal to the vast movements which are giving his life its significance. As the Commodore and the sailors serve the convoy, and as Macdonald and the navvies serve the building of the CPR, Brébeuf serves the tide of French Christianity to which he has pledged himself. He suffers in smoky hovels, he tricks the Indians with predictions of eclipses and rainfall, he faces death at the hands of the Neutrals, eats the filthy food of the Hurons, all for the enlargement of the Catholic community. Says Pratt,

> But never could the Indians infer
> Self-gain or anything but simple courage
> Inspired by a zeal beyond reproof, . . .

This is the loyalty which Pratt admires in men, the loyalty of 'simple' courage, the submission of individual will to group projects significantly greater than oneself. The glory that Pratt admires is not that of the defiant individual but that of the defiant group (his 'truant', after all, is generic), which can be vicariously enjoyed by the individual either in a sacrificial death or a participatory triumph. The cachalot fights and dies for the glory of his race; Brébeuf fights and dies for the glory of his faith; the weekend sailors at Dunkirk fight and win for the glory of England. Today this kind of glory is the kind offered by large corporations to their loyal employees. Again Marshall McLuhan can describe the process:

> Great physical and industrial power rests on a multitude of powerless individuals, many of whom are deeply resentful of their condition. The smaller and meaner the man, the more he craves to possess not limited human powers, with all the effort of cultivation and all the responsibility that implies, but superhuman power. (That is the meaning of the Squinky comic books, and of 'Superman'.) The sadistic craving for enormous physical powers to revenge or compensate for human futility will always drive such people to link themselves to vast impersonal enterprises. They will follow automatically any road which promises to bring them to that goal. So that to be a switch thrower in a *big* plant looks better to them than any lonely task, however human. Such is also the attraction of bureaucratic jobs, whether in great corporations or in government. It is by fantasy identification with the very big

power unit that the very small man obtains his self-realization as a
superman. The key to Superman is Clark Kent the useless. Therefore the more we create and centralize physical power, the more
we suppress our human nature; and then that human nature queues
up all the more to support the big physical power that crushes it.

This is the fate of Brébeuf, of the nameless sailors of Convoy
SC42, of the masses who built the CPR, even of the cachalot: to
achieve greatness only as agents of oppressively vast powers,
forces, traditions. It is a fate based on a principle very similar to
that 'old lie' of Wilfrid Owen's 'Dulce at Decorum Est'. It is a
fate which McLuhan terms 'a nightmare dream'[26] but which
Pratt consistently recommends.

Pratt's story of the *Titanic* is the story of the consequences of
man's failure to live up to tradition and duty, of his failure to
exhibit Conradian restraint and solidarity upon the sea. In Pratt,
machinery requires for its management the utmost in disciplined
civilized values. Men welded together as a unit operate the
successful K-148 ('The Submarine'), row the *Roosevelt's* lifeboats
to the *Antinoë*, lay the rails of the CPR, and save Convoy SC42.
On the *Titanic* men have become so dazzled by the qualities of
the machine with which they have been entrusted that they fail
to be worthy of this trust. They over-estimate this machine's
capabilities much as Ulysses' men over-estimated human capabilities when they 'would have slain the cattle of the sun'. Thus the
Titanic's crew believe that 'caution was absurd' and disregard the
disciplined management necessary for any ship's safety.

Throughout the poem the *Titanic*'s crew's aloofness and difference from the crews of other ships are clearly developed. While
the *Caronia, Mesaba, Amerika, Baltic, Touraine,* and *Californian* pick
their ways gingerly through the ice-field, the *Titanic* increases
speed as it approaches. And while these ships, particularly the
Californian, fulfil their social duties by warning all other ships at
sea, the *Titanic* declares itself superciliously above this moral
solidarity of all good sailors.

> Say, 'Californian', shut up, keep out,
> You're jamming all my signals with Cape Race.

The *Titanic*'s passengers share in this divorce between human
responsibility and the demands of machine and sea. The tread of
the passengers' feet, we are told, is 'rivalling the engines'. The

diners approach the ship's diningroom 'like storm troops before a citadel'. So remote are the passengers from the requirements of discipline, attention, and duty at sea that some of them suggest the crew to be superfluous.

> For all the hard work there's to do
> Aboard this liner up on deck, the crew
> Might just as well have stopped ashore.

Even less concern for solidarity and for human action in a corporate body is shown by the passengers in their relationships with their fellow men. Physical violence is latent in the wrestling and boxing displays in the ship's gymnasium. Animosity and rapaciousness only just below the level of physical violence are continually evident in Cabin D's poker game. Meanwhile the 'grey-templed Caesars of the world's Exchange' have gathered in the lounge to use their collective wisdom not for social good but to 'rock / the pillared dollars of a railroad stock'. Representative of this general non-observance of obligation to the social order is the Egyptian mummy in the hold. Stolen from a tomb in the Valley of the Kings in direct contravention not only of respect for the human dead but also of the mores of another civilization, this mummy is rumoured to carry with it 'an ancient curse' on all violators of the necessary mores which bind men together and make possible their survival on earth. It is noteworthy that Pratt does not question the credulity of the passengers who discuss this mummy and its 'curse', but presents their dialogue with the same profound fascination as he presents the other events of the poem.

Once the iceberg has punctured the illusion of the crew and passengers that social irresponsibility is a condition possible for man, there is a marked return among these people to the old loyalties. Captain Smith regains a captain's wisdom in his managing of the ship's abandonment so that panic and violence do not interfere with the orderly evacuation of women and children. In playing until the sea silences their instruments, the seven musicians exhibit a fidelity which, in the ship's officers, could earlier have saved the entire ship. Among the passengers also a selfless heroism takes hold, not only among those anonymous masses 'of unknown name / and race' who impressed Pratt in *Behind the Log* and *Towards the Last Spike*, but also among those rulers of the stock exchange, Guggenheim and Astor. Thus the story of the *Titanic* is, like Pratt's other major narrative poems, a story of the necessity of social responsibility, of group action and group heroism, of men uniting in a common cause and gaining strength and inspiration from their own communality.

This theme of *The Titanic* is clearly the single most powerful constant of Pratt's poetry. It surpasses in importance both his theme of power and his intermittent theme of Christian love in that it subsumes both of these. It is through corporate action that power, both effective power and individual power, is realized. Christianity itself, especially in *Brébeuf and his Brethren*, is merely one more means of binding men together and giving to the individual totemistic or institutional support.

The question of whether this philosophy of Pratt's was felt by him to be relevant only to crisis situations or to all of human life has been raised by Northrop Frye, who, in suggesting the former, observed that Pratt 'is almost always dealing with a society in a state of emergency'.[27] This observation seems both insufficient for the conclusion and an over-statement of the case. The everyday building of the CPR certainly did not constitute a 'crisis' to the ordinary labourer, and yet Pratt definitely expects a continuing loyalty and efficiency from him. In the case of the *Titanic*, the time period in which communality is lacking is that immediately preceding the crisis. Here Pratt's implication would seem to be that society-oriented or corporate action in everyday life is necessary to prevent states of emergency as much as to cope with them. Further, Pratt sometimes pointedly neglects to compartmentalize crisis behaviour from ordinary duties, and thus writes as if society-centred behaviour were no more than should be expected at any time from any man. Such is clearly the message of the concluding passage of *The Roosevelt and the Antinoë*, where both the mundane and the heroic are merely parts of the 'day's work'.

> The nation gave its thanks on board; and she [the *Roosevelt*],
> Soon ready for completion of her run,
> Swung out the sound, with her day's work well done,
> And in an hour was on the Channel sea.

One might conclude from Pratt's selection and treatment of subjects that to him society always lives under threat of imminent crisis.

E. J. Pratt is a committed and somewhat uncritical spokesman for the values of industrial man. He has frequently been acknowledged as a humanist. To be more specific, Pratt is a Pelagian liberal, not only casting out original sin on a torrent of words from his 'truant' but continually presenting both the machinery of technology and the machinery of social organization as man's best way to salvation. Just as human muscle successfully supplants the priest's prayers in *The Roosevelt and the Antinoë,* submarines, locomotives, and convoys supplant the early mystery behind 'the iron door', and the truant's brash optimism supplants the poet's early but frail humility. Pratt's own frequent use of the personal pronoun *we* spells out his position. Like the programmed D-503 of Zamiatin's anti-utopia *We,* Pratt typically cannot help but present himself as the voice of his society rather than as an individual man. The world of E. J. Pratt is a world where the individual voice, the lyric voice, is obligated to be silent, where gangs, crews, religions, and nations succeed, and private men die. It is a world where ships outlive successive crews, where the CPR outlives the individuals who built it. It is a world where it is indeed *dulce et decorum* to die for one's faith, *patria,* ship, or family of whales.

[No. 43, 1970]

[1] *The Poetry of E. J. Pratt: A New Interpretation* (Toronto, 1956).
[2] *Ten Canadian Poets* (Toronto, 1958).
[3] 'Editor's Introduction', *The Collected Poems of E. J. Pratt,* 2nd ed. (Toronto, 1958).
[4] 'E. J. Pratt and Christianity', *Canadian Literature* 19, 1964, 21-32.
[5] 'Introduction', *Selected Poems by E. J. Pratt* (Toronto, 1968), p. xvi.
[6] 'Editor's Introduction', p. xvii.
[7] *Ibid.*, p. xviii.
[8] 'E. J. Pratt's Literary Reputation', *Canadian Literature* 19, 1964, 9.
[9] 'E. J. Pratt and his Critics', in R. L. McDougall (ed.), *Our Living Tradition* (Toronto, 1959), pp. 123-47.
[10] 'Dunkirk', in Northrop Frye (ed.), *The Collected Poems of E. J. Pratt,* 2nd ed. (Toronto, 1958).
[11] *Ten Canadian Poets,* p. 177.
[12] 'E. J. Pratt and his Critics', p. 136.
[13] 'E. J. Pratt and Christianity', 24.
[14] 'Introduction', *Selected Poems of E. J. Pratt,* p. xv.
[15] 'Editor's Introduction', p. xvii.
[16] *Ten Canadian Poets,* p. 169.
[17] *Ibid.*, p. 167.
[18] 'E. J. Pratt and Christianity', 26-9.
[19] *Ten Canadian Poets,* p. 166.
[20] *Quintessence of Capitalism,* tr. M. Epstein (New York, 1967 [1915]).
[21] *Religion and the Rise of Capitalism* (New York, 1926).
[22] (New York, 1951), p. 33.
[23] 'Editor's Introduction', p. xx.
[24] 'Introduction', p. xxiv.
[25] 'Introduction', p. xix.
[26] *The Mechanical Bride,* p. 128.
[27] 'Editor's Introduction', p. xvii.

F. R. Scott and Some of His Poems

A. J. M. Smith

In Frank Scott we have a figure whom some Carlyle of Canada's second century might write about as The Hero as Canadian Poet or perhaps more soberly as The Poet as Man of Action. Politician, lawyer, teacher, scholar, and public figure, F. R. Scott has been in the forefront of the battle for civil liberties and social justice in Canada. He was one of the doctors presiding over the births of the CCF and the New Democratic Party; he fought and won the legal battles against the padlock law of Premier Duplessis and against the censorship of *Lady Chatterley's Lover*; he has written studies of Canada's constitution, has been Dean of Law at McGill, and is at present a member of the Royal Commission on Bilingualism and Biculturalism. And he has, since his early days as a law student at McGill, been a poet.

The main function of a poet, of course, is to write poems, and Scott has been doing that steadily for more than three and a half decades. But his energy, his generous good will, and his natural self-assertiveness that makes him an inevitable and stimulating leader, were thrown into the battle for the new poetry in Canada as soon as it was joined in the mid-twenties. The now classic satire 'The Canadian Authors Meet' was one of his first shots, while his social and editorial participation in the doings of the *Preview* group and the encouragement he has given to other poets in Montreal have kept up the good work to the present moment. There is hardly a poet in Canada who has not, passing through Montreal, made his pilgrimage to Clarke Avenue, Westmount, and been royally entertained and stimulated with wise and witty talk about poetry and poets; and all of them from the early days of Leo

Kennedy, Abe Klein, and myself, through the time of Patrick Anderson, John Sutherland, P. K. Page, and the rest, to the over-lapping and heterogeneous groups that might include Louis Dudek, Ralph Gustafson, Irving Layton, Doug Jones, and John Glassco, felt the charm, energy and good sense that animated Frank Scott and make him one of the leaders in every group.

Ralph Gustafson has expressed in an appropriate and witty piece of verse a judgement that I think every one of the poets I have named would agree is just:

> To say
> that this man is fantastic
> is to be
> Frankly wrong.
> Real
> is the right root
> for him.
> He bears history,
> the lakes
> he dives under,
> the cold hard sun
> he walks in,
> Canada perhaps . . .
>
> Praise
> he goes into,
> padlocks
> he gets well out of
> and piety . . .
>
> Mortality
> moves him,
> he goes for wrong-doing,
> never lets bad enough
> alone . . .
>
> Words
> he gets the wear out of . . .
> buried with respectable honour
> goes
> Scott-free.

'He bears history,/the lakes/he dives under . . .' These lines will take us into the first poem in Scott's new book,* 'Lakeshore', one of the finest and most characteristic pieces in the collection.

It will serve as a gateway through which to enter into an examination of some of his most striking themes and interesting techniques.

Its theme is Man's history, which extends back into pre-history and before man. Its unifying symbol is water as the source of life. The poem establishes through a specific concrete personal experience a contact in awareness with biological history, stretching back to the primordial beginnings of life and all around to the earthbound mechanical *now* of 'a crowded street'.

By the edge of a lake, the poet—or, better, the sensuous mind that is the protagonist of so many of Scott's metaphysical lyrics—contemplates water, earth, and sky. There is first 'the bevelled edge of land', then 'the fretted sands' that the eye follows as they 'go slanting down through liquid air'. Now the regard is fixed on stones below the surface of the water and held too at the surface where the stones seem to be

> Floating upon their broken sky
> All netted by the prism wave
> And rippled where the currents are.

This is exact, clear, and elegant. There is a seventeenth-century grace about these opening lines. One thinks of Cowley's praise: 'His candid style like a clean stream does slide.' It is a style that admits, indeed invites, Wit—as we see in the next couple of stanzas. The poet (Man-and-Mind) peers into the water.

> I stare through windows at this cave
> Where fish, like planes, slow-motioned, fly
> Poised in a still of gravity . . .

The windows are the surface of the water and the surfaces of the eyes. Note also the hushed gravity of the last line and the gentle punning on *still*.

But the most striking object that confronts the poet is his own reflection.

> I am a tall frond that waves
> Its head below its rooted feet

* *Selected Poems*, Oxford University Press (Toronto, 1966).

Seeking the light that draws it down
To forest floors beyond its reach
Vivid with gloom and eerie dreams.

At the beginning of the fourth stanza the sensuous mind dives down into the depths of the water and into the pre-racial aeons of the past, and for the four next stanzas we become, like the diver, liquid and loosed and silent, 'Stroked by the fingertips of love',

Too virginal for speech or sound
And each is personal and laned
Along his private aqueduct.

But this return to the all-embracing primordial womb can be only a momentary glimpse of a long-lost freedom, a long since forfeited harmony with our environment.

Too soon the tether of the lungs
Is taut and straining, and we rise
Upon our undeveloped wings
Toward the prison of our ground
A secret anguish in our thighs
And mermaids in our memories.

This is our talent, to have grown
Upright in posture, false-erect,
A landed gentry, circumspect,
Tied to a horizontal soil
The floor and ceiling of the soul;
Striving, with cold and fishy care
To make an ocean of the air.

The physical and sensuous exactness of the beginnings of the first of these two stanzas is admirable, as is the emotional and imaginative rightness of the end. The witty implications in naming our arms 'our undeveloped wings' should not go without notice either. In the next stanza, the aptness of the joke in calling mankind 'a landed gentry' adds to the laughter of the mind which it is one—though only one—of the functions of this poem to provoke.

But it is not with laughter, however philosophical, that the poem ends, but with wonder.

Sometimes, upon a crowded street,
I feel the sudden rain come down

> And in the old, magnetic sound
> I hear the opening of a gate
> That loosens all the seven seas.
> Watching the whole creation drown
> I muse, alone, on Ararat.

Here, at the threshold of his book, Scott moves from the poetry of concrete images through wit and metaphysical imagination to myth and magic. A long cool dive into Lake Massawippi and the poet comes up with a rich hoard of racial memories, dreams, desires and aspirations. All are perfectly fused: earth, water, air; science and mythology; mermaids, Venus, Noah; the I and All-Mankind; a crowded street and 'the water's deepest colonnades'.

'Lakeshore' is an excellent starting point for a consideration of Scott's non-satirical poetry. The themes and the motives of many of his most completely articulated poems are seen in it at their clearest and most direct. The fascination with water, as an element and as a symbol; the identification of the poet's Self with Man and of the sensuous perceptive physical being with Mind; and the inescapable tendency to identify or interchange the language and imagery of science (especially biology, geology, and pyschology) with the language and imagery of religion: all these are here. And they are to be found also, in varying degrees and proportions, in such deeply felt and intellectually stimulating poems as 'Paradise Lost', 'Eden', 'Journey', 'My Amoeba is Unaware', and the best of the pieces on India and the Far East—'Bangkok', 'Water', 'A Grain of Rice', and, 'On the Death of Gandhi'.

'Lakeshore' may also serve as an exemplar both of the 'candid' style derived from Imagism and of the witty metaphysical style that, without being in the least derivative, recalls Marvell and Waller—or, if you prefer, Auden. Some of the earliest poems dating from the days of the *McGill Fortnightly Review* already have a simplicity of language and an exactness of imagery which are the firstfruits of conscious discipline, control, and humility. Little pieces like 'North Stream' and 'Snowdrift' or the much later haiku 'Plane Landing in Tokyo' exhibit these qualities in miniature splendour.

A pure and naked perception alone could not, of course, satisfy Scott for more than a moment, and most of his poems that start out as an image soon become images, and perceptions soon become concepts and blossom in metaphor, analogy, and conceit. Mind comes flooding in.

Many of the early very simple verses grouped near the beginning of *Selected Poems* are nevertheless quite delightful, though their importance perhaps is mainly historical (they date from the mid-twenties) and technical (they show Scott's later style beginning to form). 'New Names' develops in a personal and indeed almost rapturous way the old thesis that writers as different as Mrs Traill and Mr Douglas Le Pan have united in expressing—that Canada is a country without a mythology. Scott suggests we must make our own anew. 'Old Song' finds and expresses an austere cadence in the almost-silence of the northern wilderness:

> far voices
> and fretting leaves
> this music the
> hillside gives
>
> but in the deep
> Laurentian river
> an elemental song
> for ever
>
> a quiet calling
> of no mind
> out of long aeons
> .   .   .
> granite lips
> a stone throat

Here we are back to the purest imagism and a style that is the ultimate in simplicity and suggestiveness. This poem has a theme and a style that are irresistibly appealing to the Canadian poet, as new poets like Bowering and Newlove show as clearly as E. J. Pratt or W. W. E. Ross. Here, as in 'Lakeshore', we have the sense of vast distances in space and time and a view of geological pre-history that goes back even farther than the ages of man-as-fish.

Another poem that rises naturally out of such telescopic prob-ings into the geologic and biologic past and therefore has affinities with 'Lakeshore' and 'Old Song' is the strange meditation called 'Mount Royal'. This is a Pratt poem with a difference. One thinks of the vivifying dynamism of the description of the Laurentian

Shield in 'Towards the Last Spike'. Here time is speeded up: the Mountain rises out of the sea; the sea subsides, leaving its deposit of silt and shells; Man walks and builds his muddled cities 'where crept the shiny mollusc', and the poet or poet-mind observes it all.

> Where flowers march, I dig these tiny shells
> Once deep-down fishes safe, it seemed, on sand . . .

The joke about the fishes building on sand and thinking themselves safe alerts us to the fact that irony and satire are this poet's chosen weapons. The satire here is directed against man's vanity, pride, and blind self-confidence as in Hardy's lines on the loss of the *Titanic*, where dim moon-cyed fishes stare at the mighty wreck and query 'What does this vaingloriousness down here?' The situation is reversed in 'Mount Royal'. It is the fish who have been stranded and passed by. Now they are cited as an object lesson that suburban and commercial man, who builds his villas on the reclaimed island of the mountain, fails to heed—blindly and foolishly, it is implied, since the forces of atomic destruction are to hand. The poem ends in angry scorn.

> Pay taxes now,
> Elect your boys, lay out your pleasant parks,
> You gill-lunged, quarrelsome ephemera!
> The tension tightens yearly, underneath,
> A folding continent shifts silently
> And oceans wait their turn for ice or streets.

There is a curious consequence of this geologic view that we can observe in some of Scott's most characteristic poems. He is a man capable of—indeed unable to refrain from—taking long views, both backwards into the past and forward into the future, an idealist in the popular sense of the word. Both in his political life as a socialist and his literary life as a poet he welcomes the new, the just, and the generous—and always in the broadest and most generous terms. Poems that embrace vast cosmic distances, both of space and time, lend themselves to thinking in abstractions. There is world enough and time for all the great abstractions to come into being, to evolve and grow, to change, to grow old, and perhaps to die. The good ones we must cultivate, preserve, and nourish; the bad ones we must kill.

There is a very peculiar class of poems in which these consequences of taking large views are quite explicit. Some of its members are 'Creed', 'Conflict', Dialogue', 'Degeneration', poems concerned with War or with Love, and a remarkable series of what for want of a better name I will call 'defining' poems—among them 'Memory', 'Heart', 'Was', 'Caring', and (with a difference) 'Stone'. Let us look at one or two of them.

'Conflict' is a rather Emersonian poem on the tragic paradox of war. It develops the thesis that men on both sides in any conflict fight for the good they know and die with equal courage for the opposite sides of truth:

> When I see the falling bombs
> Then I see defended homes.
> Men above and men below
> Die to save the good they know....
>
> Pro and con have single stem
> Half a truth dividing them....
>
> Persecution's cruel mouth
> Shows a twisted love of truth....

Here speaks the defender of unpopular causes, the idealist who loves the abstract and the universal. It is the wide application of unparticularized truth that such a poetry seeks to secure. Universals and abstractions are employed with the confidence born of an utter faith in their reality and validity. Such words as *good, wrong, bravery, love, truth, prison, ghetto, flag, gun, rack, rope, persecution, sacrifice*, whether abstractions or collective symbols, are made to glow with the vitality of an individual existence—or are used as if they did so glow.

How this is done, the eight quatrains entitled 'Dialogue' may demonstrate. In structure and language this poem is as taut and concentrated as 'Conflict', but its movement is in the reverse direction—from sensation and particularity (from the concrete, that is) to the universal, a universal which is equated with the spiritual—'spirit takes communion/From every living touch'. The progression is straightforward. 'Sense is more than mortal'. Our bodies are the gateway to a supra-sensual world. Eye, ear, and hand contribute to the synthesis of a new form 'to house a new conception'.

> Desire first, then structure
> Complete the balanced picture.
> The thought requires the form.

The poem's rhetoric is serpentine, for we have now reached—this is the fifth of eight stanzas—the point where the poem begins:

> The hour is ripe for union,
> And spirit takes communion
> From every living touch.

The end in the last two stanzas is surprising and unheroic. The serpent cannot rear back and strike; instead it sinks down and seems to collapse.

> For us, how small the power
> To build our dreams a tower
> Or cast the molten need.
> For us, how small the power.
>
> So few, so worn, the symbols.
> No line or word resembles
> The vision in its womb.
> So few, so worn, the symbols.

Truth, not wishes, hopes, or evasions, is the business of poetry; and this poem would be a lesser one if it ended any other way.

What is needed always is a new language, new images, and a new technique. Scott has been trying all his life—and sometimes with heartening success—to find these. Some of his notable successes are moving love poems that have been placed in this collection immediately after 'Dialogue'. Their newness and hence their effectiveness lies in nothing more strange than an absolute fidelity to the occasion and the emotion that has brought them into being. One, called 'Meeting', begins like this:

> If what we say and do is quick and intense,
> And if in our minds we see the end before starting,
> It is not fear, but understanding that holds us.

Here the conciseness of the syntax contributes potentialities to the meaning. It is not fear that holds us apart but understanding that holds us together.

Other poems that approach or achieve the new style are 'Will to Win'—a deceptively light and witty *jeu d'esprit* in which the lightness enables the poet to keep control of the situation and the wit serves to define it; 'Vision'—beautifully rhymed quatrains in which the 'newness' or rightness comes from the clarity with which the sharp edge of every idea is defined; and 'A l'Ange Avantgardien'— the explicit statement of a romantic view of poetic creation according to which the emphasis must always be on the making, never on the made.

One of the most striking paradoxes of Scott's poetic life is that the ceaseless flow of energy which throws up poems of all kinds and in all modes should nevertheless be able to shape them with extreme care, whether the work in hand is a piece of impressionistic and typographical experiment or a closely knit web of thought, like the fine late poem 'Vision'—a true metaphysical lyric that begins:

> Vision in long filaments flows
> Through the needles of my eyes.
> I am fastened to the rose . . .
>
> I am clothed in what eye sees.

and ends:

> Tireless eye, so taut and long,
> Touching flowers and flames with ease,
> All your wires vibrate with song
> When it is the heart that sees.

Here is song that is as well written as prose—a poem that reiterates the validity of the 'candid' style of 'Lakeshore' and the earlier imagist pieces.

This style is seen at its most purely intellectual in what I have called the 'defining' poems—lyrics that perhaps have developed out of Scott's training as a lawyer. Lawyers, like poets, are involved with words, with definitions, and with subtle quibbles. Some of these pieces, as for example 'Memory', are apt and ingenious metaphors:

> Tight skin called Face is drawn
> Over the skull's bone comb
> Casing the honey brain

> And thoughts like bee-line bees
> Fly straight from blossom eyes
> To store sweet facts in cells . . .
>
> Within the waxy walls
> Lifetimes of sounds and smells
> Lie captive in the coils . . .

Others, like 'Was' seem merely verbal, until we notice that here the universal and the abstract are made concrete and immediate, the ideal transformed before our eyes into the real:

> Was is an Is that died
>   in our careless hands
> and would not stay
>   in its niche of time.
>
> We crumble all our nows
>   into the dust of Was . . .
> forgetting Was
>
>   cannot be shaken off
>   follows close behind
>   *breathes down our neck* . . .
>
> One day we shall look back
>   into those staring eyes
> and there will be nothing left but
>   Was.

Another 'defining' poem of the same sort is the one beginning 'Caring is loving, motionless', but the lines entitled 'Stone' show an interesting difference. In these what is being defined is not an abstraction or a state but an object, a solid item, 'a still of gravity'. The method is entirely different from that of imagism. The purpose of an imagist poem is to perceive and to present perception, but here we go further in an effort to grasp the idea of the thing and of its place in history. The motion too is just the reverse of that in 'Was', where an abstraction was made concrete; here a concretion is seen in the light of thought—the remarkable thing being, however, that the thought is made to seem to radiate from the stone itself:

> A stone is a tomb
> with the door barred.

A still picture
from a flick of motion.

A stone is a closed eye
reflecting what it saw. . . .

In these distichs we come back to the sense of time in which Scott is so deeply immersed that it recurs in poem after poem. Here the mind moves from the glacial epochs of pre-history to the bursting stone that falls on Hiroshima.

Perhaps in coming to a close I should return to the personal. But actually I have not been away from it. The old dictum that the style is the man has never been more clearly illustrated than in the poetry of F. R. Scott. All his poems, from the gayest and lightest expression of delight in life through his pointed and savage satires to the profound lyrics I have been mainly considering, are informed and qualified by a sense of responsibility and an inescapable sincerity, which is serious but never solemn and rich without ostentation.

[No. 31, 1967]

Poet Without a Muse
Earle Birney

Milton Wilson

You might suppose that Earle Birney was too busy creating new poems to worry about collecting old ones. But for a writer whose old poems never stop pestering him to be transformed into new ones, the first task is hard to separate from the second. His *Selected Poems 1940-1966* isn't really a retrospective show; it challenges us to see Birney not so much plain as anew. I've read his work far too often in the past to make a fresh look very easy. What follows is at best a series of notes towards an unwritten revised portrait.

I

The more Birney you read, the less he looks like anybody else. His asymmetrical, bulky, unpredictable accumulation of poems gathers individuality as it grows. In context even the least distinguished members start to seem unlikely and even independent. For a poet so unmistakably of his own time and place, he is a surprisingly free agent. Certainly no influential contemporary has ever taught him how to iron out any local idiosyncrasies and unfashionable commonplaces that he preferred to keep. He has learned only what he wanted and at his own speed. Any inescapable influence of his generation that he found irrelevant (T. S. Eliot, for example), he has managed to escape completely. What gives his work distinctiveness, I suppose, is not so much its originality as its mixture of openness and stubbornness, of cleverness and provinciality, even the way it sometimes stumbles over its own reality, like that half-teachable bear the title of whose poem Birney sets at the entrance of this selection.

2

If the problem of Birney's education as a poet is worth a second glance, it ought to be a very careful and skeptical one, particularly now that we have these *Selected Poems*, which throw doubt on many of the old Birney legends. Take the matter of chronology. The legend of Birney the late starter may have to give way to Birney the late publisher, depending on how seriously you take the vital statistics of date and place with which he has labelled his offspring, some of them—like 'North of Superior' (labelled '1926-1945') and 'Mammorial Stunzas for Aimee Simple McFarcin' (labelled 'Toronto 1932-San Francisco 1934', but first printed in a *Prism* of 1959)—apparently twice-born or at least held in suspension for a long time. Did Birney draft a full-scale version of 'North of Superior' in 1926 or did the 1945 version just incorporate a jotted image or two from the distant past? Was 'Mammorial Stunzas', which seems so characteristic of Birney's linguistic high spirits in the fifties, entirely conceived in the early thirties or did the young Birney merely give Aimee her graffiti from Belshazzar's feast and a pun or two on her name and then wait twenty-five years for the right poem to go with them and justify publication? The dating, in this case, seems to insist on a finished product in 1934 (or as finished as a Birney poem ever allows itself to be—the format has been completely reshaped for 1966). At least I will now stop being puzzled as to why anyone would choose to write Aimee's definitive poem long after everyone else had forgotten her.

Then there's the legend of a poetic hiatus in the mid-fifties, of a Birney unproductive because he had maybe lost faith in poetry or humanity or even himself. But, from the new vantage point, any hiatus, if it existed, starts to look pretty small, the sort of thing that needed little more than a trip to Mexico for its cure. And anyway, if Birney can write and only publish twenty or twenty-five years later, who knows what piles of unpublished poems lie in his bottom drawer waiting for their public moment?

3

Simple questions of chronology may be tricky, but the difficulties are multiplied for anyone who ventures to talk about Birney's poetic development and its relation to his poetic contemporaries. Most of the obvious half-truths that used to occur to me, I now find myself wanting to qualify almost as soon as I have uttered them. The staple product of conventional up-to-date British and American poetry can (very broadly indeed) be described as having moved from a metaphoric and allusive phase in the thirties and

forties to a more linguistic—idiomatic and syntactic—one in the
fifties and sixties, from the rhetoric of the image to the rhetoric of
the voice. It's tempting to see Birney's own development following
a similar course, with *Trial of a City* (1952) as the Janus-faced
turning point. Nobody could be surprised at the date of an elaborate editorial conceit like 'Page of Gaspé' (1943-1950) or an even
more elaborate tidal one like 'The Ebb Begins from Dream'
(1945-1947)—despite Birney's difficulty persuading editors to print
the latter. Still, although they date, they aren't just dated. The
slightly later 'North Star West' (1951) seems more of a mere
period piece, the sort of inventive and readable exercise in imagery
that with luck you might be able to bring off in those days. Indeed,
if I interpret a remark in Birney's Preface correctly, that may be
part of the point of the poem. But, while some of Birney's poems
could (and in fact did) fit quite snugly into the post-war world of
Penguin New Writing, the philologist and verbal mimic didn't need
to wait until *Trial of a City* to be released. Among the early poems
for which obviously no retrospective indulgence at all is needed are
'Anglo-Saxon Street', 'Mappemounde', and 'War Winters'. Birney
is amused by those critics who thought that to write the verse of
these poems he had to be an imitator of Hopkins, instead of just a
mere student and teacher of medieval literature. Although he is
properly aware of the dangers in any academic-poetic alliance, his
own academic niche could hardly have been a luckier choice.

4

Birney's vocal virtuosity hasn't seemed out of place in the more
recent worlds of 'articulate energy' and 'projective verse', or on
the p.a. circuit. But he can't be confused with the new virtuosos of
breath and syntax, and his academic context certainly predates
structural linguistics. There's also something a bit old-fashioned
about his taste for 'phonetic' spelling; it doesn't help much for
Birney to write 'damnear' or 'billyuns', when nobody says 'damn
near' or 'billions' anyway. I suppose that it all justifies itself, in that
without it the 'Billboards' and 'Diaper' poems couldn't have been
written at all, but they remind me a bit of the easy old days when
all a writer had to do to present his readers with a recognizable
substandard dialect was to spell their own standard dialect as they
really pronounced it. Birney's phonetic technique works best with
an exotic like the speaker in that delightful monologue 'Sinaloa'.
The people who strike my ear most successfully, however, receive

no such phonetic help, like the two-tongued Colombian bookseller in 'Cartagena de Indias', which (if I had to make a choice) I would call his finest poem.

5

Birney's other notational idiosyncrasies interest me far more than his spelling. Except for a few poems (notably 'David', 'The Damnation of Vancouver' and the translations) and a few special places within poems (mainly conversations), instead of using the conventional comma, semicolon, colon, and period as rhetorical and syntactic signposts, he now relies mainly on spacing and lineation, and has revised his old poems accordingly.

He is not (so the Preface tells us) trying to facilitate immediate and accurate reading or comprehension by these changes; on the contrary, his aim is 'the art of indefinitely delayed communication —Infinite Ambiguity'. I don't know how seriously to take these last phrases; I do know that the new ambiguity is real enough, and in a few cases results in a new awkwardness. The chief problem is at the end of a line, where the distinction between endstopped and run-on lines is no longer visible, even when still relevant. One space starts to look like any other space, whether it breaks or ends a line. In 'Captain Cook', when

> flashed him a South Sea shilling; like a javelin
> it split the old shop's air.

is revised to

> flashed him a South Sea shilling   like a javelin
> it split the old shop's air

the phrase at the end of the first line can now look backwards and forwards instead of just forwards. It wouldn't be hard to defend the ambiguity of *that* revised version. But in the same poem, when

> First voyage, mouths burning
> from the weevils in the biscuits,
> charted New Zealand.

is revised to

> First voyage   mouths burning
> from the weevils in the biscuits

> charted New Zealand

the new syntactic ambiguity of the second line is a doubtful blessing indeed. It may be amusing, but the joke is at the expense of the poem.

The advantages and disadvantages of the new notation are worth weighing not just from passage to passage but from poem to poem. One fine poem that I much prefer to see in its old format is 'Wake Island': the format in the *Selected Poems* seems more confusing than ambiguous. On the other hand, while not a word of 'Late Afternoon in Manzanilla' has been altered, the poem looks twice as good and comes off twice as well in its new format. I had no idea until now what an excellent poem it is.

Of course the reaction against the clutter of punctuation in favour of the austerity of space Birney shares with a good many of his newer contemporaries. But he isn't always that austere (dashes, apostrophes, question marks, etc. are used), or, for that matter, consistent. In the new space-filled pages, even a few concluding periods still survive (I'm glad that he kept the one at the end of the 'Diaper' poem), although, so far as I've noticed, only one anomalous comma (near the end of 'Tavern by the Hellespont'):

> Between
> the individual tables   couples   uncoupled
> by the radio's decision, turn to their true oneness—

and here, although I like to think that it's an unexpected attempt to limit Infinite Ambiguity, it may be just an editorial or proofreading oversight, like the mislineation that disfigures 'The Damnation of Vanouver' on page 176.

6

Not that Birney minds anomalies anyway. Some of his best poems are sports. No one could possibly anticipate them, he has shown no desire to repeat them, but once written they are an inevitable choice for his *Selected Poems*, no matter how stringent the selection. 'St Valentine is Past' is an obvious example. One of the few Birney poems that reads like a pure gift from his muse (he is not the sort of poet whom one usually credits with a muse), it has remained virtually unchanged since appearing in 1952's *Trial of a City and Other Verse*. In these ballad quatrains, while Theseus is off on his boar-hunt, and death seems mercifully at a distance, love finds late fulfilment under a shadowless sky. The lovers, like the age-old elements of earth and water, renew their long-past youthful fertility, and, for a day at least, seem to have Time on their side.

> While he is rooted rock she strikes
>   to foam a loud cascade
> that drowns the jeering gullish wings
>   far crashings in the glade
>
> No more while lizard minutes sleep
>   around a cactus land
> they'll blow their longings out like spores
>   that never grass the sand
>
> No longer Time's a cloud of cliffs
>   unechoed by her Nile . . .

But these elemental lovers or late-coupling birds or aging Venus and Adonis (or whatever you wish to call them) are no match for dusty Time. And, as their elegiac, unkept sounds fade away, the pastness of St Valentine's Day is sealed by the return of hunter, boar, and pack.

> And yet and yet a failing rod
>   strikes only dust from rock
> while all the tune and time they breathe
>   is never kept in talk
>
> Now water sky and rock are gone
>   the huddled woodbirds back
> and hot upon the throbbing boar
>   comes Theseus and his pack

Although Birney, in his primitive or medieval or modern vein (sometimes all at once), is often a poet of myths, as such different poems as 'Mappemounde', 'Pachuchan Miners', 'Takkakaw Falls', 'Bushed', 'Ballad of Mr. Chubb' and, of course, 'November Walk near False Creek Mouth' (with its updated characters from the sagas) make evident, nevertheless the sort of Renaissance mythmaking that 'St Valentine is Past' does superbly seems to me totally uncharacteristic of him. If I had to choose a historical niche for him other than his own, the Age of Spenser would be my last choice.

And yet, in other respects, this is a typical Birney love poem, typical at least of his published range. In a recent article on Irving Layton, George Woodcock has praised our older love poets at the expense of their younger rivals. But Birney's love poems have been elegiac and autumnal from the start, or, when not elegiac, at least about love at a distance (e.g., 'The Page My Pigeon' and, in a sense, 'The Road to Nijmegen'). The very lovely 'Under the Hazel Bough' (stylistically another anomaly, but quite different from 'St Valentine is Past') is destined to this end:

> but no man sees
>> where the trout lie now
> or what leans out
>> from the hazel bough

In some recent poems the autumnal erotic note takes on a January-and-May form. I'm thinking not just of 'Haiku for a Young Waitress', 'Curacao' and 'Twenty-third Flight', but also of 'On the Beach' (which I miss from these *Selected Poems*), where the no-longer-agile speaker cries:

> I will follow in a small trot only
>> not whirling
>>> O girl from the seafoam
>>> have pity

and even of 'A Walk in Kyoto', where sex somehow triumphs over 'the ancient discretions of Zen'.

7

Perhaps all that I have just been doing is applying to his love poems the cliché that Birney is in some respects a very Chaucerian kind of poet. The cliché deserves its wider application too. To begin with, there is his basic impersonality. You can learn practically nothing about him as a private person from his published poems. Self-revelation or self-analysis is not his business. And yet, like Chaucer, and increasingly with age, he enjoys offering us a kind of persona in the foreground: the innocent scapegoat of 'Meeting of Strangers', the aging and garlanded ram of 'Twenty-third Flight', the absurdly grateful initiate of 'Cartagena de Indias'. If one of these days somebody writes a Ph.D. thesis called *Birney's Irony*, one person on whom the irony will not be lost is Birney himself.

[No. 30, 1966]

Dorothy Livesay
The Love Poetry

Peter Stevens

In her social poetry of the 1930s Dorothy Livesay is concerned principally with human fellowship and the poems call for freedom from capitalist tyranny. There is no mention of the problem of freedom for each individual: the question of the roles played in society by man and woman is not raised. I suppose that she had tackled the problem indirectly in the long poem in *Signpost*, 'City Wife', but that poem seems more concerned with the personal relationship of husband and wife, not with an examination of woman's role in contemporary life and not in any large sense with aspects of the relative freedoms and responsibilities of man and woman in modern society.

Her later poems, however, show a greater interest in woman's individuality, her need for freedom, her right to exist in her own way. Woman as herself is very much a part of her love poems, as we shall see later. The love poems in *The Unquiet Bed* are preceded by a section of personal poems in which the poet concentrates on various aspects of herself as woman. In 'Woman Waylaid' she sets up a contrast between the opposing sensitive and practical sides of her nature. In this poem the sensitive side wins out. She prefers to pick flowers, not to collect wood for the cool evenings. So she returns

> empty-
> handed
> to face
> pot-bellied stove
> its greed.

She makes her choice as individual woman and she is free to make the choice. Although it may mean that she will be uncomfortable in 'the cool evenings/by the lake', at least she has herself made the decision. Too much must not be made of this poem, but in the context of the whole book (and the arrangement of the poems and sections of *The Unquiet Bed* is an important aspect of the book), this poem, and most of the others in the second section, are directly concerned in an unpretentious way with the problem of woman's position in modern society. Dorothy Livesay still insists that woman is involved in the natural cycle of growth. In 'Sunfast' she sees herself as part of the whole life force symbolized by the sun. She takes in the sun like food; the sun refreshes and re-orders the world, just as human beings try to establish patterns. But the poet seems released to some higher mode of life than suburban pattern and order:

> I am one
> with rolling animal life
> legs in air
> green blades scissoring
> the sun.

In a general way the image of a 'sunfast' is close to images used by Gwendolyn MacEwen, particularly in *Breakfast for Barbarians*. And it is perhaps significant in this context to remember that Dorothy Livesay has written a poem 'For Gwendolyn' in which she expresses her feeling that the younger poet could have been her child.

The feeding on nature, the immersion in it as well as the recognition of one's place in it, is expressed in several poems in the second section of *The Unquiet Bed*, for instance 'Process'. 'Pear Tree' has the same notion at its centre. The tree in this poem becomes almost a symbolic mother, for it hears 'children chugging on the chains/of sound/practising language'. But the reference in the poem takes on a wider significance, for the tree connects daylight with darkness, and so perhaps foreshadows the idea of union and communication achieved through the man-woman relationship in the love poems:

> Lucky this pear tree seeped in sun
> shivering the air
> in her white
> doldrums
> taps with her roots
> the worms' kingdom.

The question of individuality in relation to the male-female principle Dorothy Livesay herself finds so prevalent in her poetry crops up humorously in the poem 'Flower Music', particularly in the section titled 'Peony'. The male neighbour grows peonies easily—the language suggests something rather brutal and violent about the male's bringing forth these flowers, an attack perhaps on the nature of the peony itself, its virgin purity. The poet herself peevishly resents his success. She has tried to make them flower by using the brute power perhaps associated with the male principle. She has been a tyrant to the flowers, but they do not blossom. The poem ends ironically, for she suggests that the man's masculinity, his power brings forth beauty 'so light/so silken'. This sense of opposition and contradiction between male and female, expressed somewhat obliquely in the poem, is very much a part of Dorothy Livesay's view of human love, and it turns up in the next section of *The Unquiet Bed* which is devoted exclusively to love poems.

But these love poems were not the first that Dorothy Livesay wrote. There are quite a number of love poems in *Signpost*, and it is interesting to look at them now to see how her views on the role of woman have changed. The love poems in *Signpost* are attempts to express the changing moods and emotions of a love affair. They are personal poems but they are also objectified to make more universal statements about love, as Robert Weaver in the Fall, 1948 issue of *Contemporary Verse* suggested. He said that the poems were poems

> about love; about the paradoxical, even tragic desire to lose oneself wholly in passion and love, at the same time retain something essential of oneself. The person, invaded, often resisted successfully, or fled. But already, in this microcosmic human relationship, Miss Livesay was being strongly drawn towards identification with something outside of the self.

Obviously these remarks in some sense could apply to her later love poems, although I think that Dorothy Livesay is much surer of herself as a woman in the later poems, so that she can afford to be more open, direct, and honest, make the poems in fact much more personal. The early poems still have some romanticism clinging to them, although some of the poems are admirable statements of the wayward passions, misgivings, deceits, and contradictions of love. And certainly they are the first attempts in Canadian poetry to express a modern approach to love, even though they are not always successful.

In 'Song And Dance' Dorothy Livesay suggests some of the literary and philosophic (if that is not too pedantic a word in this context) motivations behind these early love poems:

> Through my twenties an experimentation with sex . . . was simply [a] search for the perfect dancing partner. I had read Havelock Ellis's *The Dance of Life* and I believed of [sic] the consummation of two bodies into one, the merging of the self in other self. Also, it goes without saying, I had read *Lady Chatterley's Lover*.

The partners in love try to keep each his own individuality, in order to prevent being overwhelmed and overpowered by the other partner. The poet attempts to protect herself by keeping herself close to natural things. This she uses as 'armour' ('Weapons') because in love she feels vulnerable, but if the other merges with her own essential faith in nature, then she is defenceless. Thus, love can become a kind of struggle for power; it may be impossible to wall oneself in, for love demands openness between partners. This idea is reminiscent of that expressed in other early poems, in which the poet, in talking of the immense external reality in terms of an outer darkness, often used the image of enclosed space within which she kept the darkness at bay. But even in erecting a shell around one, one senses that it is futile. In the same way, love seems to be an enormous force in the love poems in *Signpost* and defences against it are fragile, particularly as love demands frankness and searches out the private sanctities of personality. Even if one of the partners takes refuge in nature, as the poet suggests in 'Sun', recognizing the naturalness of love, then the other partner can uncover the whole, can see everything open to his eye as he looks at nature. The poet expresses her love as a purely natural phenomenon:

> I am as earth upturned, alive with seed
> For summer's silence and for autumn's fire.

Caught in the creative urges implicit in nature, she feels unified with nature but does not wish her partner to recognize her surrender to these primal promptings: 'I am all things I would not let you know.' But this natural development beyond words is still apparent, so even as she thinks she escapes with a retention of her own self, she is caught by a lover through his acceptance of her implicit union with nature:

> I may escape—you hold my body still
> In stretching out your hand to feel the wind.

Love is all-encompassing in these poems, so the poet surrendering to it completely with candour and honesty, lays herself open to attack. The full knowledge of another individual as a necessary part of a complete love leads each partner to be at the mercy of the other. Thus, love is not all sweetness and a bringing forth through union; it can be ruthless. In 'Ask Of The Winds' the poet uses details from spring to suggest the awakening of love within her, but she senses the power of her lover, a power which so shakes her that in spite of the emergence of new life, she realizes the ruthlessness and coldness in his love. Indeed, so overwhelming is his strength that often she feels left outside his experience:

> What was it, after all,
> The night, or the night-scented phlox?
> Your mind, or the garden where
> Always the wind stalks?
>
> What was it, what brief cloak
> Of magic fell about
> Lending you such a radiance,—
> Leaving me out?
>
> What was it, why was I
> Shivering like a tree,
> Blind in a golden garden
> Where only you could see?
>
> ('Alienation')

The notion, then, of distance, a notion that crops up time and again in Dorothy Livesay's poetry, a distance between people, in this case between lovers, is part of the poet's concept of love. She seems to be suggesting that union through love is only momentary and that it includes struggle for dominance. The release from individuality through complete union seems to be too open a position, may bring about such a thorough nakedness of soul as to threaten the very basis of the personality. In 'Blindness' Dorothy Livesay uses the image of dancing as a symbol of this ecstatic release, but within the poem she expresses the idea that that release is too dangerous if seen by the other partner. It might lead to a destruction of individuality:

> You did not see me dancing,
> Even then!
> Your blindness saves my soul's integrity.

Perhaps the poet is even suggesting that the blindness is an effect of love and so paradoxically the power of love capable of dominating is denied that power because of the ecstasy of love itself. But the paradox within love becomes more complex in the context of such a poem as 'The Unbeliever', for here the poet takes up the problem of individuality again. The poem poses the question of commitment. It suggests that there must be total involvement, no holding back, the state that might menace individual integrity. Yet at the same time anything less than complete commitment leads to failure and lack of communication. As if to stress this aspect, 'The Unbeliever' develops by a series of questions. The poet asks why put no trust in the words of her lover; seemingly, she believes that she could retain her own self this way. But it has led to a breakdown. The voice she did not believe is now silent so she is 'Quiet now in these lonely places.'

In fact, three or four of the poems in *Signpost* are concerned with the loss of love, the moving apart of the lovers. In 'Consideration', for instance, the opening stanza suggests how words become weapons, destructive with 'biting analysis/Of one another.' 'A Song For Ophelia' is a simple lyric about loneliness, the sense of desolation after love has broken down. Yet love persists, if only in the memory; sometimes, in spite of the deliberate attempt to forget it, love returns, somewhat shadowy, after its 'cobweb image' ('Dust') has been brushed from the heart. The ghost of love returns, seen in objects associated with it—and at such times the anguish of the loss of love returns as well:

> Whenever I passed the house
> At far, rare intervals
> Memory stabbed,
> **The tree at the gate grieved.**

> But now, passing it daily,
> I scarcely remember—
> Pain has a too familiar look
> To need the averted head.
> ('Neighbourhood')

The same kind of feeling is expressed in a poem 'Time' which does not appear in *Signpost* but from its position in *Selected Poems* was probably written at the same time:

> I opened wide a furnace door
> And hot flame seared my face:
> I was surprised, that after breach of time
> I could not love you less.

Perhaps this discussion of the early love poems has suggested an overly schematic approach on the part of the poet. This is not so. The poems are attempts to express the varying moods occurring during the course of a love affair with images pointing to psychological states and conflicts. Not all the poems dealing with love in this volume are successful. Some retain a kind of adolescent vagueness of romantic feeling, some strive for ambivalence of meaning which results only in obscurity or, conversely, over-simplification. But on the whole, Robert Weaver's summary of these poems quoted earlier is accurate. They convince as personal statements; they are believable as notations on personal experience. At the same time, however, they reach a certain objectivity because of the tone of directness amounting in most cases to a starkness. The images are not often over-developed; the poems themselves are generally short and to the point, as if the poet—and this is somewhat surprising, considering both the age of the poet when she wrote these poems and the general poetic atmosphere in Canada when these poems were published—as if, the, the poet is determined to get to the root of her emotions in order to express them as openly and frankly as possible without making them too private in their connotation. Indeed, the closing poem in the volume, 'Protest', is in its series of questions a kind of manifesto about honesty, a pledge of openness and candour:

> Can I help it, if the wind
> Catches crows and holds them pinned
>
> Across the skyway in a row,
> Scaring off the rain and snow?

> Can I help it then, if I
> Seize forgotten ecstasy—
>
> Give away closed thoughts of mine,
> Hang my secrets on the line?

In view of the association of crows and flight in her poetry with re-birth and release, she may even be suggesting in this poem that a poetry of real honesty is a defence itself against the loss of love, that by expressing it accurately, the poet can retain a good deal of the meaning and joy of the experience of love.

Honesty and candour are essential components of the poems she wrote about her later experience of love in *The Unquiet Bed* and *Plainsongs*. These poems, stemming as they do from her maturity as both poet and woman, taking into consideration her whole-hearted concern about the position of woman in society and there-fore the integrity of woman in a love relationship, are obviously for the most part more compelling statements than those in *Signpost*.

The poet prepares us for the section devoted to the love poems in *The Unquiet Bed* by closing the previous section, which as we saw earlier concentrated on the individual liberty of woman in personal life, with two poems about the reawakening of love within woman. And again she expresses this in an intensely personal manner. The first of these poems is 'Eve'. The poet notices an old apple tree, 'the last survivor of a pioneer/orchard' which is 'miraculously still/bearing'. She stoops to pick up one of the fallen apples, to possess it, to taste it 'earth-sweet'. And the tree she now recognizes as a symbol of herself:

> In fifty seconds, fifty summers sweep
> and shake me—
> I am alive! can stand
> up still
> hoarding this apple
> in my hand.

She feels this earth sweetness developing within her as an 'unwithering' in the second of these poems, 'Second Coming'. She thinks of blossoms in autumn, colours of growth and purity. Through love she grows to another vital existence, 'coming be/

coming'. This poem prefigures perhaps the insistence on physicality in the love poems which follow. But the titles of both these poems with their general religious implications also suggest that physical manifestations of love, however momentary, may include some spiritual meaning and revelation, and in some of the love poems the spirituality does arise from the physical presences of the lovers themselves, so that the ideas of separation, darkness, silence, and distance in these poems take on weightier values because of the context in which they have been placed.

An insistent demand runs through the love poems, a demand that comes from her essential individuality but, also, a demand that comes from the masculine opposite partner. 'Be woman' is the opening line of 'The Taming', and in this poem being a woman means being submissive in sexual union, but paradoxically that basic feminity has its own strength which will take away some of the mastery of the male. In a way 'The Taming' is a poem that emphasizes the give-and-take of love in the strictest sense. The sexual experience puts her at the mercy of the partner:

> Be woman. I did not know
> the measure of the words
> until that night
> when you denied me darkness
> even the right
> to turn in my own light.

The language here suggests that love must be fully acknowledged in the open; woman must give herself in order to release her own womanhood. Although this sounds like the passive feminine element as described in 'Bartok And The Geranium', the closing lines of 'The Taming' indicate that this release through sexual union in fact gives the woman at least an equality of mastery in the experience:

> Do as I say, I heard you faintly
> over me fainting:
> Be woman.

Thus the sexual experience makes her face her essential self, her womanhood, with both its submissive qualities and its strength. Through the physical experience comes a release from physicality. Woman is not to be considered merely as a physical piece of property. Love must give her freedom to remain herself even within the gestures of submission. 'I'm not just bones/and crockery,' she says in 'The Unquiet Bed'. She wants the freedom to be part of a unity, a loss of one kind of freedom in order to release a true individuality. She has held to the idea that

> love
> might set men free
> yet hold them fast
> in loyalty.

So love must always 'make room for me', the 'I', the individual human being, even in the act of union.

In spite of the ecstasies and freedom of love, in spite of the joy she experiences in rediscovering love at this point in her life—see particularly 'A Letter', which repeats the image of the tree used in 'Eve' and 'Second Coming'—the poet acknowledges the terrors, failures, and paradoxes of love. She sees its creative joys but also its abysses, gaps, and silences. 'And Give Us Our Trespasses' can be seen as a poem about the dark kingdom of human love.

It is a poem coming out of darkness, involving the darkness and the silence in itself. Love is the swaying form; the first section shows the room of love shaking and quaking. This movement dispels the darkness 'at midnight':

> a socket
> was plunged in the wall
>
> and my eyes sprang open.

Love is beyond words, perhaps a parallel with poetry which tries to catch the more complex beat beneath ordinary language. Speech in love is 'out of turn'. One must listen. 'I heard only your heartbeat.' The poet recognizes her inadequacies, a sort of recognition of the impotence of language even in the act of using words. The movement and the image of light breaking returns in the poem's fifth section:

> quivering water
> under the smite
> of sunlight

But after this epiphany there is the return to words, to make sense of the silence and darkness. 'The telephone' is 'always available/for transmitting messages', but to make the effort to speak is like trying 'to push the weight/of a mountain', so the poem closes with an acceptance of that large area of silence 'between the impulse to speak/and the speaking' for in that area 'storms crackle'. So we are finally apart in love because of our inadequacies, just as we finally have to rely on the silence beneath words because our use of words is always inadequate. There is distance between lovers; there is distance between silence and speech:

> Forgive us our
> distances.

Images of dream and sleep figure a great deal in the love poems in *The Unquiet Bed*. The poet sees the experience of love as something other-worldly and dream-like ('A Book of Charms'), something beyond words as in a dream ('The Dream'), but at times sleep and dream represent loneliness and distance, as in 'The Vigil'.

Some poems in *The Unquiet Bed* and *Plainsongs* attempt to describe the momentary blisses and fearful transient qualities of human love. 'Old Song', in *The Unquiet Bed*, expresses in controlled and resigned tone the passing of love, the impermanence of a human relationship even though it may achieve harmony and union. 'You cannot hold/what vanishes.' Humans must accept transience in love, 'Your bones may melt/in me/or in another woman', but that acceptance of momentary things is of the essence of love, for 'the essence is/to catch the bird in season'. In a later poem in *Plainsongs*, 'Con Sequences', Dorothy Livesay uses images drawn from nature to suggest the distances between lovers and also the growth and violent surge of love. When there is no desire in the lovers, then a face 'is stone/carved bone' but this hardness can crack and disintegrate through love:

> I wait for lightning
> an avalanche
> to tear the hillside

Underneath the placid surface, love rests, waiting for growth:

> Kick the leaves
> aside

> yellow roots
> cry for greening.

So love is a kind of undersurface that rises through the union of sex. Love, paradoxically, is there, both in lack of desire and in passionate response:

> The sun shines
> on the bald hill
> or the lush valley
> equally fiercely.

'Four Songs' (*The Unquiet Bed*) expresses Dorothy Livesay's personal explanations about her need and desire for love as a mature woman. She assesses frankly her indulgence in sexual love, trying to counter superficial arguments:

> People will say
> I did it for delight
> you—for compassion

but she establishes in the first song that it was indeed a matter of give-and-take:

> *Give me the will,* you said
> *and in return*
> *take from my fill*
> *of passion.*

In those terms, then, people's opinions about this affair were wrong, for

> You did it from design
> I—from compulsion.

She recognizes the dangers of mere indulgence in passion, but she cannot reject the passion, even though it may be quenched for both herself and her lover. The fire of her desire 'envelops' her lover; 'attracts the moth/and the murderer too'. She realizes the double-sidedness of insistence on passion:

> Dido knew
> this fire

and chose
that funeral.

She finds her passion urgent and insistent, a 'hunger'. Her body is
'blunt' and needs 'the forked light/ning of tongues'. Her passion is
assuaged, but 'thirst remains' for the gentleness and calm of love. In
this third lyric there is an indirect return to the idea of words in
'tongues' and the fourth lyric gathers together the images of fire,
thirst, and words. The inexpressible experience of human love is
cooled to the level of words, giving a taste of the sensual pleasure
just as a poem in a way gives a sense of the ineffable experience
which may give rise to the poem:

> I drink now
> no fiery stuff
> burning the mouth
> I drink the liquid flow
> of words   and taste
> song in the mouth.

'The Touching' is another series of lyrics which describes the sexual experience more explicitly. The image of coldness and warmth
is repeated as love is seen as a protection against coldness. Love as a
kind of violence, a union of entrance and submission ('pierce me
again/gently'), leads to completion, to a merging in new life. The
joining of man and woman in the sexual experience enlarges the
individuality of woman, for the 'steady pulse' of the penis she feels
as 'my second heart/beating'.

The second lyric plays with concepts of light and dark, revelation and darkness, submergence in warmth 'under the cover' so
that love lightens that darkness.

The third lyric repeats the notion of growth, for the poet
acknowledges a kind of re-birth beyond words through love. It
releases her into new elements; she becomes 'part of some mystery'.
She is swallowed within her lover, but although she loses her own
individuality; she feels herself within a larger, more basic and elemental self:

> I drown
>   in your identity
> I am not I

                        but root
                    shell
                        fire

so that at the moment of climax, that moment of completion and
union, she is somehow alone, deep in some underworld of darkness
from which she struggles to be born anew. At this epiphany she
becomes both mother and child at the moment of birth:

>   I tear through the womb's room
>   give birth
>   and yet   alone
>   deep in the dark
>   earth
>   I am the one   wrestling
>   the element re-born.

Here again is the image of isolation in a dark world, the image of
violent struggle leading to a break-through to creation. This same
image is repeated in 'The Woman' (*Plainsongs*), in which she cries
for relief, for 'the fearful knot of pain' to be untied. She wants
release through the climax to the urgency of love:

>   When you make me come
>   it is the breaking of a shell
>   a shattering birth
>
>   how many thousand children
>   we have conceived!

Through love she lives on the tips of her senses. Through submission to her lover her whole sensual life is opened, even though she
recognizes that she is in some way held and lost to herself:

>   never thought me bound
>   until one night all night I lay
>   under your will and mind
>   and heard you play my secrets
>   over and over in your hand
>   ('The Cave', *Plainsongs*)

so that

>   over all
>   my body's fingertips

> day breaks
> a thousand crystals
>> ('At Dawn', *Plainsongs*)

The idea of loss of self, of complete submission in order to reach to the elemental life in which a new self is released opens 'The Notations Of Love' (*The Unquiet Bed*). The poem moves into the area of silence in the sense that at one point the poet is accused of being unable to speak of love. There is only cruelty, but she sees love as being hard in its strength and asks her lover to take love 'the hard way'. Then in 'facing the rock' he will feel 'the fountain's force'. This force of love goes beyond age and time. Of the senses it is touch, the joining of flesh that offers its secrets. A finger may trace crows' feet round the eyes but

> the lips stay fresh
> only the tongue
> unsheathes its secret skin
> and bolts
> the lightning in.

Thus lovers come to union through experience beyond words; they are joined across silence and darkness, and even when separated by distance, the substructure of their love can seem to join them at almost a physical level:

> especially around
> these absences
>
> our minds are twins
> they circle and unite
> my left arm is your right arm
> bound   even in flight

The physical union of lovers continues even after the act of love, and 'The Notations of Love' closes with the idea of continuance beyond sexual love. Out of 'the dead/of night' comes light; she has lost one kind of individuality but has gained a new understanding of her essential elemental self:

> day or night, I
> am undressed
> dance
> differently.

Paradoxically, the poem following 'The Notations of Love', which closes on the idea of new release and a kind of continuance, is a poem that hints at the break-down of love. 'Moving Out' uses the dismantling of a house as a symbol of the paring away of love. The physical features of the house make the house, just as the physical love of the lover makes the love, so that now she can only

> find an upright bed
> between your bones—
> without the body of your house
> I'd have no home.

The poem, then, contains an allusion to the possibility of parting, to the disintegration of love, and indeed in *Plainsongs* there are poems which offer a bleak statement of the gradual collapse of love. In 'Auguries' the poet drops into the darkness—perhaps that darkness that love can lift her from. Here, however, she waits in the dark and has ominous dreams, waiting perhaps to be broken by love like 'a shell in your hand'. She finds herself alone in a dark garden, the trees shrouded and black around her. After the presentation of these dismal dreams, there is a stark statement of the denial of love: 'you have said no'. The poem ends with a series of questions, listing her hopes for a return to love. In the future she wants the dark garden of her dream to become 'a green place', where she will be held again in a landscape where 'your hands were the sky itself/cupping my body'. She waits hopefully to be lifted 'on girders of sunlight' out of the gloom of her present state.

Two other poems in *Plainsongs* give indications of the loss of love. In 'The Sign' there is a reference to separation, though there is 'yet touching'. The progress of a log rushing along with the flow of a river, whirled and battered against the banks, sucked under the surface, then swept out of sight, represents the vicissitudes of their love, so that, even though the poem ends in a joining of hands, the emphasis in the poem has been on separation, distance, and disappearance. 'The Uninvited' also suggests that the shadow of a third lies between the lovers, and the poet is conscious at the end of the poem of 'another voice/singing under ice'.

The closing pages of *Plainsongs* seem to concentrate on the separation of the lovers and the attempt by the poet to assess her situation, to come to terms now with the absence of love. In 'Another Journey' she sees herself as escaping from the captivity of love. She recognizes signs around her in nature that might make her cling to the past: a switchback trail that almost turns back on itself, but she moves steadily upwards, her eyes fixed resolutely in front of her. She may be moving in a darkness, but the poem closes with a glint of light, a return to life:

> Night
> spills stars
> into the valley
> I am aware
> of cedars   breathing
>   turning   the trees
>   move with me
>   UP   the mountain.

Throughout the love poetry in *The Unquiet Bed* and *Plainsongs* Dorothy Livesay emphasizes the physical aspects of human love, so it is not surprising that the poem 'The Operation' *(Plainsongs)* connects her experience of love and her recovery from it, together with a general reassessment of her situation of her life as she found it at that time.

'The Operation' opens with a sense of crisis. The poet has reached a crucial point in her life, this crisis made all the more emphatic in her mind because it happened after her tremendous experience of love:

> And I too
> after the blaze of being
>   alive
> faced the wall
> over which breath must be thrown.

Her view of the doctor corresponds to her view of her lover. He is one who uses violence, a knife, to save her. She is a 'victim/ grateful to be saved', so she gives herself completely to him.

After the operation the doctor watches over her with 'silent white precision' and with solicitude until there grows between them an 'intimate flashing bond'. So far in the poem the hospital experience is a kind of parallel with her experience of love, so that her emergence from the hospital is in a sense a re-birth. She must learn to live again; she must learn to face the world of external reality: 'I have to breathe deep here/to be alive again.'

The second section is devoted to a meditation about her response to love. She tries to evaluate it. Just as she has to rely on herself to effect a complete physical cure after the operation, so she must assess her chances in the aftermath of love, which she now sees as 'a sickness' which the lovers attempted to cure in many ways: by separation or even by physical indulgence. The disease racked them and at times their sexual union was an effort to effect a cure. Eventually their separation has led to some kind of cure, at least for her lover, as she now watches him, 'a well man', though she herself is still trapped in gloom: 'rain/smirches the pain'. This image suggests that she cannot face her new situation in a clear-sighted fashion, and the poem adds further details of poor vision:

> I face
> wet pavement   distorted
> mirrors

A picture of her lover suddenly breaks into the poem but she dismisses it by the choice of an act of violence:

> I decide to complete the operation
> tear myself into four quarters
> scatter the pieces.

This will lead to re-creation, a new life, in 'uncoiling/animal sun—/ another kingdom'.

The last section of the poem returns to a key image in Dorothy Livesay's poetry—a doorway—used generally as an entrance to new experience, as a release, a revelation or emergence into some new world. Here, as she stands in a doorway, she takes stock of herself in specific physical terms. She realizes that by an acceptance of what she is now she can rebuild a life. She can now see her lover in an objective light, enabling her to concentrate on her own life:

> for now the *he*   the   *you*   are one
> and gone
> and I must measure me.

Thus she imperatively exhorts herself to grow again, to stretch for the life force of the sun, 'reach a dazzled strangeness/sun-pierced sky'.

The process of recovery and the stoic insistence on individual growth are expressed again in two poems as yet uncollected in book form. Both were published in the magazine *First Encounter*, which appeared in 1970. It is significant that both poems repeat images that have been part of the love poetry. 'Rowan Red Rowan' takes up the tree image previously used in 'Eve', 'Second Coming', and 'A Letter'. She sees herself here somehow like a tree

> winter enclosed   crystal
> pale mouth   stiff
> and the smile   frozen

But there are bright berries on the tree. Still, the numbness she feels is perhaps a kindly numbness, because spring, like a time of new growth, may release her frozen tears:

> I cannot cry till the far green time
> when the hills loosen
> and the tears in streams rove through my veins
> into frenzied blossom.

The long hard look she has been forced to take at herself is the subject of the other poem, 'Fancy!'. Her self-regarding has revealed some undesirable features to her. It has made her more aware of her 'burdened body/the shrivelling eyes/the withered chin'. Yet the poem closes with an image of life:

> Yet still I live! move with the dancer
> stamping within.

So she has emerged from crucial experiences not unscathed but with knowledge and with a stoic evaluation of her own life. The sequences of the love poems in *The Unquiet Bed* and *Plainsongs* are the most candid revelations of the experience of love as seen by a woman in Canadian poetry. Some poems fall short of their aims because the poet seems more concerned with poetic theories about form and lining. Sometimes the structure of lining seems arbitrary, although in most cases the use of broken short-lining, together with rhyme, half-rhyme, and assonance, mirrors the changing and breathless quality of the experiences themselves, as well as rendering some sense of the spirituality of the experience, for the best poems in the sequence seem enclosed in suspension, caught in an ecstatic calm. At other times the poet mars a poem by making the reader too conscious of an image, so that it becomes for him a conceit, a rhetorical device that militates against the tone of honesty and directness in most of the poems. There is occasional over-emphasis and repetition, even (though rarely) an indulgence in romanticism and sentimentality. But these are only minor blemishes in an otherwise distinguished set of poems. These are examples of the very best in Dorothy Livesay's later work, in which she is not afraid to be intensely personal and frank because she is able to express her feelings immediately and yet objectively, so that she herself is subjected to the appraising and critical apparatus she uses in her own poetry.

[No. 47, 1971]

A Grab at Proteus
Notes on Irving Layton

George Woodcock

Many writers are best read out of their own settings. This is so especially in Canada, where the literary world is small and inbred, and where the self-dramatizing activities of authors are often unnecessarily forced on one's attention by the publicity man-oeuvres of publishers. To strike the point of this essay, Irving Layton is a poet whom one reads at his best with delight, and at his worst with a puzzled wonder that so good a poet could write and —even more astonishing—could publish such wretched verse; he is also a rather boring showman, and one wishes often that his public self could be shut off like television so that one might have the silence to listen for his real voice. The only way to begin to appreciate such a poet without distraction is to get away from his immediate presence—even when 'immediate' means three thousand miles across Canada, to escape from the antics of poetry readings and the shadow boxing of literary feuds, and to read his poetry where nothing else reminds one of his less attractive masks.

It was by chance rather than deliberation that I took Layton's *Collected Poems** on a journey which led me far from the stamping grounds of the Canadian literati. I carried the fat little gilt-covered volume, with its portrait of the author looking tough, half across Asia. I read Layton in the sweating humidity of the Malabar Coast, in the archaically English clubhouses of tea planters in the Western Ghats, and among Jesuit missionaries in the jungles of the Wynad Hills, with the tribal women howling outside like jackals as they danced to the tapping of monkey-skin drums. I dipped again, read-ing and re-reading the poems that pleased me, in Delhi, Isfahan, Shiraz, Byblos, Tyre, Sidon, Baalbek, Rome, and in the final vil-lage in the South Tirol where I at last settled down to outline this

* Irving Layton, *Collected Poems*. McClelland & Stewart (Toronto, 1965).

essay. The result was a revelation to me of the extent to which involvement—however remote—in an author's world can limit one's reactions; my dislike of the arrogance with which Layton tries to bully his readers into acceptance had provoked a resistance which I only shed when I was able to perceive, away from the aura of his public personality, the extent and character of his private achievement as a poet.

'To have written even one poem that speaks with rhythmic authority about matters that are enduringly important is something to be immensely, reverently thankful for—and I am intoxicated enough to think I have written more than one.' So claims Layton in the Foreword to his *Collected Poems*, and for once he is modest. After my several readings, I made a list of the poems which still seemed to me complete and moving achievements; there were thirty-five of them. The whole volume contains 385 poems, and thus one poem in every eleven aroused either my delight or my extreme admiration; this left Layton with a better score than most of the poets now writing in either North America or Britain.

The poems which have been selected for the retrospective collection are, of course, those which Layton now, at the beginning of his fifties, has decided are worth retaining; like all such volumes, it is a reckoning with time, a summation of achievement, a placing before the poet's contemporaries—and, by implication, before posterity—of the works by which he feels he should be remembered. Many a shoddy piece of doggerel which astonished one in an earlier volume is left out; many writers who were the subjects of personal attacks will feel half-relieved and half-disappointed that Mr Layton has chosen to withdraw their certificates of vicarious immortality. The mass of poems which will please those who critically admire Layton as a poet forms an impressive achievement; many more than half the 385 pieces are sufficiently interesting and craftsmanly to be worth preserving, even if they are not among the thirty-odd first-rate poems. At the same time there are still enough injudiciously chosen fragments to provoke those Layton-baiters whose comments will in turn provoke the poet into delighted reprisals. For all his flamboyance of manner, Layton is capable of some extraordinary lapses into mere triteness and triviality:

> To guard her virtue
> this woman

resorts
to needless stratagems
and evasions.

She doesn't
realize
her face
is ample
defence.

He can also perpetuate, with a coy archness that seems out of character, some of the weakest jokes that can ever have been given the shape of verse:

He lifted up the hem
of her dress
but being intellectual
and something of a painter
he quickly let if fall
again, saying
with an abruptness
that dismayed her:
I never did care
for Van Dycks.

It is, of course, something that Layton should have practised a modicum of self-criticism by making a selection at all, but his editing is perfunctory and eccentric. He is one of those half-fortunate writers who have a way with words and phrases, an almost fatal ability to make a statement on any subject in a heightened rhetorical manner, without necessarily producing more than a chunk of coloured prose chopped into lines or a doggerel jingle; when he cannot write a poem on a theme that stirs his emotions, he produces one of these hybrid verse compositions. With the curious purblindness that afflicts people possessed of such facile gifts, he seems unable to realize that his good poems are something quite different from his bad verse, and defends both with equal vigour.

By a convincing exhibition of his ferocity as a ring-tailed roarer in the little zoo of Canadian letters, Layton has in fact successfully embarrassed most of the critics into a kind of numbed evasiveness. In the seven years since I have been editing *Canadian Literature*, while two or three reviewers have made brief forays with bows-and-arrows into the fringes of Layton territory, no critic has submitted a complete and satisfactory study of Layton as poet, mainly because no critic has so far relished the task of considering a body of work by a notoriously irascible writer which varies so remarkably from the atrocious to the excellent, and which shows a failure of self-evaluation as monstrous as that displayed by D. H. Lawrence, who in so many ways resembled, anticipated, and influenced Layton. To grasp Layton is rather like trying to grasp Proteus. But Proteus was grasped, and so must Layton be, for behind the many disguises an exceptionally fine poet lurks in hiding.

To begin, one has to re-unite the poet and the public figure whom I found myself dividing from each other in my oriental journey through Layton's *Collected Poems*. When a writer so undoubtedly good in his better manifestations as Layton takes a certain view of himself, and develops a life style in accordance with it, one ignores the fact in the last analysis at peril to one's criticism's completeness. 'It's all in the manner,' as Layton says:

> Manner redeemeth everything:
>   redeemeth
> man, sets him among,
> over, the other worms, puts
> a crown on him, yes, the size of a
>   mountain lake,
> dazzling   more dazzling!
>   than a slice of sun

From the beginning Layton shows a romantic absorption with the poet as personality as well as with the poetry he produces. He sees himself as the vehicle of the divine frenzy of inspiration.

> I wait
> for the good lines
> to come . . .
>
> When the gods
> begin
> to batter me
> I shall howl
> like a taken
> virgin.

And the writing of poetry involves for him not only a kind of inspirational possession, but also other elements of the magical vocation of the shaman; particularly joy and power:

> And me happiest when I compose poems.
>   Love, power, the huzza of battle
>   are something, are much;
> yet a poem includes them like a pool
>   water and reflection.

Possession, indeed, gives the poet a special, privileged status; he is different from other men, and his powers bring responsibilities that go beyond the mere production of good poems. He is the prophet, the philosopher, the leader of thought, and Shelley's unacknowledged legislators of the world are never far from one's mind when one reads Layton talking in this vein, as he does in the Foreword to the *Collected Poems*. The poet, he tells us, has a 'prophetic vocation to lead his fellow men towards sanity and light.' But it is precisely this vocation which turns the poet into the misunderstood and persecuted rebel-martyr with whom Layton identifies himself.

> A poet is someone who has a strong sense of self and feels his life to be meaningful. By insisting on that self and refusing to become the socialized article that bureaucrats, priests, rabbis and so-called educators approve of, the poet offends the brainwashed millions who are the majority in any country. His words, his free manner of living, are a constant irritation to the repressed, the fearful, the self-satisfied, and the incurious. His refusing to wear the hand-me-down clothes of outworn philosophies and creeds; his resolve to see the world afresh and to see it from his own personal angle; his wry, unsleeping awareness of the ambiguities, the dark subtleties that plague the human soul; these will always make him suspect to the conformist taxpayer and his pitchmen in the universities and the churches.

I applaud Layton's desire to flout conformity and attack its supporters, and if this were all I would gladly stand shouting beside him. But I cannot see any necessary connection between rebellion of this kind and the vocation of the poet. That vocation, surely, is no more than to write poetry, and a good poet can even stand for insanity and darkness, as Yeats sometimes did, can even retreat into the darkness of literal insanity, and still continue his vocation. The social and moral rebel is something different, though the two may be and often are united. Layton takes it for granted that they *must* be united; this, to be necessarily paradoxical, is the classic romantic stance, and Layton, in upholding it, is a traditional wild man according to conventions laid down early in the nineteenth century. His essential neo-romanticism crops up in many other ways: in his 'anti-literary' stance when his poems are as crammed with literary and classical tags and allusions as the prose of any despised man-of-letters; in his 'anti-academic' attitude when, unlike many of his fellow writers in Canada, he is a university graduate who—as his poems about lectures and students show—has been lurking for years in the underbrush of the academic groves. It manifests itself also in the archaic images and phrases which embellish even Layton's most recent poems with an undeniable tinge of antique poeticism. In the final pages of the *Collected Poems* one finds him talking of

> The shadowy swaying of trees
> Like graceful nuns in a forbidden dance;
> The yearning stillness of an ended night . . . ;

telling us of his meeting with a faun (predictably conceived to point up the evils of a conformist world); and ending the volume with lines that are heavy with nostalgic echoes from the past of English romanticism:

> Meanwhile the green snake *crept upon the sky*
> Huge, his *mailed coat glittering with stars that made*
> *The night bright,* and blowing *thin wreaths of cloud*
> *Athwart the moon*; and as *the weary man*
> Stood up, coiled above his head, *transforming all.*

There is, of course, nothing intrinsically wrong in using again the phrases and images I have italicized; they belong to the accumulated stock-in-trade of poets in the same way as Shakespeare and Sheridan belong to the accumulated stock-in-trade of actors, and the way they are used is what matters most. But the fact that Layton not only acts but often writes as a latter-day romantic becomes important when we grapple with the relation between the two levels of his poetic activity.

The concept of the romantic poet provides, to begin, a justification for Layton's Saint Sebastian attitude. In fact, it is nothing more than a logical extension of the illogical idea of the poet as prophet; if the poet is really inspired, if it is really the gods (whatever they represent) who make him howl, then he is one of the chosen, against whom criticism or even competition is not merely an act of presumption but also something very near to religious persecution. Such an attitude cannot simply be waved way. Layton is talking with conviction and passion when he says that if the poet 'offers his hand in friendship and love, he must expect someone will try to chop it off at the shoulder.' He feels his isolation as a poet and a man deeply, so deeply that it has inspired not only such malicious attacks on his fellow poets as figure in the 'Prologue to the Long Pea-Shooter'* but also such a powerful vision of the fate of the rebel in the world of conformity as 'The Cage'. More than that, this feeling plays its ultimate part in the compassionate self-identification with the destroyed innocents of the animal and human worlds which inspires those of his poems that touch nearest to greatness and which pleads pardon for his arrogance towards his peers.

But there is another side to the idea of poetic inspiration. If it is blasphemous for others to criticize what the poet has written in the fine fury of possession, may it not also be an act of *hubris* for the poet himself to reject or diminish the godly gift? The whole vision of the poet as prophet denies not only the function of the critic; more seriously, it deprives the poet of the self-critical faculty which in all artistic activity is the necessary and natural balance to the irrational forces of the creative impulse. Once a poet sees himself as a vehicle for anything outside him, whether he calls it God or the Muse or Truth or, in Layton's words, 'sanity and light', he abdicates power of rational choice, and it is only logical that he should cease to discriminate between his best and his worst works, that he should seriously publish, in the same retrospective collection, a poem like 'The Predator', where pity and anger magnificently coalesce in the final verses:

> Ghost of small fox,
> hear me, if you're hovering close
> and watching this slow red trickle of your blood:
>
> Man sets even

---

* 'But if you have the gifts of Reaney / You may help your verse by being zany, / Or write as bleakly at a pinch / As Livesay, Smith, and Robert Finch; / And be admired for a brand-new pot / If you're as empty as Marriott; / I'll say nothing about Dudek; / The rhyme's too easy— speck or wreck . . .'

> more terrible traps for his own kind.
> Be at peace; your gnawed leg will be well-revenged . . .

and a joking jingle, like 'Diversion', of a kind which any versifier might whip up at two for a dollar.

> Whenever I'm angry with her
> or hold up my hand to slap or hit,
> my darling recites some lines I've writ.
>
> The crafty puss! She thinks that she
> diverts my anger by vanity,
> when it's her heaving breasts that does it.

If the lines she recites are anything like these, the breasts of Mr Layton's darling must put on a very spectacular exhibition!

But nothing is so simple where Proteus is involved. The problem of Layton's switchback career as a poet, which makes one's reactions to his *Collected Poems* take the form of a wildly dipping and climbing seismograph, cannot be solved merely by suggesting that he is deliberately unselective or incapable of selection. That might be argued for a poet whose successes, when they came, were obviously the product of deep irrational urges which rarely and unexpectedly broke into the dull cycle of an undistinguished existence and produced a masterpiece that astonished its creator; there have, very occasionally, been such writers, but Layton is not one of them. On the contrary, on reading the *Collected Poems* one is left with the impression of having been in the company of a trained and versatile craftsman liable to sudden fits of contempt for his public, in which he tries to palm off on them fragments of worn-out fustian instead of lengths of silk.

Perhaps the matter can be made clearer by bringing in an illustration from another field of art, and comparing Layton with Picasso. There is a verse at the end of his poem, 'Joseph K', which suggests that he will not find the comparison offensive.

> Then let him rise like a hawk.
> Fiercely.   A blazing chorus
> Be, or like a painting by Picasso
> Drawing energy from its own contours.

Picasso, to my mind, connotes enormous energy, and a flexible craftsmanship which has enabled him to paint and draw in many styles, and to select and use ruthlessly from past forms of art anything that might suit his purposes. No modern painter has spread such magnificent confusion, by the display of his talents, among those academic critics who originally damned the post-impressionists with the argument that they knew neither how to draw nor to paint. At the same time, as the collection of second-line material enshrined in the museum at Antibes has shown, Picasso's very energy has led him to produce a great many minor works which a more fastidious artist would have discarded or kept as mere exercises. Finally, there has always been a touch of the clown about Picasso, as became very evident in at least one of the films in which he performed as the impresario of his own art. He enjoys mystifying his more naïve admirers, and many of his works must be regarded as mere *jeux d'esprit* carried out to amuse himself or fox his public. But it would be foolish to assume that because of this Picasso is nothing more than a mountebank.

In one sense at least Irving Layton cannot be compared with Picasso. Picasso was the moving spirit in a trend that revolutionized our views of art, and it is hard now to imagine what painting would have been like anywhere in the world if he had not lived. So far there is no evidence of any real revolution that Layton had led in poetry; his work at its best has its own originality, but it breaks into no really new territory, and his followers among the younger Canadian poets have so far shown neither the vigour nor the talents of their master. In other respects, however, the resemblances between Layton and Picasso are striking. Layton, too, is an artist of great energy—in terms of quantity alone a formidable producer. And, like Picasso, he combines the ability to work in a variety of styles and to borrow freely from the past with a craftsmanship which at its best is so good that one cannot possibly attribute his worst productions to the mere inability to do better. A different explanation has to be found.

Let us hold the comparison at this point for the moment so as to consider the versatility which, from the earliest examples published in the *Collected Poems*, characterizes Layton's art. He is adept at the lyrically descriptive vignette:

> The afternoon foreclosing, see
> The swimmer plunges from his raft,
> Opening the spray corollas by his act of war—

> The snake heads strike
> Quickly and are silent.

He can make a compassionate statement in well-turned verse of almost Marvellian grace and graciousness, as in 'Mrs Fornheim, Refugee', his small elegy for a former language student who died of cancer.

> I taught you Shakespeare's tongue, not knowing
> The time and manner of your going;
> Certainly if with ghosts to dwell,
> German would have served as well.
> Voyaging lady, I wish for you
> An Englishwoman to talk to,
> An unruffled listener,
> And green words to say to her.

He presents, on occasion, mordant examples of epigrammatic wit, quite different from the snickering jokes of some of his later poems; 'Lady Enfield', for example:

> Be reckless in your loving,
> Her grace makes no one poor
> For only bullets issue
> From such an iron whore.

And he shows a fine adeptness in that admirable practice game of the young poet, the parody.

> Although I have written
>   of venery
> (and of men's hates, too, my masters!)
> and of the sun, the best thing in the cosmos,
> for it warms my bones
> now I am old and no woman
>   will lie with me
>   seeing how wrinkled
> my hams are, and my bones decrepit . . .

In this early Layton the craftsmanship is usually careful and deliberate: at times, even almost excessively precise and mannered:

> The passive motion of sand

Is fluid geometry. Fir needles
Are the cool, select thoughts
Of madmen; and
Like a beggar the wind wheedles
Pine cones from the pines.

Here Layton appears as a young man trying very hard and often very successfully to write well in an idiom derived largely from the English twenties and thirties. Later, as he turned away from this source of influence and began to feel his place within an American rather than a British tradition (in so far as his militant individualism allowed him to feel part of any tradition), he expressed his dislike of Auden and presented Eliot as something of an anti-poet ('a zeal for poetry without zest, / without marrow juices; / at best, a single hair / from the beard of Dostoevsky'). But, though there are obvious temperamental reasons why he should in the long run have reacted against both Auden and Eliot, the lingering—if diminishing—echoes of their styles which sound throughout the *Collected Poems* make it clear that Layton, whose eclecticism is—though he might resent the suggestion—one of his virtues as a writer, learnt all he could from them before he rejected them. Without such predecessors he would hardly have written lines like these:

Your face
tilts towards the gay edifice
through whose casements
birds might go in and out;
and your elbow is,
to be sure,
a gesture that makes known
your will—yet hardly more;
the flexures of your breast and skirt
turn like an appetite also there.

Evident from the beginning, among the experimental styles and often borrowed manners of the earlier poems, is an unfailing vitality and inventiveness. When Layton forgets to argue, when he lets his fancy go, and then holds it to its course with the reins of careful technique, we get his best work. It can be as luminously coloured and dreamlike as a painting by Chagall.

To the movement then of dark and light

A Byzantine angel slid down from the smoky wall
Hovering over me with his wings outstretched—
But I saw the shape where the flat tiles were not—
Before I could make a salt out of my astonishment
There was a meadow of surf in the bay at my elbow
And while the hungry robins picked at the air
White blossoms fell on their sad faces
Held in a frame of grass and ground for sentimental poets
Who weep when they are told of such things.

And at another time it can combine those two strong Laytonian elements, the pastoral and the apocalyptic, in a vision of the natural world as concentrated and intense as 'Halos at Lac Marie Louise'.

Presently I heard a stir
　　Of flying crows that came
And spread themselves against the sky
　　Like a black plume.

One like a detached feather,
　　Falling westward, stranded
On the topmost prong of a tree,
　　The tree was dead.

It was a white skeleton
　　Of a tree ominously gnarled;
And around the singular crow
　　The stark crows whirled.

The heaven split, the dark rain
　　Fell on the circling hills;
The thick gouts dropped beside the oars
　　Like melting skulls.

The boat fell with the waves
　　Into a still opening;
The halo of green hills became
　　A black pronged ring.

With the growing assurance of Layton's later phases comes a limbering of the rather stiff rhythms which mar some of the earlier poems, and this change is one of the liberating elements in his more interesting works, in the sparkling fluency of that extraordinary erotic fantasia, 'The Day Aviva Came to Paris', and, on a completely different level, in the questioning sombreness of 'Fornalutx', a ballad of disappointment with a Spanish town.

> Who thought of the heat-stained cobblestones?
> The damned who shuffled on the street?
> And cheeks made pallid by a vile sun,
> And rotting matter under one's feet.

Even in 'Fornalutx' one sees, at least to a degree, the negative aspect of the greater assurance with which Layton has written as the years have gone by. The verse is inclined to be loose rather than limber, careless rather than carefree. A little more work, one feels, and it could have been a much more concentrated and more effective poem. But 'Fornalutx' has still, within its limitations, something to say. Many of the other poems which Layton has written in recent years are not merely slipshod; they are also pointless—superficial versicles, empty jests, malicious, misfiring jibes. Layton recently expressed his annoyance with a critic who had accused him of favouring 'a loose, slapdash style of writing'. Perhaps he does not deliberately *favour* such a style, but he undoubtedly uses it on occasion. How else can one describe some of the bad poems I have already quoted?

Here one returns to the central comparison with Picasso. If we dismiss the Philistine explanations, that the poet cannot write any better, or does not know the difference between good and bad writing, how are we to explain the fact that Layton persists in publishing verses which he knows the critics will condemn, and often condemn with justification? As in the case of Picasso, I think the explanation is to be found in the relationship between Peter and Petrushka, between the poet-prophet and the romantic clown. In a fine poem which greatly illuminates his attitude towards his own role, he begins with the title statement, 'Whatever else poetry is freedom', and, having thus taken licence, presents himself as the clown of such freedom.

> . . . And now I balance on wooden stilts and dance
> And thereby sing to the loftiest casements.
> See how with polish I bow from the waist.
> Space for these stilts! More space or I fail!

> And a crown I say for my buffoon's head . . .

> And I know myself undone who am a clown
> And wear a wreath of mist for a crown . . .

The romantic idea of poetry as 'freedom' suggests that the poet should be liberated from any limits his own conscious craftsmanship or the requirements of the critics may impose (thus bringing us back in a disguised circle to the idea of the poet as the vehicle of an inspiration which it is blasphemous to criticize) and it establishes the reign of Saturn in which the respectable, the acknowledged, the established shall all be brought down, and all standards of behaviour (poetic in this case) shall be disregarded. The clown becomes the king in this Saturnalia. There is a curious fantasy poem in which Layton imagines two poets entering Toronto at the end of a Christmas parade and thinking the cheers and the civic welcome are for them.

> But the acclaiming thunders
> Were all for a clown . . .

It is unnecessary to identify the clown-hero; Layton does it in those poems in which he deliberately exaggerates what he imagines other people say or think of him, and in the process presents the figure of the traditional comic ugly man.

> Who is this butcher, you ask,
> with his nose
> broken and twisted
> like a boxer's?

> Look, you exclaim,
> at the mat of hair
> that covers his neck
> and his heavy gait
> like that of a startled bruin's (*sic*) . . .

In romantic tradition the clown represents rebellion against human conventions; he suffers from his fellows, but he has also the privilege of flouting and playing tricks on them, and it is under this mask that Layton presents those of his poems which, according to any recognizable criterion of quality must be rejected, but which he demands should be heard in the name of the poet's sacred freedom.

The figure of the clown is related to two other of Layton's *personae*, the lover and the misanthrope. Layton's erotic poems—which do not compose so large a proportion of his work as he and his detractors have conspired to make us believe—must be taken seriously, but not solemnly. For Layton sex is a matter of comedy, of joy and zest, and sometimes of laughter as loud as that of Apuleius or Rabelais. He recognizes the paradox of its glory and its absurdity, that the gods have so made man

> . . . that when he sighs
> In ecstacy between a woman's thighs
> He goes up and down, a bicycle pump . . .

Today it is our older, or at least our middle-aged poets who in Canada write best about sex—Layton, Purdy, Birney. They lack the lugubrious solemnity with which the younger writers cloddishly trample with rough cries in the obsessive dance of Venus.

This is not to say that Layton's erotic poems—any more than his other works—are uniformly successful. Some are shockers, though Layton has much less of a predilection for four-letter words than his legend suggests; some are boastful . . .

> Hell, my back's sunburnt
> from so much love-making
> in the open air.

But others, like 'Song for a Late Hour', have a marvellous singing lyricism:

> No one told me
> to beware your bracelets,
> the winds I could expect
> from your small breasts.
> No one told me
> the tumult of your hair.
> When a lock touched me
> I knew the sensations
> of shattering glass.

And some of the best are those in which the eroticism is not obvious, but which in tender sadness explore the complexity of human relationships that spring from the early raptures of love. 'Berry Picking' is a particularly good example. The poet watches his wife picking berries, and reflects on the changes marriage has brought in her attitude; now he can only 'vex and perplex' her.

> So I envy the berries she puts in her mouth,
> The red and succulent juice that stains her lips;
> I shall never taste that good to her, nor will they
> Displease her with a thousand barbarous jests.
>
> Now they lie easily for her to take,
> Part of the unoffending world that is hers;
> Here beyond complexity she stands and stares
> And leans her marvellous head as if for answers.
>
> No more the easy soul my childish craft deceives
> Nor the simpler one for whom yes is always yes;
> No, now her voice comes to me from a far way off
> Though her lips are redder than the raspberries.

In poems like this the comic view of sex is suffused with darkness, and the mood merges into the tragic view which Layton, clown and prophet alike, takes of Man, the creature whose own flaws destroy him. Here moralist and misanthrope come together in Layton as they did in Swift; the suffering poet, victim and thus exemplar of human perfidy, joins them. Beginning with the old radical ideals of brotherhood and, to use his own words, 'sanity and love', Layton suffers the radical's disillusionment. Man, as he is now, has damned himself by his rejection of life. The poet, who still stands for life, must retreat into solitude.

> Enter this tragic forest where the trees
> Uprear as if for the graves of men,
> All function and desire to offend
> With themselves finally done;
> And mark the dark pines farther on,
> The sun's fires touching them at will,
> Motionless like silent khans
> Mourning serene and terrible
> Their Lord entombed in the blazing hill.

At its height, as in 'The Improved Binoculars', Layton's rejection of humanity in his time and world reaches the level of apocalyptic vision, where he sees a city in flames and all its inhabitants seeking not merely to save themselves but also to profit from the delightful fact that their fellows are suffering.

> And the rest of the populace, their mouths
> distorted by an unusual gladness, bawled thanks
> to this comely and ravaging ally, asking
>
> Only for more light with which to see
> their neighbour's destruction.

In this world of apocalypse the poet appears as victim, slaughtered by the well-bred and cultured killer in a scene of Kafkaesque politeness and malice ('The Executioner').

Here he becomes identified with all those victims of man, and particularly those innocents of the animal world, for whom his compassion issue in a series of remarkable poems, 'The Bull Calf', 'Cat Dying in Autumn', 'The Predator'. To my mind 'The Bull Calf' is not only one of Layton's best poems; it is also one of the most moving poems of our generation. The calf, only just born, yet shapely, full of pride and 'the promise of sovereignty', must be slaughtered because, as the farmer says, there is 'No money in bull calves'. A clergyman sighs, and the murder follows.

> Struck,
> the bull calf drew in his thin forelegs
> as if gathering strength for a mad rush . . .
> tottered . . . raised his darkening eyes to us,
> and I saw we were at the far end
> of his frightened look, growing smaller and smaller
> till we were only the ponderous mallet
> that flicked his bleeding ear
> and pushed him over on his side, stiffly,
> like a block of wood.
>
> Below the hill's crest
> the river snuffled on the improvised beach.
> We dug a deep pit and threw the dead calf into it.
> It made a wet sound, a sepulchral gurgle,
> as the warm sides bulged and flattened.
> Settled, the bull calf lay as if asleep,
> one foreleg over the other,

> bereft of pride and so beautiful now,
> without movement, perfectly still in the cool pit,
> I turned away and wept.

It is not only the animal world in its suffering that Layton cele-brates with such eloquent compassion. He dedicates it also to those men and women who in some way show, in misfortune, qualities of dignity and feeling that place them outside the herd of hostile humanity: to the idiot who shames him by showing a pitiful under-standing of a dog's suffering ('The Imbecile'); to an old cripled man defying his fate as 'Death's frail, quixotic antagonist' ('Ballad of the Old Spaniard'); and, in one of his most complexly haunting poems ('Das Wahre Ich'), as a Jew to a woman who was once a Nazi.

> The terrible stillness holds us both
> and stops our breath
> while I wonder, a thrill stabbing into my mind:
> 'At this moment, does she see my crumpled form against the
>   wall
> blood on my still compassionate eyes and mouth?'

In fine, Layton is a poet in the old romantic sense, *a Dichter*—flamboyant, rowdy, angry, tortured, tender, versatile, voluble, ready for the occasion as well as the inspiration, keeping his hand constantly in, and mingling personal griefs and joys with the themes and visions of human destiny. Lately a somewhat negative element seems to have entered his poems. He is conscious of time beginning to sap the sources of life; he adjusts reluctantly to his own aging; he dwells on the unhappier aspects of sex, suspicious of the infidelity of women, of the untrustworthiness of friends. He is obviously at a point of transition, but his vigour will carry him over this and other weirs. Whatever happens we shall have to take Layton as he comes and wishes, the good and the bad together; but that is better than not having him at all. For my last feeling, after journeying through Asia with Layton in the form of his *Collected Poems*, was that of having been in the disturbing company of one of the men of my generation who will not be forgotten.

[No. 28, 1966]

The Cruising Auk
and the World Below

Lawrence W. Jones

George Johnston is surely an anomaly among the present generation of Canadian poets. His work defies classification, refuses to fit
any of the dominant patterns such as that of metaphysical exploration (as exemplified by Margaret Avison) or that of verbal and
intellectual subtlety (as exemplified by Stanley Cooperman), yet in
its own curious way it is every bit as effective. It is also, for the
most part, a more truly 'Canadian' poetry than that of his contemporaries in the images it evokes and the way of life it describes (a
fact which must please Mr Johnston's militantly pro-Canadian col-
leagues at Carleton University).

Although much of *The Cruising Auk* (1959) and *Home Free*
(1966)* is about the city of Ottawa and its people, George Johnston consistently finds elements in our country's capital (as does
Raymond Souster in Ontario's capital) which are symptomatic of
some confusing, often sickening tendencies in urban life. It is this
which places his work outside the pale of the merely 'regional'.
Evidence of this is perhaps the very popularity of *The Cruising Auk*,
which, for a collection of poetry, has sold rather widely across
Canada and is presently going into its seventh printing.

However, for those of us who know George Johnston, it is
perhaps difficult to square away his incisive poetic comments, his
function as a cultural seismograph, with the man himself. For he is
both a scholar of some repute (his translation of the Old Norse
Saga of Gísli was published by the University of Toronto Press in
1963) and a Quaker whose views on pacifism are both well known

---

*All the poems in these two books, which are out of print, are included (with thirty-two
additional poems) in *Happy Enough: Poems 1935-1972* (Oxford University Press, 1972).

and well exemplified by his life. The scholarship would seem inimical to the folksy charm exuded by his lyrics (although not to the starched black humour which underlies them); the pacifism, although it appears in many of his poems ('Under the Tree' in *Home Free* is the best example, 'War on the Periphery' and 'The Hero's Kitchen' in *The Cruising Auk* being others), would seem out of keeping with his unrelenting attack upon certain types of people. But Johnston manages to avoid either unsophistication or blatant indictment by a technique most often used in fiction—that of the microcosm.

The world he portrays, taken *in toto*, is a self-enclosed one. The people who populate it and the actions which take place in it are *reflections* of the real world, as though the poet were making his observations from the surface of a pool, which means that things are often grossly distorted, grotesque, absurd. Like the goldfish in 'Life from a Goldfish Bowl', the poet himself 'notes the goings-on with goggle face / Of all the world around about in air', and draws for us a serio-comic picture of its insanities. I would like to look briefly at this microcosmic world Johnston details, at the almost Swiftian satire which arises from his portrayal (which has its undercurrent of serious commentary), and finally at the peculiar style the poet employs in order to frame his lyrical pictures.

The first striking thing I notice about Johnston's world is the presence in it of a great number of weird people. Their names are chosen with Dickensian care: Mr Goom, Mr Boom, Mrs McGonigle, Mr Murple, Miss Decharmes, Mr Byer, Dr Gay, Joad —the list seems endless. And most of them seem to be less individuals than personifications of traits which belong to identifiable groups in our society: middle-class businessmen, spinsters in their second childhood, giggling young things, bachelors who seem to be eternally out 'on the town'. In 'Escape', for example, we hear of a belated affair between the conscience-stricken Mr Smith and the vulture-like widow Mrs McGonigle:

> Fleeing from Mrs McGonigle, Mr Smith
> Took refuge in a public telephone booth
> Whence he rang, as he always did, forthwith,
> The gospel tabernacle, home of Truth.
>
> Mrs McGonigle meanwhile searched the streets
> Asking herself as she did so why she did.

His life with her she knew was a nest of sweets
From which he beat it, now and again, and hid.

The poet, tongue-in-cheek, sums up the situation neatly:

Truly a man is never lonely here
And least of all at the moment of wild escape
In the telephone booth, a moment of bliss and fear
Between this world and the next, between fire and rape.

The last line of this poem is evidence of a technique George Johnston constantly uses in evoking his microcosmic world—the inflation or elevation of the inconsequential and seemingly ordinary. The denizens of his world become mock heroes and heroines. In 'Fun' we clearly see a parallel with the story of Snow White; Elaine 'sleeps in her maiden bed' while across the street the seven boarders dream about her. In 'Music on the Water' a modern-day Cleopatra

comes in her little boat
When the air is warm on the smoky river, afloat,
Making her presence felt in her flickering oars:
A journeying wound between the fragile shores.

Nights of splendour she's been to splendid men,
Swallowed them whole and spit them up again,
After which they've forgotten her perhaps—
As though she might have remembered them, poor chaps.

Rather than an Egyptian lullaby, the song she sings is a 'Pentecostal hymn',

According to which Earth's glories are rather dim
Whereas the rewards of the just are very bright;
Low kind of song, but it serves her turn all right.

Some of the poems' titles even reflect this mock-heroic dimension. In 'Queens and Duchesses' the subject is the promiscuous life of one Miss Belaney who 'doesn't remember who kissed her last / But he did it good, all right', but around whose head shines a 'haze of gold'. If Miss Belaney's pleasures make her a queenly sinner, Mr Boom is 'A Saint' because

> his sufferings
> Put him in the know of things,
> Teach him what is what and what
> In spiritual things is not.
> And when he looks upon us all
> His heart contracts into a ball
> Which is the perfect form of grief;
> Its perfectness provides relief.

In these cases and so many others we are confronted with recognizable character-types whose attitudes towards life are satirized, never directly condemned.

The activities in which these delightful people engage, although utterly human, even mundane, are also blown out of proportion. In 'Art and Life' the poet describes the artistic ablutions of Sadie McGonigle who has

> spent the afternoon with suds and water
> And creams and mud; her lines and points are put
> And every inch is tender to the view—
> Elegant work of art and artist too.

but who has dressed up only to be undressed:

> Sweet love, that takes a master piece like this
> And rumples it and tumbles it about,
> Why can he not be happy with a kiss?
> He turns the shimmering object inside out
> And all for life, that's enemy to art.
> Now where's your treasure, little scented heart?

Again, in 'Mail-Order Catalogue' the comprehensiveness and unfailing regularity of the contents cause the poet to remark that

> In spring and fall, when serious young men
> Comfort themselves that all that lives must die,
> Tax and the teeming catalogue again
> Come round, and give mortality the lie.

The same kind of satire can be seen in 'Mrs McGonigle on Decorum', 'Home Again', and 'Dust', and it brings to mind the sardonic humour with which James Thurber always viewed domestic life.

Significantly much of the activity so satirized throughout Johnston's poetry is city-related. For, as I mentioned earlier, the city is
really the cosmic entity which the poetry reflects. Occasionally this
is obvious, as in 'The Alderman's Day in the City' and 'Love of the
City'. In the former the fairy-tale pattern of the poem almost, but
not quite, covers up the fact that this lazy city official is lining his
pockets at the city's expense:

> Up at his desk the alderman
> Wags with his tar-warm feet;
> He puts his boots in the city
> Whose own back yard is sweet.

In the latter the poet makes a more general comment about the
artificiality and the suffocating nature of urban life. In this city that
has 'moved us in',

> The yellow sky comes down and fills the room;
> Dirt on the floor is kind, the walls are kind,
> Everyone's kind to us wherever we go.

And the poet asks the rhetorical question:

> . . . truly when death comes where will he find
> A better room than here, better arrangements,
> More courtesy, more eager friendliness
> Than in this excellent street-scattered city,
> This home, this network, this great roof of pity?

Clearly there is a serious side to all of this Thurber-like light-
hearted satire. There is always a meaningful comment made by
effective satire or parody, and it seems to me that George Johnston
is very concerned about the passivity of people in the urban *milieu*,
about the non-commital nature of people's lives in the city. There is
a general feeling of helplessness conveyed in Johnston's descriptions
of his McGonigles and Murples, a feeling which comes across
openly only infrequently, as it does in 'Flight', where the poet
watches a crow taking off from one barren tree in search of another:

> Caw! he cries, as though he knew
> Something worth his while to do
> In an empty tree elsewhere;
> Flap! he takes his blackness there.

> Me too! I would like to fly
> Somewhere else beneath the sky,
> Happy though my choice may be
> Empty tree for empty tree.

Much the same feeling is articulated in the final stanza of 'In It', where the poet declares:

> The world is a pond and I'm in it,
> In it up to my neck;
> Important people are in it too,
> It's deeper than this, if we only knew;
> Under we go, any minute—
> A swirl, some bubbles, a fleck . . . .

The submission to the 'destructive element' which is implied here may come in the form of routine drudgery which holds us captive in the city's grasp. This is the problem with 'The Queen of Lop' who

> works all day at a big machine that lops and lops and lops;
> At five o'clock she does her face and the big machine it stops;
> Home again on a public bus she goes to her little flat,
> Cooks a chop and forgets the lop and the wash-up and all that.

Even in her dreams, as the poet tells us later in the poem, when she tries to find some vicarious excitement in 'a boat on the ocean dark and queer' she finds that 'the big machine is aboard the boat'— there is no escape. Not only is there this routine of the work-a-day world, but there is the smug complacency of the settled routine of marriage, as we see in 'Domestic':

> A man should build himself a house and put himself inside
> And fill it full of furniture, and get himself a bride
> To fill it full of cooking smells and pickle smells and wit
> And all in pleasure breed it full and make a nest of it.

The repetition of 'full' here only serves to emphasize the emptiness of the way of life being described. Likewise, the mock-heroic nature of Johnston's people serves to point up the unheroic, unchallenging nature of their lives, which is perhaps the whole point of the satire.

In any case, if this reading of much of *The Cruising Auk* is correct, we might ask whether the poet suggests any alternative to the frothy existence he portrays. While it is not the poet's function to offer solutions to society's problems (indeed, poets are notoriously bad at that), I think George Johnston suggests at least one possibility: that we need consciously to seek our *own* freedom from slavish routine, perhaps by the use of our imagination. In 'This Way Down' the poet admits that 'my roof is wide to Heaven' and asks the vital question: 'Why am I not then airborne?' This is where the cruising auk of the title poem comes in. The bird is simply a symbol of the imagination which has freed itself; his virtue is that he *is* airborne, and this is why we must 'rejoice in him, cruising there'. We must strive to extricate ourselves from the life which the bird sees as he looks down upon us:

> Our unheroic mornings, afternoons
> Disconsolate in the echo-laden air—

To change this life, the poet seems to be saying (as does Raymond Souster in 'Good Fortune' in *The Colour of the Times*) we must take charge of our own lives rather than waiting passively for something to happen. This much is clear, I think, in the final poem in *The Cruising Auk*, 'O Earth, Turn!', which I quote here in its entirety:

> The little blessed Earth that turns
> Does so on its own concerns
> As though it weren't my home at all;
> It turns me winter, summer, fall
> Without a thought of me.
>
> I love the slightly flattened sphere,
> Its restless, wrinkled crust's my here,
> Its slightly wobbling spin's my now
> But not my why and not my how:
> My why and how are me.

Ways in which we may exercise our whys and hows are suggested in some of the more serious lyrics in *Home Free* (a book which has unaccountably not lived up to the promise or popularity of its predecessor). In the stylistically superb 'Under the Tree', for example, we are exhorted to recognize our complicity with the judge and the rest of society when a man is condemned to hang. 'We hardly know each other,' says the poet, 'But here we meet, under the hanging tree.' In subsequent sections of the poem various individuals and groups are described—the judge himself, religious people, the condemned man's relatives and friends—and we can see how each of them avoids having to *think* about capital punishment. The religious folk justify the hanging by soliciting the will of God, by placing their emphasis upon the 'mean and casual' murder itself and not upon what led up to it; the man's aunt and his erstwhile cronies drown any serious considerations in small talk, in 'notions soaked in beer'. Finally, the poet says, we must consider the paradox that although the Earth is the 'pit whence we were dug', it is also by necessity 'the garden in which we grope / For love'.

In the book's title poem, 'Home Free', Edward is given a chance to break the bonds of a deadening life, but refuses to take the chance:

> Edward sweats for a fortnight, the salt is in his shoes.
> Who knows about angels until he hears the news?
> Who knows about gardens until he smells the pit?
> Edward is holding a pass, and he's afraid of it.

What Edward cannot understand is that the world is a garden only if you make it so in spite of the ugliness; in 'Love in High Places' he prays that

> in Canada there must be
> Somewhere
> Surely a pleasant, sheltered garden,
> Green and fair,
> Maybe even way down in the city
> In its own air,
> Where there would not be births or dreadful pain,
> And fun
> Would have no exquisite hook inside it;

Edward does not feel himself part of what the poet calls elsewhere (in 'The Creature's Claim') the 'creatureliness of Earth', and so in the final poem in *Home Free* we find him 'asleep where brown stalks fuss and wave / And a squirrel has planted oaks beside his grave.'

Although the poetry of *Home Free* is not generally as effective as that of *The Cruising Auk*—Johnston seems much more at home when dealing with his little microcosmic world of Murples—all of the poetry is consistent in style. Unlike other Canadian poets, Johnston eschews experimentation with rhyme and phraseology. But the very presence of rhyme and regular metre gives emphasis to the routine he often describes. Occasionally he resorts to couplets, as in 'A Little Light' in *The Cruising Auk*; but most common is the rhyme scheme a-b-a-b and its variations, which is apt for what Johnston has to convey. Where the poet is most inventive (and here his vast knowledge of the history of the language is useful) is in the matter of diction. He is fond of creating words to match sounds—as seen in the 'kechunk' of anchored boats in 'Poor Edward' or the 'kaplink' of falling hairpins in 'Dust', and of simply creating words to fill his lyrical needs: 'gogglesful' in 'Elaine in a Bikini' and 'emplaned' in 'Dust'. Often slang is used to give a clearer idea of the level of life being described: 'neither I suppose I ain't' ('A Saint'), 'no dice' ('Domestic') and 'shot down' ('On the Porch') are examples.

I began by saying that George Johnston is an anomaly among Canadian poets. But as I have tried to point out, his is a unique kind of poetry with its own values, with its own valid statement to make. Taken together, the poems of *The Cruising Auk* remind us of the urban dilemma we are faced with and with which we must cope. The symbolic people and events in George Johnston's little world shed light on their counterparts in our real world. And we are forced to ask ourselves, as we watch the auk cruising overhead: 'Why am *I* not then airborne?'

[No. 48, 1971]

The Poetry of P. K. Page

A. J. M. Smith

Of the Canadian poets who led the second wave of modernism in the forties and fifties, P. K. Page holds a curious and somewhat anomalous position; she had certainly not received the critical attention that the remarkable fusion of psychological insight and poetic imagination which characterizes and individualizes her poems would lead one to expect. Perhaps the effort to discriminate between the subjective and objective elements of her work, or between image and symbol or memory and desire, has been thought by the critics too unprofitable or found too fatiguing. There is no doubt that she is a difficult poet—at least I have found her so—and the difficulty is not intellectual. Her moons are not reason's, so that what the reader who is to get the maximum enjoyment needs—or the critic who is to get the maximum comprehension—is a sensibility and an intuition that have to be nourished and educated by the poems themselves as he reads and re-reads them. Though I feel a certain presumption in approaching this subject, I can say that I have found the experience of trying to come to terms with it an absorbing one. Her gardens may be imaginary, but more than the toads in them are real; and are not her angels also?

Of course the fact that P. K. Page has not received the attention that has been given to some other poets of her generation can be partly accounted for more charitably and more prosaically. Her output has not been large. She published only three volumes of verse at rather long intervals—*As Ten, As Twenty* (1946), *The Metal and the Flower* (1954)—which won the Governor-General's Medal—and a retrospective selection, *Cry Ararat!* (1967), which contained seventeen new poems. For some ten years of the fifties and the early sixties she was out of Canada with her husband, who was in the Canadian diplomatic service in Australia, Brazil, and Mexico, and for much of this time she gave up writing (or publishing) poetry for painting. 'Gave up', of course, is not really true; her painting and her poetry complemented one another; each, I think, made the other better, or made it more deeply what it was, which is much the same thing. And then the immersion in the language, landscape, and mythology of the strange, intense, and perhaps intensely unCanadian places had a stimulating and enriching influence on all her latest poems. One does not have to rely on the evidence of the poems alone to corroborate these remarks— though that would be ample. In the tenth anniversary issue of this journal, she wrote her own account of her experiences during the years of fruitful 'exile', and in an article entitled 'Traveller, Conjuror, Journeyman' in *Canadian Literature* 46, she gave an account of her philosophy of composition and of the part played by memory, dream, sensation, and technique in both her poetry and her painting. These essays and her recent poems will mark, I believe, the beginning of a new, far juster, and far higher estimate of her standing among our poets.

The comparative lack of attention given to P. K. Page's early work, published in the little magazines of the thirties and early forties when she was an active member of the *Preview* group in Montreal, is due partly no doubt to the fact that they were over-shadowed by the flashy political poems of Patrick Anderson and the simpler satirical or amatory verses of Frank Scott. Even when she was most herself she was associated in the mind of a critic as alert as Milton Wilson with Anderson as a writer of 'decadent pastorals . . . , whose glass-tight but vulnerable aquarium leaves me gasping for air'.[1] This did not prevent Professor Wilson from giving us some just, discerning, and generous analyses of one or two of the most striking of the early poems.

No critic or literary historian, however, has made any serious attempt to deal at length with Miss Page's poetry or to define, illustrate, and evaluate her psychological symbolism and her strongly personal treatment of the universal themes of isolation and frustration—much less point to their transfiguration in certain epiphanies at the close of some of her remarkable poems. This, for want of a better workman, I shall try to do.

I begin with a few generalizations and then shall turn immediately to a close reading of some of her finest and most characteristic poems. This will perhaps enable us to isolate the special quality of her excellence and help place her in the developing pattern of modern poetry in Canada.

There are certain themes that occur over and over again in her poetry and a number of archetypal images and symbols that stamp their impress on most of the best poems in each of her three books, and in her work as a whole.

Her subjects are:

Childhood, its innocent eye, its clarity of vision, and its imaginative richness of invention, all leading to the discovery of a new and other reality than that of adulthood and reason;

Love, either faithful, happy, and unifying, or faithless, disillusioned, and lonely—the end-point of self-regarding love—that must be mastered by a conscious effort of the will;

and lastly, Dream, where child, poet, artist, and wit live and have their being in what in some poems is a garden of innocence, Eden before the Fall, and in others a briary wilderness or a sinister painted arras.

Her images and symbols are White and Green, images of snow, winter, ice, and glass; or of flowers, gardens, leaves and trees; or else glass again, and salt, the transparent green suffocating crystal sea. Her symbolic world seems mostly mineral or vegetable, but there are symbols also of birds, the swan and the peacock especially, and fish. And there are breathing human creatures also: girls, adolescents, lovers, and some selfish, isolated, lonely men. But what most vividly lives and breathes here is the Eye, the Lung, the Heart, and the feeling and perceiving Mind.

What is most strange and most revealing in this world is that the workings of its Mind are almost unconscious, often as in dreams, and that even the wit is controlled from Elsewhere. Hers is in its final effect a poetry of vision, and it demands a quality of sympathy in the reader that its poetic richness helps to create. Indeed, to speak for myself, it casts a spell that has made it possible to value it not as vision only but as revelation.

I would like, then, from the point of view of theme and imagery, to discuss, analyse, or perhaps just talk about some of the poems that have impressed me most deeply. A rough classification might go something like this:

Poems in which images of winter predominate, where White is

the colour, and ice, snow, glass, and a breathless cold make the mind and sense tingle—among these are 'Stories of Snow', 'Photos of a Salt Mine', 'The Snowman', 'Now this Cold Man', and many lines or stanzas of other poems, such as the last few disillusioned or awakening lines of 'Images of Angels'.

Poems of flowers and gardens, where vegetable dominates mineral, and Green is the primal symbol; many of these are dream gardens, and there are two opposed or contrasting gardens, gardens of innocence and grace, and gardens of imprisonment or exile, or perhaps they are one garden, before and after the Fall. Until its close 'Images of Angels' is of this group; so in part is 'Stories of Snow'. In this group also are many of the poems that deal with childhood and some of the newer poems such as 'After the Rain', 'Giovanni and the Indians', and 'The Apple', which is followed by its sad and desolate retrospective sequel, 'To a Portrait in a Gallery'. The garden songs of innocence give way to songs of experience, and here are the most intense and powerful of all the poems. Close to these in theme is 'The Metal and the Flower', though perhaps the antidote for the poison it contains is found in the much later 'This Frieze of Birds'.

Along with the poems centred around snow and ice, or green gardens of pleasure or terror—not too strong a word for 'Arras' or 'Nightmare'—are those where image and symbol are derived from the sea—the sea of poet and psychologist, where sleep is a drowning and the submarine world is the world of the unconscious. Among the most striking of these are 'Element', 'Portrait of Marina', 'Boy with a Sea Dream', and 'In a Ship Recently Raised from the Sea'.

Other classifications might list poems under such heads as Childhood, Love, Self-love, and Dream; but in all of them the same dichotomy of innocence and experience, happiness and despair, or good and evil could be discovered. Classification carried too far defeats its own end; it is time to come to a close reading of some of the poems I have named.

'Stories of Snow' grows out of memories, reveries, and dreams of childhood—'some never-nether land'—where snow storms are held 'circular, complete' in the crystal globes kept in a high tall teakwood cabinet. Encapsulated here are evocations of innocence and perfection opening 'behind the sprouting eyes' caught in the 'vegetable rain'. The conciseness and allusive richness of the language and imagery of the brief opening stanza set the tone at once and imply as a leading theme the contrast between childhood's innocence (or ignorance?) and the safe and changeless purity of the sterile snowflakes imprisoned or preserved in the small glass globe where the child (or poet) may shake up a storm. The major contrast in the poem, however, is that between the white world of innocence and art and the lush tropical landscape of 'countries where the leaves are large as hands / where flowers protrude their fleshy chins / and call their colours', which stands for the natural world of instinct and appearance, of uncontrollable organic growth, that strangles and betrays but which child and poet, or poet as child, can escape from into what the couplet that ends the poem names 'the area behind the eyes / where silent, unrefractive whiteness lies'.

This somewhat esoteric ending is led up to through a series of anecdotal pictures that seem like a multiplication of the famous ice-locked swan of Mallarmé—but with a richness and dramatic variety that needs more room than the sonnet can offer.

The illustrative central part of the poem begins with the lines 'And in the early morning one will waken / to think the glowing linen of his pillow / a northern drift, will find himself mistaken / and lie back weeping'. The dreams of this wakened sleeper in a land of fleshy flowers proliferate out of the opening stanza, become the whole poem, and lead to its climax. In Holland, in winter—we realize now that the 'never-nether land' of the opening was the embryo of a pun—hunters, their breath in plumes, 'part the flakes' and sail in their white winged ice-boats over the frozen lakes to hunt the swan. All the images here are of whiteness and no-colour, of snow-flakes and ice, and we see that the innocent world of the child's glass globe has taken on a new, beautiful but sinister significance.

> And of the swan in death these dreamers tell
> of its last flight and how it falls, a plummet,
> pierced by the freezing bullet
> and how three feathers, loosened by the shot,
> descend like snow upon it.
> While hunters plunge their fingers in its down
> deep as a drift, and dive their hands
> up to the neck of the wrist

> in that warm metamorphosis of snow
> as gentle as the sort that woodsmen know
> who, lost in the white circle, fall at last
> and dream their way to death.

'Stories of Snow' is the outstanding success of P. K. Page's first volume, comparable in magnificence and complexity to 'Images of Angels' in her second. These are perhaps the finest of the many very individual poems that seem to grow like beautiful flowers out of childhood memories, recurring dreams, and a crystal clairvoyance. Innocence and experience, illusion and disillusionment, find expression in an overflowing of powerful emotion, remembered not in tranquillity but with a craftsmanly excitement and an exquisite shiver that sets the rhythmical pattern of all her most moving poems.

'Images of Angels', like 'Stories of Snow', 'Photos of a Salt Mine', and some of the newer poems, 'After Rain', and the finest of all, 'Cry Ararat!', is a kind of sentimental education—*sentimental* not in any pejorative or ironic Flaubertian sense—that, recognizing worlds without love, seeks to explore ways of transforming them or coming to terms with them. Here images of ice and snow give way at the beginning to the daisy fields of childhood. This is the sharpening contrast to the close of 'The Snowman', the poem immediately preceding 'Images of Angels' in the inclusive volume of 1967. Here are the concluding lines of 'The Snowman':

> And as far as I could see the snow was scarred
> only with angels' wing marks or the feet of birds
> like twigs broken upon the snow or shards
>
> discarded. And I could hear no sound
> as far as I could hear except a round
> kind of an echo without end
>
> rung like a hoop below them and above
> jarring the air they had no need of
> in a landscape without love.

And here is the beginning of 'Images of Angels':

> Imagine them as they were first conceived:
> part musical instrument and part daisy

in a white manshape.
Imagine a crowd on the Elysian grass
playing ring-around-a-rosy,
mute except for their singing,
their gold smiles
gold sickle moons in the white sky of their faces.
Sex, neither male nor female,
name and race, in each case, simply angel.

This gives us the traditional almost Sunday-school picture-card of the Angel, innocent, whimsical, happy, but it is done with the wit and knowledge of the mature and *critical* grown-up poet. The angels are white, and gold, and holy; but they are to be pitied— they were made (by Whom?) 'never to be loved or petted, never to be friended'. Almost at once a sinister note intrudes. Somehow the angels are realized now to be 'mixed with the father, fearful and fully / . . . when the vanishing bed / floats in the darkness . . . '

In the body of the poem we have three witty and dramatic characterizations—representative figures who might be thought of as imagining angels: the 'little notary', the financier or business man,[2] and 'the anthropologist, with his tidy science'.

For each the Angel is a special symbol. For the little notary—the scene is surely Québec—'given one as a pet', it is his private guilt, and might, if discovered, be his private shame, and he keeps it 'behind the lethal lock / used for his legal documents', guiltily shut up. Reading this today one thinks of the legal and political repression of the Duplessis days before the Quiet Revolution, an allusion impossible to have been in the author's mind when the poem was written in the early fifties. This is an illustration, I think, of the growth into an even wider significance that some poems undergo with time.[3]

The eleven-line stanza devoted to the business man is lighter in tone than the rest and more frankly witty. Could this be the reason it has been omitted from the reprinted version? 'Angels are dropping, angels going up.'

What business man would buy as he buys stock
as many as could cluster on a pin?

But the stanza ends by humanizing the business man by filling his heart with uneasiness and shame as he remembers childhood tying a tinsel angel to his children's Christmas tree, and the poem returns for a moment to the world of such innocent poems as 'Christmas Tree—Market Square'.

For the anthropologist, the Angel is the miraculous transcendence and perhaps the condemnation to futility of all his classifiable observations. Where in the writings of philosophers or poets has the triumph of imagination over reason been more brilliantly and wittily put than here?

> The anthropologist with his tidy science
> had he stumbled on one unawares,
> found as he finds an arrowhead, an angel—
> a what-of-a-thing
> as primitive as a daisy,
> might with his cold eye have assessed it coolly.
> But how, despite his detailed observations,
> could he face his learned society and explain?
> 'Gentlemen, it is thought that they are born
> with harps and haloes,
> as the unicorn with its horn.
> Study discloses them white and gold as daisies . . .

as they were described, indeed, at the beginning of the poem. This is the tone and language of light verse and intellectual prose, but the poetry rises out of the thought as naturally and inevitably as in Marvell. The union of the homely and the profound is so quietly accomplished that hasty readers may never notice it. Somewhat in this vein the poem ventures other perceptions: 'Perhaps only a dog could accept them wholly / be happy to follow at their heels . . .' and again, 'Or, take the nudes of Lawrence and impose / a-sexuality upon them; those / could meet with ease these gilded albinos.'

The next and penultimate stanza returns to the child's world and the child's faith of the beginning, where the sphere of consciousness and imagination is reduced to something as small and self-contained as the glass globe of 'Stories of Snow'. This prepares us for the close of the poem—unexpected and very strange: the summer imagery of daisies, sun-dazzle, and lamb-white gives way to the white of cold and snow. The child, '*this* innocent' (the poet herself), 'with his almost unicorn' (his imaginary angel, the poem up to this point), 'would let it go . . .'

and feeling implicated in a lie,
his flesh would grow
cold
and snow
would cover the warm and sunny avenue.

Does this ending repudiate imagination, faith, and the fairytale world of childhood so convincingly recreated not only in this poem but in many others such as the beautiful 'Christmas Eve—Market Square' and the pieces gathered in the last book under the title of one of them, 'The Bands and the Beautiful Children'? I do not think so. These closing lines are an affirmation of sincerity and of an integrity that is moral as well as aesthetic—a look at the worst as the images in so many poems of flowers and sun and summer are an attempt to find the best.

Before attempting an analysis of 'Arras', which I think is the finest, if among the most difficult of the poems, let me jot down a few notes on some in which imagery and symbol are drawn from the sea and from salt or metal. In some the sea is clearly, like sleep, a symbol of the unconscious and, indeed, for the sensitive and perhaps easily hurt spirit of the poet a dark place of refuge. This is the theme of one of the shortest but most explicit, the beautiful and touching 'Element': 'caught and swung on a line under the sun / I am frightened held in the light that people make ·/ and sink in darkness freed and whole again / as fish returned by dream into the stream.' Although the key statement is the line 'I am not wishful in this dream of immersion', the poem ends with the agonizing image of 'gull on fire or fish / silently hurt—its mouth alive with metal'.

Much more objective and therefore free to be more witty, but inevitably less intense, is 'Boy with a Sea Dream'. Here are images of masts of ships, ancient hulls, and keels rusting in the iodine air—a dream of immersion again 'where like a sleep / strange men drown drowsily / spiralling down the sea's steep underlip...' Once again the sea is a symbol of dream as the cinema of the unconscious, but without any of the jargon of the clinical psychologist. For the critic, who like the poet ought to have a poetry-crammed head, the associations are with the music and imagery of 'Lycidas', 'Full Fathom Five', and the 'Voyages' of Hart Crane.

The end is strange and subtle, a sort of inside-outside reversal, recalling—distantly, of course—some passages in Jay Macpherson and Robert Graves.

> . . . like the perfect schooner which is pushed
> through the slim neck to fill a bottle's shape
> his dream has filled the cavern of his head
> and he, a brimful seascape,
> a blue brine,
> with undertows and sudden swells
> which toll his bells
> and watery laws to be obeyed
> and strange salt death to die

Images of sterile salt and metallic cold are found in a number of poems that analyse self-love with what can only be described as a kind of cold fury. Among these are 'Isolationist', 'Only Child', 'Foreigner', 'Man with One Small Hand', 'Mineral', and 'This Cold Man'. The last three are particularly impressive for the concentrated angry wit that turns experience into a new universal and instant myth.

A striking quality of many of these poems is the sudden immediacy of perception and emotion.

> Look, look, he took me straight
> to the snake's eye . . .

begins 'The Apple'—a magnificent opening, equalled only perhaps by Anne Hébert's awakening in 'La Chambre fermée'—

> Qui donc m'a conduite ici?
> Il y a certainement quelqu'un
> Qui a soufflé sur mes pas . . .

It is these quick exclamations of bewilderment, horror, or agony that give so much of its intensity to the haunted dream garden of 'Arras'. Here the perfection and purity of the classical Eden have been violated by a strange and somehow sinister intruder:

> . . . a peacock rattling its rattan tail
>   and screaming
> has found a point of entry. Through whose eye
> did it insinuate in furled disguise . . . ?

The agonizing questions come thick and fast: 'Who am I / or who am I become that walking here / I am observer, other . . . ?' 'What did they deal me in this pack?' Alice's looking-glass garden has grown menacing and lonely. 'I want a hand to clutch, a heart to crack . . . the stillness is / infinite. If I should make a break . . . ' Then the truly terrifying line:

> The stillness points a bone at me.

And now the prisoned dreamer breaks under the reiteration of the self-imposed questioning:

> I confess:
> It was my eye.
> Voluptuous it came.
> Its head the ferrule and its lovely tail
> folded so sweetly; it was strangely slim
> to fit the retina . . .

This fearful magnificence gives way to a simple homely cry, which in its context has a grandeur beyond the reach of rhetoric—'Does no one care?'

This poem alone would be sufficient to place P. K. Page among the fine poets of this century, and it is good to know that, while it is perhaps the high point of her achievement, it is also the high point of a school of symbolist Canadian poets among whom I would name Anne Wilkinson, Anne Hébert, Jay Macpherson, Daryl Hine, and Gwen MacEwen.

These are the poets in Canada who write not for the immediate moment alone. They are the poets who will live when the urbanized hitch-hiking social realists or the lung-born egoists of instant experience have been long forgotten.

Postscript

That great man, Frank Underhill, once sent me a collection of his political essays, not ironically but too modestly inscribed, as to a poet, 'these prosaic offerings'. When I read the poems of P. K. Page and her equally profound notes[4] on poetry, painting, and magic I am conscious of how prosaic *this* offering is. My hope, however, is that it may lead other critics to write of her work with their own perceptions.

[No. 50, 1971]

[1] 'Other Canadians and After', in Masks of Poetry, ed. A. J. M. Smith (Toronto, 1962), p. 126.

[2] The stanza on the business man has been deleted from the poem as it appears in Cry Ararat! (Toronto, 1967). I enjoyed the passage and cannot feel that it is out of keeping with the rest of the poem.

[3] Poems by Shelley, Auden, Anne Hébert, and Frank Scott might be cited in further illustration.

[4] The article in Canadian Literature 46 referred to above, and the earlier and brief 'Questions and Images' in Canadian Literature 41.

Proteus at Roblin Lake
Al Purdy's Transformations

Mike Doyle

Recent commentators have suggested that Al (or A. W., Alfred, Alfred W.) Purdy is a poet of 'many over-lapping self-created versions', in Margaret Atwood's phrase. George Bowering, in his Purdy monograph,* says of the earliest version, perpetrator of *The Enchanted Echo* (1944), 'he seemed to think that the poet had to be a sort of Emily Dickinson, maybe with a moustache'. Mention of Emily Dickinson in the same breath as *The Enchanted Echo* is gross flattery to that jejune conglomeration of verses, yet Bowering has a point. He cites a quatrain which does *sound* like Emily Dickinson, the resemblance deriving from the fact that Purdy, too, seemed to need to make poems in fixed stanza forms, many of them standard in nineteenth-century hymnology. *The Enchanted Echo* demonstrates two things about Purdy, both crucial. First, even in the formal strait-jacket he provided himself, he has an ear. Second, perceptible when *The Enchanted Echo* takes its place in the Purdy *oeuvre* , this is the initial promulgation of poet Purdy—Purdy Mark One (so to speak, since we are in the Air Force) at 'a sort of moral attention'.

That last phrase comes from the narrator of *The Great Gatsby*. Scott Fitzgerald told us that Jimmy Gatz (i.e., Jay Gatsby, earlier version) derived from 'his Platonic conception of himself'. *The Enchanted Echo* reveals what conception of 'the poet', and himself as poet, Purdy developed from the age of thirteeen, when he began to write the stuff, up to his mid-twenties when he was unwittingly (unDuchampishly) a mustachioed Emily Dickinson. One can think of numerous examples of poets whose first books are awkward or amateur beyond belief (two well-known examples: John Crowe Ransom, William Carlos Williams). The closest parallel to Purdy

* *Al Purdy* (Studies in Canadian Literature, Copp Clark, 1970).

among 'colonial' poets is his New Zealand near-contemporary Louis Johnson, whose *Stanza and Scene* (1945) bears the same relationship to Johnson's mature work as *The Enchanted Echo* does to Purdy's. Some poets, from their beginnings, produce highly developed and beautifully finished work, usually in small quantities. Dylan Thomas is a fine example. Others, and Johnson and Purdy are two, grow and metamorphose in public. Such poets are more available to negative criticism, often known for their mistakes and limitations, but they seem to need publication for growth. Today Purdy rejects that first public version of himself, regarding the work of that phase as 'crap'. No wonder, for both technique and substance are routine, mechanical, stock-response. The large gestures of the verse bear no relation to Purdy's day-to-day life. They introduce us to someone apparently plugged in to the whole range of 'king and country' clichés.

We know today that Purdy was never really like that. Part of him was, of course, if *The Enchanted Echo* has any truth to it at all, but all of him—no! He did not even begin to get all the possibilities of himself into that early book, which was an act of homage to an outdated and extremely provincial conception of 'the poet', and which shows only that (like Jay Gatsby) he had to begin somewhere. Seemingly he began from a position of extreme cultural poverty and met the need to externalize his sense of vocation in a book—an echo, perhaps, because of a sense that he was talking only to himself.

What happened next may seem surprising. As far as book publication goes, nothing happened for more than a decade. A first book, apparently, rid Purdy's ego system of a need. He submerged. A restlessness, physical and psychological, showed itself in his way of life: running a taxi business in Belleville, Ont., and working in various factory jobs, just as in the thirties he had ridden the freights across country. That, says Bowering, is 'the stuff literary legends . . . are made of', but such a legend had already been preempted at least a generation earlier by the old Georgian poet, W. H. Davies, who told us about it in *The Autobiography of a Supertramp* fifty years ago.

Who knows what inner reasons Purdy had for his courses of action? But the 'legend', when matched up against the poetry of the late 1950s (such things as the pervasive archaisms and 'poetical' language of *Emu, Remember!*) gives a distinctly schizoid impression. As far as the craft of poetry is concerned, Purdy had simply gone further into the British tradition. He had exchanged the Quiller-Couch schoolboy stereotype of the poet for another and livelier one, but still a stereotype. Yet there are signs of growth: a developing consciousness of sound and language, a sense of the immediate environment—of what is actually and physically around him, and of the poem as part (an important part for him) of the process of being alive. He has begun to choose better models, in particular Hopkins, whose device of hyphenated phrases he adopts in (as Bowering acutely observes) a 'striving for openness and the natural motion in freedom'.

During the late 1950s the new influence of William Carlos Williams was being felt among Canadian poets. Up to this point Purdy had shown himself to be a typical colonial poet (easily matchable with poets in Australia, New Zealand, South Africa, and elsewhere) but now he too began to show signs of Williams' influence —in his explicitly stated concern with particular objects, in the run of his lines, and in his conscious concern with craft (though he labelled it, less than happily in the circumstances, 'the crafte so longe to lerne'):

> I forget whether I ever loved you
> in the past—when you enter the room
> your climate is the mood
> of living, the hinge of now,
> in time the present tense.
> Certainly you are the world
> I am not done with
> until I dispense with words—

Yet Purdy was already too much himself to be confined by another artist's conception of reality and the poet's relation to it, even one as seminal as Williams'. Purdy's eclecticism, his protean personality, first shows itself markedly in *The Crafte So Longe to Lerne* (1959), sometimes destroying the particular poem, as in 'Whoever You Are', with its metamorphic sentiments, which curdle at the end into 'romantic' melancholy. Underlying a number of the poems of this period is a strange fear of disintegration (see 'Whoever You Are', 'After the Rats', 'Vestigia', 'At Evergreen Cemetery', and even 'On the Decipherment of Linear B', which portrays the work of Michael Ventris as a threat to a cherished perception of history. A half-submerged 'romantic' nostalgia is betrayed here both by the theme and the poem's closing cadences.)

In contrast, Purdy shows himself as Alfred W. Purdy, somewhat learned but tongue-in-cheek, in 'Gilgamesh and Friend', where he uses controlled lightness of tone to interfuse condensed mythology with contemporary details and tone of voice. Equally successful, and more important, is 'At Roblin Lake', introducing the locus of so many future poems, which was to give Purdy a central fixed point in the local. Several facets or versions of Purdy merge—the bookish Alfred W., the self-oberver, the punster, the vulnerable:

> . . . wondering at myself, experiencing
> for this bit of green costume jewellery
> the beginning of understanding,
> the remoteness of alien love—

From some poems in this volume one has a sense of disintegration— already mentioned; from others 'the beginnings of understanding'. Seen in the long perspective of three decades of published work, perhaps the key moment of *The Crafte So Longe to Lerne* is in the conclusion of 'At Evergreen Cemetery':

> Myself, having the sense of something going
> on without my knowledge, changes taking place
> that I should be concerned with,
> sit motionless in the black car behind the hearse
> waiting to re-enter a different world.

An admirer of Purdy's has described him as being 'very Canadian without being provincial', offering an unconsciously backhanded compliment. Why has Purdy become so significant a poet for Canada today? To an outsider Canada must present a somewhat puzzling international image: innocent yet canny, straightforward yet oblique, open and yet shut in, eclectic and yet groping for a single image of itself. Some or all of these characteristics apply to Purdy, who seems as much as anyone writing today to sense what it is, the Canadian thing, the local thing, and whose work may be seen as a slow unpeeling, a groping towards the core of that thing.

Years ago, reviewing *The Crafte So Longe to Lerne*, Milton Wilson suggested that, 'Purdy has to find his directions by indirections; poetically he needs to be devious'. Part of the explanation may be in Purdy's intuition of the gap between his fellow Canadians' daily experience and his own vocation ('Canadian without being provincial'):

Now I am a sensitive man
so I say to him mildly as hell
'You shouldn'ta knocked over that good beer
with them beautiful flowers in it'
So he says to me 'Come on'
so I Come On
like a rabbit with weak kidneys I guess
like a yellow streak charging
on flower power I suppose
& knock the shit outa him & sit on him
(he is just a little guy)
and say reprovingly
'Violence will get you nowhere this time chum
Now you take me
I am a sensitive man
and would you believe I write poems?'
But I could see the doubt in his upside down face
in fact in all the faces
'What kinda poems?'
'Flower poems'
'So tell us a poem'
I got off the little guy but reluctantly
for he was comfortable
and told them this poem
They crowded around me with tears
in their eyes and wrung my hands feelingly
for my pockets for
it was a heart-warming moment for Literature
and moved by the demonstrable effect
of great Art and the brotherhood of people I remarked
'-the poem oughta be worth some beer'
It was a mistake of terminology
for silence came
and it was brought home to me in the tavern
that poems will not really buy beer or flowers
or a goddam thing

First, an aside on provincialism. I do not believe a poem such as this could have been written by an English poet until the rise, in recent years, of live poetry in centres such as Liverpool and Newcastle. It could, however, have been written by any number of Australian or New Zealand poets in the last forty years. More to our present point: the energy with which this incident is portrayed locates the great advance of Purdy's work in the early 1960s. At its worst, such energy and self-mockery result in a leer, a display of knowingness, but the best work in *Poems for all the Annettes,* for example, is due to a tension between energy and watchfulness, energy and diffidence, energy and skepticism. An earlier introversion has been superseded by something more positive. Sometimes the new energy is manifest in sweeping declarations, catalogues of whole masses, but in such instances the energy is largely of the surface and largely lost. Where it really counts is in the exploring of a relationship with one other person, a situation at once open and closed, tentative and yet assured. This is why the whole notional framework of *Poems for all the Annettes* is a happy one.

Simultaneously Purdy seems to grapple with the shape of a human exchange and the shape of a poem, as in 'Encounter', a (finally unsuccessful) piece about loosening a screw in a pantry door which had been fixed in place by another man a hundred years earlier. The poem's very occasion demonstrates Purdy's sensitivity and alertness, but he lets it diffuse into stridency, first betrayed by a verbose elongating of the line and finally by capitalization. Yet there has been an encounter and it is precisely revealing of Purdy's strength that he can realize he is talking about 'the metaphysical notion about how we're all interconnected', but makes us feel the palpable human reality of his nineteenth-century counterpart. (This poem too, incidentally, has its provincialist element: the poet imagining what others must think of his being a poet—'a phony'.

With recurring amazement and admiration one meets Purdy's sensitivty to 'the one important thing among so much meaningless trivia / the one thing that always eludes you', of which he meanwhile professes, 'Nothing is said or can be said'. Elusiveness is directly related to life's limitless possibilities, the quality of experience, the process, painful enough and yet open:

> every decision, word, thought, positive act,
> causes the sum of the parts of a man's self to change
> and he betrays himself into the future day after day

But this is 'talking about it', one reason why this poem, 'Collecting the Square Root of Minus One', appeals to me less than the finely realized concreteness of 'House Guest', where Purdy combines the texture of a two-way relationship (the guest is Milton

Acorn, I believe) with the fabric of his own mental interests and experiences. Technically hardly more than a list, an enumeration, much may be learned from 'House Guest' about Purdy's skill in handling his materials, his adroit use of line breaks and conjunctions, his laconic eloquence, and the absurdity and yet appropriateness of detail:

> Every night the house shook from his snoring
> a great motor driving us on into daylight
> and the vibration was terrible
> Every morning I'd get up and say 'Look at the nails—
> you snored them out half an inch in the night-'
> He'd believe me at first and look and get mad and glare
> and stare angrily out the window while I watched 10
>   minutes of irritation
> drain from his eyes on to fields and farms and miles
>   and miles of snow

Since the guest spent so much time there pounding nails, the psychology of this is acute, and, indirectly, is a strong expression of affection for the guest, who is close enough to the poet to be included in his characteristic self-mockery.

As its title suggests, many of the two-way relationships in *Poems for all the Annettes* centre on women. 'The Old Woman and the Mayflowers' epitomizes what Gary Geddes (in a recent article on Purdy) calls Canadian 'orneryness', portraying the end of a woman who, 'after almost 80 years of bitchiness', had died in a field:

> She'd picked maybe a dozen mayflowers
> before dying, and a goat ate them
> out of her hand.

Ending in understatement and diminution, yet Purdy has made a local myth, thereby giving Ameliasburg Township a meaningful name. Once again the reader is aware of a closeness, poet to subject, and perhaps the old woman is even a surrogate for the poet.

A woman is also the focus of 'Archaeology of Snow', frequently seen as centrepiece of *Poems for all the Annettes*, with its complementary statements:

> we encounter the entire race
> of men just by being
>   alive here

and

> a few more moments
> to hang in a private gallery
> of permanent imaginings

Here we perceive another element of the tension which gives Purdy's work its vitality. He is public, he is the globetrotting Canadian who makes pronouncements about public events, but one feels in the texture of his work that he is also intensely private, and that, in the end, may be the more interesting thing about him. Of course encountering 'the entire' human race is not, of itself, just public. Again, the poet feels himself part of a vast process; but the meat of the poem is a human encounter and its reverberations.

Open form, particularly the fragmented beginning, establishes the poem's exploratory nature. The protagonist has lost his girlfriend, Anna, laments the loss, but does not romanticize it. Something, at once comical and beautiful, ephemeral and tangible, remains with him:

> Day after next day
> > I found her
> > heavy buttocks
> > in the snow
> printed there
> > like a Cambrian trilobite
> Except the girl was not there
> but was there also somehow

Later he refers to her as 'Helen of Illyria with the big behind', at once humanizing the myth and mythifying the human. Chill weather helps retain the lost girl's imprint, as though in some sense she is invisibly there; but with warmer weather, a new season, spring, she will disappear inevitably, because the large process of the universe continues. But has she gone? Purdy's 'Platonism' intervenes to save her:

> the form is HERE
> > has to be
> > must be
> As if we were all immortal
> in some way I've not fathomed

and the poem resolves itself into a sense of the 'grandeur' of the interpenetration of all things into one, including the humans, of whom 'there's no end'.

Purdy's strength shows here in his correlation of a sense of the immensity of flux and the fleetingly possessed and mock-heroic human, in the antithesis implied by the title—'Archaeology of Snow'—that man leaves traces though almost everything melts away. One thing I have not perhaps sufficiently stressed may be indicated in these opposites: Purdy's inclusiveness, his capacity to bring to bear many facets of his personality. This, as much as anything, serves to make *Poems for all the Annettes* a landmark in his career and in Canadian poetry.

When *The Cariboo Horses* was published in 1965 it confirmed Purdy's public status, but more than one commentator remarked that no poem in the volume is the kind of 'finished structure which focuses and holds attention'. Mercurial as Purdy is, that is not surprising. The most significant pieces in *The Cariboo Horses* have not a memorable façade but a presence, a texture, which permeates. Some features of Purdy's craftsmanship at this stage will show what I mean.

My first-year English grammar text informs me that, in verbal structure, 'The continuous forms denote an action, an event, or a condition that is incomplete and still continuing':

> At 100 Mile House the cowboys ride in rolling
> stagey cigarettes with one hand reining
> restive equine rebels on a morning grey as stone
> —so much like riding dangerous women
>   with whiskey coloured eyes-

Purdy is attached to objects, particularly what Williams once called 'the raw beauty of ugliness':

> the football players
> ride in colourless convertibles their
> upholstery worn down
> to foam rubber quivering tho it
>   is still
>   quite beautiful—

But despite this he is a poet of the verb, and many poems in *The*

Cariboo Horses gain their immediacy and emotional force from the verb-form (responding to Heidegger's dictum that the human condition is *to be there*). Poem after poem moves in the continuous form, even ('My Grandfather Talking—30 Years Ago') remembered incidents, are recreated as if happening now.

Such technique is one index of Purdy's sophistication, but other methods also contribute to the poems' momentum. In many instances the poem is a continuum, its forward pressure developed through the deployment of verbs, on the one hand, and link words, conjunctions, transitions, on the other. Used at line ends or beginnings, such devices can control the pace:

> dreaming not of houris and other men's wives
> but his potash works and the sawmill hearing
> only the hard tusked music of wheels turning
> and hardly ever heard anything soft he
> did not know one March that June was early . . .

Gary Geddes asked Purdy, in an interview,* whether the openendedness of his poems is merely a 'device'. Acknowledging some debt to Olson, Purdy agreed, but said it is also 'a philosophy'. If so, it is indicative of one more version of Purdy. Casting our minds back, momentarily, to a phrase in 'Archaeology of Snow', I suggested that 'the form is HERE' carries 'Platonic' overtones (i.e., that one element behind Purdy's experiences is a vision of an ideal experience), but more deeply felt is the sense of the leaving of human traces. Their qualities of presentness and movement make Purdy's mature poems highly dramatic. We are immediately involved in the process of his responses. We may then ask: what is the nature of those responses? What answers does Purdy have? I tend to disagree with those who suggest that none is offered; gradually coming into the work is a feeling for the specific occasion, person, object. Instead of Plato's chair:

> I see the myth of God
> is a kitchen chair
> full of wormholes
> and fall down and worship

The flux itself is for Purdy an answer, and a sufficient answer. His

* *Canadian Literature* 41, Summer 1969.

grandfather tells him 'you don't dast stop / or everything would fall down', and all indications are that Purdy believes him, profoundly. Life is that and nothing more, the movement through—though his imagination longs for it to be more, as he suggests in 'Method for Calling up Ghosts', with its wish image of the dead leaving white-painted trails. Meanwhile, experience is of 'fumbling to stay alive / and always the listening'. Stoppage is death for Purdy, as is revealed even in a casual phrase such as 'television's awful semi-colon' (an informative sidelight on his technique).

To return to the kitchen chair. Cast up in the flux it has particularity, but it is also common, and representative—of what one lives with day by day, 'full of wormholes'. Such an attitude is movingly captured in 'The Country North of Belleville', a poem of the harsh farmlands, which shares something with such 'provincials' as Williams, and Patrick White in his great novel of pioneer farming, *The Tree of Man*. Deeply conscious as he is of the countryside in question, 'the country of defeat', where 'Old fences drift vaguely among the trees', Purdy speaks as one whose restlessness has drawn him away, but who is drawn back albeit reluctantly to 'the same / red patch mixed with gold'.

Time and space, spartan time and empty—or snow-filled—space, predominate in *The Cariboo Horses*. If *Poems for all the Annettes* marks the moment when Purdy's creative energies gathered into a cohesiveness which comes through, at its high points, as fierce joy, *The Cariboo Horses* follows up by confirming that he is a *Canadian* poet. Purdy's answer to Northrop Frye's (and Margaret Atwood's) question, the Canadian question, 'Where is here?', is now in the *texture* of almost every poem. One could argue *ad nauseam* about the meaning of 'provincialism' (as I would argue that, seen from London or Paris, Canada is 'provincial', but then I do not consider 'provincial' to be a term of derogation), but I note simply that many foremost Commonwealth writers continue to feel the need to come to terms with European culture. Purdy is manifestly Canadian partially because his consciousness is a link-point between past and present, between European (but also North American) history and 'the country of defeat':

> Here we are
> Euclid and Ptolemy and I
> walking along the dusty road

From this point on Purdy will be much preoccupied with the

question of how, in what manner, Canadians dwell in their home-
land.

Something of that manner he offers in himself—a mixture of
understatement, self-mockery, pathos, and comedy, beautifully evident in the two poems 'In the Wilderness' and 'One Rural Winter', both narrative in their basic thrust. In the first, his encounter
with the Doukhobors at Agassiz is an encounter also with Canadian history. Admiring the spiritual strength of these people, he
knows throughout that he is not one of them, but merely taking
notes in 'a steno's notebook'. The resulting complex stance is fruitful and revealing. Objective and yet self-mocking, he perceives
both the grandeur and comedy of 'the nay-sayers and spirit-
wrestlers of the Kootenay'.

Self-mockery controls 'One Rural Winter', miniature mock-
epic of a 'journey', to a distant outdoor john in the midst of
snowbound winter:

> The earth is frozen
> the beautiful trees are frozen
> even the mailbox is frozen
> & I'm getting a little chilly myself

He journeys between Muse and everyday reality, between the girl
he goes out to meet ('my most delicate imagining') and the dwell-
ing held together by pounded thumbnails, his necessary haven (the
journey too is necessary!) On his return:

> the WIND
> steals all my internal heat
> my heavy body is doped with wind and cold
> and the house door
> drags me into the hall
> and the door knob
> is a handle I hold onto the sky with

Purdy is not a poet of 'gems' (his discursiveness alone would
make that difficult), but *The Cariboo Horses* is a rich book of which
much more could be said. A grasp of the central image in 'One
Rural Winter', however, may convey the book's substance and the
core of Purdy's work, the quality which endows the best of it with
its peculiar excellence. A lone figure struggles with a harsh environment to reach the goal where he can commune with his imag-

ination? Or is it just a guy answering the need to relieve himself, in difficult conditions? In entering Purdy's world it is hazardous to forget the necessary existence of either the shithouse or the sky.

Today a common feature of Canadian poetry is the book with the single, explicit (usually factual) theme: Louis Riel, the mounties. Some good books have been produced this way, some very dull, but the interesting thing is the desire to shape a book of verse around a significant theme, often the pioneer quality of Canadian life in the not-too-distant past. Al Purdy, still in his fifties, anticipated much of this in the explorations of his own work, and perhaps his *North of Summer* (1967) started the whole trend.

Never particularly conscious of the poetry of epiphany or the lyric moment, he travels, steno's notebook at the ready, going after poems. The assumption seems to be that, given contact with his sensibility, there are poems everywhere. His task is to draw them forth. In *North of Summer,* using a familiar figure, he evokes his own role:

> listening
> reaching under the stone
> to the far side of the world
> into space and beyond space

He is both maker and medium. In a 'Postscript' to *North of Summer* he details the external circumstances of his 1965 Arctic visit, starting from Frobisher Bay, going north to the Arctic Circle, journeying by canoe to the Kikastan Islands in Cumberland Sound (merely recording the names here gives the project a degree of concreteness). Writing at every stage of the way, afterwards, as he tells us, he 'worked on the poems for more than a year'. Thus we may adduce at least two distinct stages of deliberateness, of calculation in working these poems, which have been described as 'journalism'. Yet there is a further element in which,

> On the country road these spring days
> odd things happen
> brown men in mukluks climb
>   the snake fences
> with Norris Whitney's sheep
> near Ameliasburg

and I'm afraid to mention it
at the village store

Purdy knows his facts, and carries them lightly, but his *attention,* concentration, does not stop there. He absorbs first the book information, next the on-the-spot details. He does not pretend to be other than what he is, a traveller come to look and listen, but his opening lines (above) should warn us that something more will emerge. When he ponders, 'About the poems: they seem to me like a set of binoculars thru which you can view the Arctic . . . What I'm doing here is providing my own particular kind of optic glass', the remark has more range than may seem so at first, for everywhere he is conscious of the Arctic in the perspective of Western history, of 'the Innuit / The People / these unknowable human beings / who have endured 5000 years / on the edge of the world', who yet fit into the world of Achilles, Picasso, Odysseus, and Maple Leaf Gardens.

Purdy carries the book with ease, enabled by a verse-line which he handles consummately well. Capturing the bleak, brooding quality of the landscapes, he is never pretentious and his characteristic self-mockery does not desert him (see, for example, the witty 'When I Sat Down to Play the Piano', another outhouse story). Notebook-carrying Purdy sees himself as one of the 'white men / who were also visitors / and thought to be human', for better or worse bringing the twentieth century to this arid outpost. If this were all the book has to offer it would be thin pickings indeed, but behind the cultural ambassador is another Purdy, the one whose vision may on occasion stretch to 'the other side' of things:

> the sea crowded with invisible animals
> the horizon full of vague white shapes
> of icebergs in whispering lagoons where
> Old Squaw ducks are going
>   'ouw-ouw-ouw'
> And I think of the other side of that sound
> I have to
>   because it gathers everything
> all the self-deception and phoniness
> of my lifetime into an empty place
> and the RUNNER IN THE SKIES
> I invented
>   as symbol of the human spirit

crashes like a housefly
my only strength is blind will

to go on

A pity, perhaps, that the latter part of this passage is over-explicit
to a degree, but the lines touch on something notable: first, Purdy's
image of the spirit as 'runner', second his puritanical conception of
life as 'blind will', pitted against 'self-deception and phoniness'. As
ground for such a struggle he has a preference for spartan landscapes and there may be more than a touch of resemblance between
this 'empty place' at 'the edge of the world' and the country
around Belleville.

'I don't think the poet is ever not looking for subjects.' — Al Purdy

Like Earle Birney, to whom *Wild Grape Wine* (1968) is dedicated,
Purdy has taken to travelling a great deal. He told Gary Geddes
'somehow or other one uses up one's past', and later added, 'I like
to think of a continual becoming and a changing and a moving'.
Wild Grape Wine (as its blurb tells us) includes poems on Mexican
poverty and post-revolutionary Cuba, but the book's considerable
strength derives largely from Ontario poems such as 'Wilderness
Gothic', 'St Francis in Ameliasburg' or 'Skeleton by an Old
Cedar', or from the pre-history of the North American sub-
continent in 'The Runners'.

Since 1968 four major Purdy collections have appeared. Two of
these together, *Love in a Burning Building* (1970) and *Selected Poems*
(1972), are a substantial retrospective. The others, *Wild Grape Wine*
and the recent *Sex and Death,* (1973) are both extensive and wide-
ranging. The moment seems propitious for a summing-up, but this
is not easy since Purdy is both elusive and multi-faceted. Joker,
traveller, mythographer, political commentator, wine-maker, common man, archaeologist, poet— all these versions of Purdy have
been ably touched upon by MacCallum, Bowering, Lee, Atwood,
Geddes, and others. Something beyond these Purdy *personae* is at
issue. Margaret Atwood perhaps located it when, reviewing *North
of Summer,* she said: 'One of Purdy's specialities is catching himself
in the act.'

Purdy has proved many things: among them, that a boy from
Hicksville with the worst, most platitudinous and tum-ti-tum sense

of poetry can become a subtle and sensitive craftsman, and that through the imagination it is possible to see Canada clearly and see it whole (however spreadeagled and sectarian it may seem geographically and politically). To my sense, however, he has one major problem to solve before moving on.

Wallace Stevens put it that the distinctive characteristic of good poems is 'the presence of the determining personality'. In that sense Purdy is very much present, but often *too much* and too self-consciously. Sometimes he is too obviously the succinct recorder: details with moral, as in 'Beothuck Indian Skeleton in Glass Case (St. John's Museum, Nfld.)', which opens, flatly, 'Six feet three inches / a man of 40'. This kind of economy may easily be justified (and, in fact, is essential), but it can also have a certain air of banality, like the TV ads in which the husband lies beside his wife in bed at night after having taken his indigestion pill. Dialogue: *She:* 'Feel good?' *He:* 'Feel great!' Of course thousands of dollars depend on the omission of those pronouns, etc., but the outcome is a travesty of honest conversation. When Purdy's notebook is more evident than his spark, his efficiency more obvious than his insight, his work can resemble that ad. This plus a certain discursiveness prevents *Wild Grape Wine* from being as satisfying as *The Cariboo Horses*. Yet there is much excellence in the book: the almost uncanny depth and rightness of 'The Runners' (a touchstone, as Dennis Lee notes in his eloquent response to the poem), the zest of 'The Winemaker's Beat-Etude' (with its 'GREAT JEROBOAM / that booms inside from the land beyond the world'—presumably the land of the Sky Runner, found in a moment of earthly release), and the crucial discovery of *a tone of voice* in such cornerstone poems as 'Wilderness Gothic', 'Roblin Mills', 'The Runners', and 'My Grandfather's Country', in which Purdy appears to be establishing Canada's psychic bearings.

That he could not do with vague generalizations, and he achieves his tone partly by knowing a great deal, factually. Avid bookstore browser and collector of Canadiana, Purdy has grounding in Canadian history, ancient history, world affairs, art, myth, psychology. Since the basis of most of his verse now is story-telling (note how, in recent books, the characteristic poem length is two to three pages), he can deploy a great deal of *information*. A resulting journalistic element in the poems is an added dimension of self-consciousness. Self-admittedly, he goes looking for poems the way another man would go on safari. *Sex and Death* contains great slabs of poem got from a trip to South Africa. Nothing wrong with that, except that it presents a paradigm case of the risks involved. Going to South Africa one is, inevitably, the liberal visiting fascist/racist stronghold. From such a preconception, the poems can begin to write themselves.

Purdy's Ontario poems *feel* (I, as immigrant, can suggest no more) as if they have a deep rightness not present in his South Africa / Cuba / Etcetera 'trips'. In *Sex and Death* particularly one encounters the journalist who goes to the places he writes about in order to authenticate his 'literary product' ('At Acayucan we stopped / to water and feed / the engine's horses').

Deliberately sought 'experience' has as its corollary in this instance the poet as observer at a distance, able to throw in an occasional knowing aside ('I'm being too clever about it of course'). Purdy seems to have given up, for the most part, the participatory verb-forms of *The Cariboo Horses*. Often a static, ponderous quality has seeped into the verse. One cannot but admire 'Hiroshima Poems', for example, for their competence and unexceptionable sentiments, as a man's offering of 'a part of himself not even original' but necessary. Necessary obeisances to the horrors of our world, such poems are not the true depths of Purdy. Rather the essential tone of voice (the voice as essence), the equally essential participation, reach us again in, say, 'The Horseman of Agawa'. Here we are not buzzed by overt reference to 'identity questions', but watch a reaching out for a 'secret knowing' beyond words. Purdy is beginning to grope not only with the problem of 'Where is here?', but with the ontology of selfhood.

What I am saying, I suppose, is that many poems *display* too much Al and Co., but *reveal* too little Purdy. Perhaps it is churlish, however, to ask for an artist attributes he does not wish for himself. Purdy ends the main part of *Sex and Death:*

> And we the third persons
> are a kind of privileged children
> suspend judgment sometimes
> and not loving ourselves
> love the mystery
> and do not understand it

The poem is called 'Observing Persons'. But what mystery is this? As I have worked with Purdy's poems, ranging from doubt as to their value, to the excitement of fully discovering a zestfully genuine poet, to the sense of some elusive element in the work (a depth glimpsed, fleetingly, occasionally, then gone, gone), I have been reading also the new edition of Merton's *Seeds of Contemplation:* 'Contemplation . . . is the experiential grasp of reality as *subjective,* not so much 'mine' (which would signify 'belonging to the external self') but 'myself' in existential mystery'. What has this to do with Purdy?

Here and there in his work of the past few years are poems in which Purdy the personality and pundit is completely submerged, where the sense of subject is totally empathetic:

> And I do not know why
> whether because I cannot hunt with the others
> and they laugh
> or because the things I have done are useless
> as I may be useless
> but there is something here I must follow
> into myself to find
> outside myself in the mammoth
> beyond the scorn of my people
> who are still my people
> my own pain and theirs
> joining the shriek that does not end
> that is inside me now
> The shriek flows back into the mammoth
> returning from sky and stars
> finds the cave and its dark entrance
> brushes by where I stand on tip-toes
> to scratch the mountain body on stone
> moves past me into the body itself
> toward a meaning I do not know
> and perhaps should not . . .

Far deeper than surface coruscations, fluid in movement and of the exact tonal essence, in such poetry participation and self-definition merge in a way which suggests (through vibrations as much as words) that Purdy may yet take us to realms unexplored. Thoreau once said, 'I have travelled much in Concord'. Purdy may have the means to do likewise around Ameliasburg. A year or two ago he professed to be 'running out of places' to travel to. But then he was referring only to places *out there.*

[No. 61, 1974]

Poet as Philosopher
Louis Dudek

Douglas Barbour

Louis Dudek, along with Irving Layton and Raymond Souster, was one of the prime movers of modern Canadian poetry in the 1940s. As members of John Sutherland's *First Statement* group, these writers brought a new excitement to the poetry of the time, a brash vulgarity which revealed their proletarian adventurousness. Layton and Souster are today very popular with the poetry-reading public. Dudek has failed to attract a similarly wide readership, and during the poetry explosion of the past decade, has managed to publish only one book (*Atlantis*, 1967). To most younger readers and poets he is known less for his poetry than for his élitist statements about recent Canadian poets, like those which fill his *Canadian Literature* 41 article on poetry in English during the sixties. The recent publication of his *Collected Poetry*[1] is thus a most welcome event, for it provides the needed opportunity to read and assess the whole body of his poetry.

For a reader not very familiar with Dudek's work, the overwhelming fact about *Collected Poetry* is the way in which it demonstrates how much of a piece his poetry is. Dorothy Livesay[2] has said that Dudek had not yet found his voice in the early poems of *Unit of Five* (1944), *East of the City* (1946), and *Cerberus* (1952). This is true, of course, as true as such a statement can be about any young apprentice artist. What struck me, however, as I read through this book, was the way in which certain approaches to subject matter, certain ways of articulating what can only be called arguments, form a part of his poetic *content* right from the start. Although he doesn't find the proper form for his 'statement' right away, he is always striving for an intellectually tough poetry. Even in the early poems, where his control of 'voice' is weak, the philosophic tone that marks all his serious poetry is present.

One of Dudek's continuing interests has been the *process* of thought. His poems often provide paradigms of that process, or icons of the results of that process. They move from a formal, traditional metric towards a prose-like, argumentative, 'open' metric, which often resolves (in the longer poems, and especially *Atlantis*), into a near-prose of short maxims which remind me of La Rochefoucauld. Dorothy Livesay, writing before the appearance of *Atlantis*, noted this tendency towards prose statement but concluded that his 'prose content, like his prose syntax, is a kind of disguise.'³ But such an early poem as 'On Poetry', for example, is full of abstractions and presents a definite argument; it is not merely a disguise of those things:

> The flame of a man's imagination should be organic
>   with his body,
> coincident with an act, like an igniting spark.
> But mostly, he fails in the act
> and expels his bad humour in visions. A man curses,
> seeing the thing he hates in pain, cursed by his vision:
> this is poetry, action unrealized:
>   what we want most we imagine most, like self-abusing boys.

Later in this poem, Dudek suggests Shakespeare 'should have been all his monarchs', an argument closely analogous to Borges' in 'Everything and Nothing'. The point of this comparison is that Borges, too, is presenting a subtle, philosophical, aesthetic argument, and he does so in prose: the medium considered most proper for that kind of *intellectual* subtlety.

'On Poetry' is interesting partly because it is an early poem in which Dudek essays the open form. But he does not stick with it, and many of the poems of the next few years (I think they are from the forties and early fifties) are in traditional forms, like the quatrains of 'Flower Bulbs'. This very interesting poem, which is a love poem of sorts, is yet very reminiscent of metaphysical poetry in the way it uses an image from nature as a basis for a closely argued and witty proposition. The argument is just as important as the lovely image which informs it, if not more so.

The poems about the city, usually New York, from this period, relate to the social-consciousness poetry of the thirties, but once again reveal the philosophical interest with which Dudek approaches all his subjects. They are socio-political meditations, and would be entirely suitable to a book of essays by a left-wing historian. 'Line and Form' is one of the most interesting of the pre-*Europe* poems, because it is so obviously an essay in the aesthetics of universal creation. Aesthetics is one of the major areas of philosophy that interest Dudek, and the concerns of this poem will reappear throughout all his later poetry.

> Eternal forms.
> The single power, working alone
>   rounds out a parabola
>   that flies into the infinite;
> but the deflected particle
>   out of that line, will fetch a frisk
>   of sixes and eights
>   before it vanishes:
> an ocean arrested
>   by sudden solid
>   ripples out in the sand.
> So this world of forms, having no scope for eternity,
>   is created
>   in the limitation of what would be complete and perfect,
> achieving virtue only
>   by the justice of its compromises.

This is only the final third of the poem, but that last sentence, with its opening 'So', the 'Thus' or 'Therefore' of this particular demonstration, perfectly illustrates the argumentative method Dudek is using.

Even in such an obviously philosophical poem, however, Dudek makes use of what is an obsessive image in his work, and that is the great Sea itself. Here the line 'an ocean arrested' is both a major link in his argument and a reference to the vast chaos of possibilities that the sea has always represented to man. It is a natural reference for Dudek to make, for he has always been possessed by the sea; it appears in all his work, from the early tone poem, 'The Sea', through *Europe* and *En Mexico*, to *Atlantis* and beyond. Although his poetry tends to be intellectual and lacking in obvious emotionalism, the sea always provokes emotional outbursts from him. It is his true muse.

Dudek wrote a lot of short poems in the fifties, including the formal and philosophical love poems collected under the heading

'Pure Science' and the various humorous poems and parodies that were published in *Laughing Stocks* (1958). Personally I find few of Dudek's 'humorous poems' funny, and I don't think his sense of humour is amenable to poetry. Too often such poems telegraph their punchline and utterly fail to provide the 'surprise' of a good joke. Arthur Koestler says that the 'unexpected' climax to a good joke must be 'both unexpected and perfectly logical—but of a logic not usually applied to this type of situation.'[4] It is precisely this 'logical unexpectedness' which is missing in Dudek's poems. His parodies of Canadian poets, however, especially those of A. J. M. Smith, A. M. Klein, and Irving Layton, are often dead on, and reveal an acute *critical* wit.

The fifties are crucial years in Dudek's career, however, because during them he wrote the two long poems, *Europe* (1955) and *En Mexico* (1958). It was in these poems that he came into full command of his voice, and it was there that he truly became a philosophical poet. *Europe* is an extended personal essay, a travelogue by a philosopher with a gifted and far-ranging eye. The branches of philosophy which engage Dudek's mind—philosophy of history, politics, aesthetics (and art-history), and ethics—all appear in *Europe* and in *En Mexico*. All will reappear in *Atlantis*.

I think it is important to note that Dudek is a student of modern poetry and a follower of Ezra Pound. Unlike many of the younger practitioners of the popular poetry of primitivism he lashed out against in 'Poetry in English', he is a highly educated student of poetic tradition, especially of twentieth-century modernism. To him the following point has the force of a prime-directive:

> Integrity, we should remember, has been the prime virtue of the great twentieth-century poets. The entire modern movement was a retreat from the idols of the marketplace to the private household gods of art and knowledge.[5]

I think there can be little doubt that Dudek has practised that kind of integrity and faithfully served those gods. He is the only one of the three *Cerberus* poets even to attempt a truly long poem. He has walked the paths of his art alone. If he has not been completely successful in his poetic quest, surely one of the reasons is that he had to do it all by himself: he had no other poets in Canada to share his particular problems and efforts.

Europe is an oddly likeable piece of writing. Although I am not at all sure that it fully succeeds as poetry, I find myself completely won over by the man behind the work. This says a great deal for the poem, for I began the *Collected Poetry* with a definite bias against him, based mostly on my disagreement with many of his criticisms of his fellow poets in 'Poetry in English'. In *Europe* the poet shows such a genuinely and engagingly interesting mind, uses that mind to deal with such interesting materials, and expresses his opinions with such a refreshing forthrightness, I found it impossible to dislike him. In this he is like Ruskin, another traveller in Europe, to whom he refers occasionally in the poem. As he continues to speak on various subjects during the poem's progress, he wins our respect because his intellectual engagement with them is so clear and intelligent. He is also like Ruskin in creating a series of little personal essays, even if they appear to be parts of a poem. Although they contain many richly poetic images and metaphors, the very stuff of poetry, to bolster their various arguments, they are basically essays, as, for example, the lesson in art-history that is No. 50:

> The Greeks were fine, but French classicism
> using the Greek for its own purpose,
> smooth hypocrisy, conceit, & the display
>   of that corruption, *le bon goût,*
> —the worst taste in manners or in art
>   the world has ever seen—
> spoiled two centuries of European art,
> opened the arts to worse corruption still—
>   the monstrous sugar teeth
> of 'money' and 'amusement': here you see
>   in Chartres
> art is no entertainment, it does not amuse;
> money paid for it, but it paid for
>   something that the sculptor really preferred;
> pride was satisfied, but it was pride
>   in objects, the full scale
> of human performance—they worked for this, gladly.
> The wedge of ignorance entered Europe
>   with a blind idolatry
> of Greece and Rome; you can see it
>   as a straight line from the 15th century down,
> 'art for art', copying the Greek forms,

shape without sense, imitating
          imitations, dramatic motion, sensuality
for the boudoir, decorativeness
to make room for gold, for size.
After this, there was no honesty
whether in art or trade, to fight off the incisor
of the pure profiteer, the hog
with his snout in the mire, his belly in shit.
The Gothic tower had fallen,
          the last craftsman
dropped his hammer; it has come
to all of us, poets, advertisers,
dance hall singers and all,
we make our pilgrimage to Chartres, without praying beads;
look at the Virgin helpless, and up to the great dome
          where the light seems to rise and fall.

This is witty, and provocative of thought, but despite its appearance, and the rhythmic control of certain parts, it would strike many readers as very different, at bottom, from what they know as poetry. This reaction may merely reveal their ignorance of certain aspects of modern poetry, as Dudek suggests, but the periodic sentences and the syntax of those grand periods, are surely qualities normally associated with scintillating prose. This is also true of the discussion of the true meaning of Greece in No. 70, and the marvellously allusive politico-historical commentary on the nature of evil in No. 78. I kept reading them for their prose values, despite their appearance on the page. It would appear that Dudek has carried Pound's dictum, 'that poetry should be written at least as well as prose',[6] to its limit. Pound also said, 'The prose artist has shown the triumph of his intellect and one knows that such triumph is not without its sufferings by the way, but by the verses one is brought upon the passionate moment. This moment has brought with it nothing, that violates the prose simplicities. The intellect has not found it, but the intellect has been moved.'[7] What one misses in so many of Dudek's poems are the 'passionate moments' that would lift us out of ourselves. What we find, however, are qualities of meditative vision and intense ratiocination that are seldom to be found in any other Canadian poet.

In *En Mexico* Dudek continues to work with the open form, the long, discursive, essay-like 'canto', and the philosophical voice he had developed in *Europe*. *En Mexico* displays a new mastery of rhythm, however, in many of its parts. In 1958 Dudek wrote a fascinating article for his magazine *Delta* entitled 'A Note on Metrics'. It is an obvious development from the early essays by Pound on the subject and reveals the depth of Dudek's concern with metrics. The Note is his major statement on the uselessness of traditional forms for the contemporary poet. Although he continued to use those forms in the fifties, he has not used them in any of his published work since 1958. It appears that the Note was the final nail in the coffin of traditional verse, as far as Dudek was concerned, for in it he insists that if you write in one of the formal metres, especially iambic, you 'thus neglect the essential music, which is that of your sounds, *as they fit the content of your poetry*, and you produce for the most part an empty rattle of sounds.'[8] *En Mexico*, and all the poems following it, are written in the light of that statement. Dudek's rhythmic achievements in this poem have been pointed out by Dorothy Livesay in *Canadian Literature* 30. His achievements in *content* are every bit as important. *En Mexico* is a more successful whole than *Europe* because of Dudek's new mastery of rhythm, but the centre of interest in the poem remains the philosophizing that the trip to Mexico engenders.

No. 3 of *En Mexico* is a commentary on religion, full of the short maxims that I find so fascinating in his poems:

> Optimism is foolish. Life can only be
> tragic, no matter what its success . . .
>
> Knowledge is neither necessary nor possible
> to justify the turning
> of that huge design.

He achieves here a kind of juxtaposition of epigrams which is far more powerful than mere statement could be. The mixture of the maxims and the images of life in Mexico creates a powerful commentary on contemporary civilization, just as Dudek wants it to. Because the whole poem provides such a resonant context for them, these short aphoristic statements have a power and interest that is entirely lacking in Irving Layton's 'Aphs' from *The Whole Bloody Bird*. There is a decorum to Dudek's epigrams which the boring and boorish statements of Layton lack, and that decorum is provided by the unity of tone of the whole poem. It is also interesting to see, as in so many philosophical works, the statement, again

justified by the whole context, that 'Knowledge is neither necessary nor possible'.

No. 4 is a description of life in the people, of 'America, the
Continent, dancing'. Here Dudek displays another technique, that
of 'borrowing' the voice of another poet to make a point. In a
sequence climaxing with the lines:

> *now!* say the strings in singing consummation
> we have touched the life-giving current,
> > making a relay!
> Take it from us, you swarming futures!
> Sing, as we now sing!

he uses the voice of Whitman to further the argument of his poem.
These 'vocal borrowings' serve the same purpose as quotations
would in a literary or philosophical discussion. Finally he reaches
the philosophical climax of the poem, flowing in the way of logical discourse out of what came before:

> Form is the visible part of being.
> We know the logic of its adaptations,
> a signature of individuality, of integrity,
> the end of perfect resolution—
> but not the inner stir.
>
> Rest. Rest in that great affair.

The ending is a fitting one for such a poem, and it attains a
powerful philosophical intensity. In many ways *En Mexico* stands as
Dudek's most successful poem: an organic, unified whole.

'Lac En Coeur', another fairly long poem of the time, is a quiet
meditation full of questions about life. It is a lovely small personal
poem, an essay from 'the mind and heart of love' of the natural
world around the poet. But it is a philosophical meditation, shar-
ing, as do parts of *Atlantis*, the concerns of such poems as Yeats's
'Lapis Lazuli' and the later *Cantos*, but without their 'passionate
intensity' (which may be a good thing, but 'passionate intensity' in
'the best' is not the same as it is in 'the worst').

Dudek the poet seemed to drop out of sight from 1958 until 1967
(although excerpts from *Atlantis* began appearing in *Yes* as early as
1965), the very years when Layton and others were reaping their
first major popular successes. *Atlantis* (1967) showed that he had not

retired from the field but had engaged his muse in a lengthy and difficult struggle.

Atlantis is not the unqualified success that *En Mexico* was. It is Dudek's longest piece of sustained writing, gathering all his themes and ideas into a single massive argument. Yet in the final analysis it fails because he is unable to incorporate everything he wants in quite the manner he wants. Had he paid attention to W. C. Williams' *Paterson*, rather than just the *Cantos*, he might have learned an invaluable lesson: that if you do use actual prose, it can mix with your own poetry without much trouble, so long as you juxtapose with care, but, if you merely make your own poetry too prosaic in places, the obviously 'poetic' parts of your poem will clash with the rest. This is what happens in *Atlantis*, and it is a definite fault in the poem.

The tone of *Atlantis*, from the very beginning, is that discursive tone that presents the personal essayist, once again *en voyage*, once again looking around and noting with great precision and wit what he sees, and then reflecting upon it. The casualness of the speech ('Speaking of coral, the white whirling wave / behind the ship / is like a Japanese painting of a wave') does not mask, but subtly underlines the wide range of allusions and ideas the speaker commands. This tone, this manner of speaking, allows for a great breadth of material, but not for everything. In fact it is a curious paradox of this poem that the sections of 'pure poetry' are both the most powerful, and the most out-of-place, parts of it. Near the end of The Prologue, Dudek catches hold of the idea of Atlantis itself, and he is moved to write some lovely and evocative lines:

> Here nothing is real, only a few
>   actions, or words,
> bits of Atlantis, are real . . .
> One day at sea, at sunset,
>   when the long rays struck the water,
> it seemed to me the whole sea was living
>   under the surface motion;
>
> the waves moved like a great cosmic animal
> twisting and turning its muscular body
> under the grey glistening skin.

Yet even here, in the midst of such writing, he feels the need to inject some moral reflections on the very next page. These lines contain the 'voice' of the rest of the poem, the Ruskinian figure reflecting upon Nature ('it seemed to me'), but they soar above the prosaic philosophizing that is that figure's usual mode of address.

In the body of the poem Dudek continues to reflect upon things; he discusses town planning, moral philosophy, aesthetic history, the concept of pity, the reasons for art, and much else. He even goes in for a very esoteric aquarium list, which he then transforms, through some very precise description, into a lyrical celebration of the many varieties of ocean-going life-forms. All these discussions are fascinating as discussions; some of them fall terribly flat as poetry. One need only compare his reflections on the nature of evil with Auden's 'Musée de Beaux Arts', for example, to see this. The concentration of the Auden poem gives it a force that is entirely lacking in Dudek's rather abstruse, though very interesting, discussion. Or take his comment,

> This voyage is almost over. I think
> how everything will go on here
> as before. As it must. And yet I know
> that somehow I am a part of it, in it
> for good—or I do not live at all.

and compare it with the sardonic and yet loving appreciation of the same fact in George Johnston's concentrated epics, 'In It' and 'O Earth, Turn!'. This statement should be a 'passionate moment' and yet it isn't, quite.

The Epilogue to *Atlantis* almost saves the whole poem. This is a poetry like that of the late *Cantos*: pristine, the language pure and magnificent as it apotheosizes 'Atlantis', that region of the human / divine soul for which Dudek has quested through all his poems. The first two pages of the Epilogue shine with the very 'Light' they celebrate, but the effort of such an ecstatic flight proves too great, and the poet returns to earth, except for a few leaps of a line or two, for the remaining five pages of the poem. Still it is beautiful; it is a passionate moment, however brief, and yet it does seem somehow out of place in this particular poem. It is not that Dudek is wrong in his approach to poetry; he is following a major modern tradition, one whose value has been proven time and again. It is merely that in *this* poem he has failed to weld all his various elements into a harmonious sculpture of words.

Since the publication of *Atlantis* Dudek has written a number of short 'Jeux & Divertissements'. They are all poems with a point to make, many of them about our sexual lives. 'Erotic Tropes', for example, perhaps the best of the lot, is full of a wit reminiscent of Oscar Wilde's prose. Dudek obviously does not consider these poems important. The groups of longer poems, collected in the section 'Reflections After Atlantis', are important to him, I think.

Basically they continue the approach worked out in *Europe, En Mexico*, and *Atlantis*. 'The Demolitions', an elegy for destroyed architecture, is essentially a lyrical autobiographical essay. 'Canada: Interim Report' is a bitter politically oriented polemic. There are some rather neat juxtapositions but the tone is too angry, the bitterness too diffuse; it all sounds like a variant on the poems Souster and Layton had in *The New Romans*, and that kind of poetry is something Dudek has always, until this poem, had the good sense to ignore. The philosopher ranting can provide little pleasure or stimulation, for he is using language in a manner, for him, meretricious. 'A Circle Tour of the Rockies' is a mistake from start to finish, but not for the same reasons as 'Canada: Interim Report', and it is a mistake of major interest, which also differentiates it from that poem. It is another very good essay, and one could imagine Ruskin, or even Dr Johnson, writing it in prose. But to even *think* that such language would work in a poem about mountains betrays the kind of one-sidedness Dudek's preoccupations have led him to. There is absolutely no sense of a response to the overwhelming (*emotionally* overwhelming!) *grandeur* of the Rockies.

> Clear it to the peneplane of un-being,
> an empty consciousness, space-time, a blank page,
> and something begins again. God knows
> maybe just a new area of suffering. Of experience.

Is this all he can say? These words are refractory in this context, they are not the right material for a poem. Compare Ralph Gustafson's 'Rocky Mountain Poems' in *Ixion's Wheel*: by a variety of strategies they immerse the reader with the poet in the many experiences the mountains offer the sensitive observer. Where Dudek's poem discusses all kinds of things *around* the basic and absolute fact of the mountains, refusing to confront them in their being, almost as if they were unnecessary to the discussion, Gustafson takes us right into the experience of them with all the 'visceral drive, committed passion'⁹ Dudek has accused him of lacking. If the mountains were unnecessary, they should never have been invoked at all. The point is that Dudek failed to recognize the limitations of his poetic; he did not understand that it was not meant to deal with the kind of grandeur (the Awesomeness that the great Romantics felt in the presence of mountains) the Rocky Mountains are. His refusal to use image or metaphor to any extent in the poem is the measure of that failure of recognition.

The last poem in the book is the beginning of what may become another very long poem called 'Continuation I'. It is another attempt to use 'only a language / to contain the essentials that matter, in all the flux of illusion' to construct an artifact of words. Once again a man of rich philosophic experiences is reflecting upon all the things which interest him. I hope he will keep it going.

There is a fascinating aside on the poet in 'Continuation I': 'O the poet that incredible madman,' says Dudek. 'He is possessed with possibility.' These are strong words, yet they have authority. Dudek has always, like his mentors, especially Ezra Pound, been 'possessed with possibility'; that is why his philosophizing has been so rewarding, to him, and to his readers. But he is no 'incredible madman'; all too plainly the opposite. I see him as a product of the Enlightenment who has been forced to cope with certain aspects of humanity (the 'Evil' of the twentieth century which he has written so many pages about) the eighteenth century did not have to face. But he seems somewhat out of place, really, in a world which is still living in the Romantic Age, for Romanticism has touched him only slightly, if at all. Perhaps that is an overstatement, but I think it helps to define him and his art. Pound was just such a madman, but Dudek pleases us most when he is rational, meditative, the philosopher to be listened to and argued with, but not possessed by.

We are overburdened these days with 'possessed' and 'incredible' madmen in poetry. But there is no one else to speak to us in the reasonable, honourable, voice of intellectual integrity that is Louis Dudek's. Too many younger writers have been ignorant of his work and the possibilities for poetry that it represents.

[No. 53, 1972]

[1] Delta Canada (Montreal, 1971).

[2] 'The Sculputre of Poetry', *Canadian Literature* 30, 1966, 26-35.

[3] *Ibid.*, 30.

[4] *The Act of Creation* (London, 1969), pp. 33-4.

[5] 'Poetry in English', *Canadian Literature* 41, 1969, 114.

[6] 'The Prose Tradition in Verse', *Literary Essays*, ed. T. S. Eliot (London, 1954), p. 373.

[7] 'The Serious Artist', *Ibid.*, p. 53.

[8] 'A Note on Metrics', *Delta* 5, October 1958, 17.

[9] *Ibid.*, 120.

Search and Discovery
Margaret Avison's Poetry

Daniel W. Doerksen

In 'Love (III)', the poem which concludes his 'picture of many spiritual Conflicts', George Herbert portrays the culmination of the religious quest in unexpected discovery. Unaware that she herself will one day describe such experience, the Margaret Avison of *Winter Sun* feels intrigued into envious comment. Having probed about in a world of Heraclitean flux and materialistic preoccupation, she marvels that

> George Herbert—and he makes it plain—
> Guest at this same transfiguring board
> *Did sit and eat.*[1]

And indeed Miss Avison's own poetical achievement in *Winter Sun* (1960) and *The Dumbfounding* (1966) merits consideration as spiritual quest and discovery. The first of her books is marked by a continual seeking, while the second speaks of fulfilment in lyrics which have been hailed as 'among the finest religious poems of our time'.[2] Aside from sheer literary excellence, what makes the two collections remarkable is that, far from being tacked on as a 'Christian' afterthought to her previous verse, Miss Avison's later poems seem to grow out of her earlier searching ones in a sequence which, if not that of simple cause and effect, is yet that of authentic experience.[3] Search and discovery are thus like two sides of one coin, or like two main parts of that one thing Claudel declares every poet is born to say in the totality of his works. In this essay I propose to examine Margaret Avison's poetry of search and of discovery, noting the way in which search leads into discovery.

If to be secular means to be fully engaged in the world of the 'here and now', then all of Miss Avison's poetry is secular. If to be religious means to care about meaning, to have (in Tillich's language) an 'ultimate concern', little of her poetry is not religious. The search for the ultimately significant in life stands out as a main feature of *Winter Sun*, but it is not always obtrusive. 'The Apex Animal' manifests a leisurely, playful curiosity as to the nature of 'the One . . . Who sees, the ultimate Recipient / of what happens.' Fancy suggests to the poet, as it surely could not to a Christian, that this ultimate being is none other than a cloud formation shaped like a horse's head, since after all the latter has a commanding view of things in its 'patch of altitude / troubled only by clarity of weather' and seems free of matters in 'mortal memory'. Under the fanciful surface of the poem, and hidden away before the parenthetical conclusion, there lurks a note of concern about the human individual, in this case the clerk whose 'lustreless life' has been touched by the 'ointment of mortality'.

'Dispersed Titles', both more serious and more profound, also displays an ambivalence as to the spiritual nature of its quest. The 'titles' of the title form a poem of their own, which aids in threading together the central metaphor of flight in its various transformations:

> [FLIGHT]
> [HAS ROOTS]
> BUT IS CUT OFF
> EXCEPT FROM ALL ITS SELVES
> THE EARTH HAS OTHER ROOTS AND SELVES
> THE NAMELESS ONE DWELLS IN HIS TENTS
> AND 'UP' IS A DIRECTION.

The 'flight', beginning as the modern scientific conquest of the air, is soon traced back to that other flight made possible for Kepler by his 'Orpheus', the Danish astronomer Tycho Brahe. The escape from the old cosmology ('the defiant break / with cycles') has left a 'weird hollow under the solar architrave', and the repeated invocation of Tycho Brahe (suggesting man's Narcissistic self-worship during the Renaissance and later) is accompanied by a feeling of corresponding emptiness within man himself:

> Something wrought by itself out of itself
> must bear its own

ultimates of heat and cold
nakedly, refusing
the sweet surrender.

For Tycho Brahe's sake I find myself,
but lose myself again for
so few are salvaged
in the sludge of the
ancestral singular.

Miring the person in the past rather than freeing him for flight, the new humanistic religion has apparently reversed the old paradox, 'he that loseth his life for my sake shall find it' (Matt. 10:30). But such awareness of modern man's plight does not in itself set him free, and while the poet senses something beyond the known ('Things I can't know I smell / as plainly as if invisible campfires / smoked'), the conclusion of the poem reveals no joy of discovery, but at best the musing of one who wishes there were a Christian reality, yet feels compelled to conclude that 'up', as the post-medieval cosmology demonstrates, is after all only a 'direction'. Thus, in the final twist of the basic metaphor, Christianity is seen as a 'flight' from reality. Still the vividness with which the poet depicts man's persistent idea that the world is a cosmic 'stage' betrays, despite the overt rejection, a quest for a reality beyond scientific humanism.

Much poetry of religious search reveals a potentiality for 'finding'. Paul Claudel once said that the past is 'an incantation of things to come, . . . the forever growing sum of future conditions.'[4] A Christian outcome may be implied but not necessitated by these poems. For the time being, the overt religious references point chiefly to frustration. The 'waste land' quality of the 'gardenless gardens'[5] in 'Not the Sweet Cicely of Gerardes Herball' is aggravated, strengthened by the allusions to myrrh and to 'rams-horn thickets', which like the gardens themselves mock the very thing they seem to promise. It is the very bleakness that is religious. Disheartening scenes are frequently encountered in *Winter Sun*: the 'Fallen, Fallen World' is a world of 'breathing murk and apprehension of / Slow sure estrangement from the sun', and 'enforced passage' through 'vacant corridors'. Life often seems like a 'choked day, swollen to almost total swamp'. Just as the piled-up consonants in these phrases help convey the sense of obstruction, the prevailing complexity of surface and structure throughout Miss Avison's first book reflects the difficulties of an as yet unrewarded search.

The quest proceeds under a variety of moods. The gentle speculation of 'The Apex Animal' yields to a more despairing note in the descriptions just given, and even to something like rebellion: 'Since Lucifer', the poet says, 'waiting is all / A rebel can.' Yet since there is still the search, questions are raised in 'Atlantis and the Department Store' as to whether she really is a rebel, and if so, what she is rebelling against. She proceeds to describe what she elsewhere calls 'dull repudiated house'—the earlier religious ideas which she 'did not hate' but nevertheless has rejected in favour of a secular world. The latter's 'splendid / Echoing stairways' she contrasts with the 'steady escalators' of organized religion.

But while the religious emporium's 'stunned' hierarchies ignore the life behind 'soiled concrete walls', the inquiring poet is only too much aware of the problems of modern society. 'The World Still Needs', Miss Avison entitles one poem, and the incompleted transitive verb suggests the endlessness of the need. She sees not only the 'communal cramp of understanding' which produces suburbia, and the masses, their eyes 'swimming with sleep' at a concert, but the lonely and confined housewife suffering literally and symbolically from 'Sore throat and dusty curtains' and the engineer 'watchful and blank' who 'had no Christmas worries / Mainly because it was the eve of April.' Colloquial phrases here mark an occasional movement towards simplified expression, which is to be more fully exploited in the poetry of discovery, and is in this poem accompanied by hints of coming harmony in the allusions to 'piano-tuners' and 'another spring'. But the lucidity and lyric power of another 'social problems ' poem is both witty and grim: the pun in the title of 'Mordent for a Melody' cleverly suggests just that combination of pungency and lilt that perfectly describes the poem itself. Fully alert to modern developments in science and society, Miss Avison adroitly mocks man's unthinking enthusiasm about them. However, it seems more typical of the searching poet to express a tragic realization with sympathy, as in 'Apocalyptic?' (the question mark in the title is significant), where the poet explores the possibility that a 'luminous' doom may be what frees us from the 'treadmill' of life.

Facing man's situation is an indispensable necessity, but, as the poet of *Winter Sun* realizes, what matters beyond that is how one responds to it. In these poems of search, Miss Avison explores various alternatives, but does not advocate any particular response —she is not ready yet, and the search itself, together with her hopes or fears, is all that she can share. In 'Unfinished After-Portrait', a poem of mourning, the poet expresses her own dissatisfaction with the repeated frustrations of her quest:

> Start-and-stop despairs of
> that royal moving
> keeps trying other sleights
> as rockets roar for the interlunar
> only to piffle out in
> the oceans suds.
>
> This trip and gamble cannot be
> the best, the looked-for.

The continually varying line-lengths, emphasized by indentation, reflect the erratic course of the searchings. Most of the remaining lines consist of just such 'Start-and-stop', such 'trip and gamble', and if the conclusion does not 'piffle out', it is only because the poet is willing to settle for a somewhat vague feeling of a 'human presence'.

An increasing sense of urgency in the quest seems to develop in some poems of *Winter Sun*. 'The Mirrored Man' articulates this increased intensity with artistic power. The opening rhymed quatrains (I quote the second and third) state the paradox of man's search, which is at once a refusal to search:

> So now we flee the Garden
> Of Eden, steadfastly.
> And still in our flight are ardent
> For lost eternity.
>
> We always turn our heads away
> When Canaan is at hand,
> Knowing it mortal to enjoy
> The Promise, not the Land.

This re-statement of the gist of George Herbert's 'Miserie' leads through a brief Miltonic evocation of a flaming sword and curse to a thoroughly modern yet, one feels, timeless picture of man's existential self-confrontation:

> So each of us conceals within himself
> A cell where one man stares into the glass
> And sees, now featureless the meadow mists,
> And now himself, a pistol at his temple,
> Grey, separate, wearily waiting.　　　　.

In the succeeding lines, alternative responses to the dilemma are pictured: ignoring the 'burden' of self and thus turning the quest into 'trivial ramblings'; despairing, and choosing actual or virtual suicide; or deliberately inculcating illusion in an exploitation of the self. Realizing the futility of each possibility, the poet sums up the search in haunting, poignant lines:

> All of us, flung in one
> Murky parabola,
> Seek out some pivot for significance,
> Leery of comets' tails, mask-merry,
> Wondering at the centre
> Who will gain access, search the citadel
> To its last, secret door?
> And what face will the violator find
> When he confronts the glass?

The passage itself mirrors the enigma that is life, its beginning and ending shrouded in mystery (implying some unknown Other in 'flung' and 'violator'), and even the relatively known element partaking teasingly of 'murk' as well as of precise mathematical pattern ('parabola'). The central lines beautifully sum up the search itself, suggesting its purpose, hopes, fears, and protective disguises. Such is man's quest, seen from the point of view of one who has not found—not basically, though sensitivity to everything observable makes possible moments of calm and wonder such as that recorded in 'Easter'.[6]

A delightful poem which strikes one as being earlier than the more serious ones in *Winter Sun* is 'Meeting together of Poles and Latitudes (In Prospect)'. This poem of search comments on the seeming unlikelihood that active energetic seekers should ultimately 'encounter at the Judgment Seat' the more relaxed, ambivalent explorers of life, who want 'for death that / Myth-clay, though / Scratch-happy in these (foreign) brambly wilds'; yet the poem implies that such a 'curious encounter', will take place. One feels that the poet herself in *Winter Sun* partakes first in the leisurely playful search, then in the more earnest kind. Of the latter kind are her poems on death. As the quest becomes more serious, she begins to think of ultimate judgement as a cataclysmic 'singeing-day' or a 'universal / Swallowing-up'. The poems 'Jael's Part' and 'Span' both, in carefully non-theological language, probe into divine judgements on sin.

Gradually in this first volume of Miss Avison's there begins to emerge a realization that some radical renewal, some transforming rebirth might be possible, and might, if attained, turn out to be the true goal of the search. In one poem the struggle to 'win belief in a new burgeoning' is, as the context shows, written off as idealistic, and impossible for the learned or the rebellious. The conclusion of 'Apocalyptics' is chiefly ironical and yet somewhat sympathetic to the idea of actually discovering a yet-not-evident harmony of the worlds:

> Bewildered
> Each broods in his own world
> But half believes
> Doctrines that promise to,
> After some few suppressions here and there,
> Orchestrate *for* all worlds;
> . . . . .
> Don't you suppose
> Anything could start it?
> > Music and all?
> > > Some time?

In 'Voluptuaries and Others', a very Auden-like poem in its long lines and blend of clinical precision with casual tone, Miss Avison speaks of two kinds of discovery, one being like that which occasioned Archimedes' 'Eureka':

> The kind of lighting up of the terrain
> That leaves aside the whole terrain, really,
> But signalizes, and compels, an advance in it.

The accumulation of human experience 'makes the spontaneous

jubilation at such moments' of scientific discovery 'less and less likely though', since genuine significance is only to be found in that 'other kind of lighting up / That shows the terrain comprehended, as also its containing space.' This latter illumination, then, is the object of the poet's search.

A poem of quest pregnant with hints of future discovery is 'Intra-Political: An Exercise in Political Astronomy'. The questions at its outset—the interrogative is appropriately frequent in these poems—concern the basic order (or disorder) of life, and man's right (or lack of right) to make judgements on the matter. The poet decides that 'nothing we know / who do know fearful things', yet feels the pressure of a 'precreation density':

> our darkness dreams of
> this heavy mass, this moil, this self-
> consuming endless squirm and squander, this
> chaos, singling off
> in a new Genesis.
> (Would it perhaps set swinging
> the little horn-gates to new life's
> illumined labyrinths if, released
> from stifling,
> creatures like us were planet-bathed
> in new-born Light?)
> (Glee dogs our glumness so.)

Such 'Dreams, even doubted, drive us', but the actual experience of being put to use by some power beyond us would be enough to break the pattern of life as a series of purely materialist transactions —to 'change this circular exchange'. Quite seriously, now, the poet, taking into account George Herbert's testimony, considers whether man, by 'daring to gambol' (i.e., to take himself less seriously as well as to risk), might yet call forth 'an immense answering / of human skies? / a new expectant largeness?'

Actual experiences, some vicarious, tend to confirm the expectation of impending transformation. In the half-allegorical poem 'Our Working Day may be Menaced' an acquaintance, Madeleine, is observed to undergo a remarkable spiritual experience:

> It was
> As if a spoke of the final sky
> Snagged her suddenly.

> For what seemed only one
> Queer moment, she was swept
> In some sidereal swerve,
> Blotted sheer out of time; then spurned
> Back to the pebbles of the path.

(The passage suggests one of the 'timeless' moments in T. S. Eliot's *Four Quartets*.) All who know Madeleine are skeptical, but the speaker muses: 'A calling from our calling?...Can they have appointed / A locus elsewhere for us?' and goes on to ponder a possible

> universal
> Swallowing-up
> (Proceedings against Madeleine alone
> Clearly being absurd).

Despite the secular language (which in fact registers engagement), the increasing impetus towards a new and perhaps Christian outlook is evident.

An experience which seems more than vicarious is described in one passage of the long poem which concludes *Winter Sun*, 'The Agnes Cleves Papers':

> One evening, just a year or two ago,
> The simple penetrating force of love
> Redeemed me, for the last perhaps. I've
>   seldom dared, since,
> To approach that; not that it would go out,
> But it might prove as centre of all
> Revolutions, and, defined,
> Limn with false human clarity
> A solar system with its verge
> Lost, perhaps, but illumined in
> A mathematical certainty
> And for my secret I would have a universe.

The experience seems real enough, but there is still a holding back —for fear, apparently, that this illumination or discovery might prove to be a 'false human clarity', as ultimately disappointing as that of Archimedes or that inspired by Tycho Brahe, but on a more sweeping scale. It is only much later in the poem, after 'Telling it in plain words', that she realizes that she had 'feared the wrong thing':

> The other centre, the known enigma—
> All eyes I do not own, contours
> That force familiarity where I would
> Tumult and spurn like Pan—were the mountain
>   passes
> Pure out of thought . . .

God's way, though demanding self-renunciation, is the true way to freedom. What she *should* fear and give up is the world she has loved till now, since it is 'scarfed in dreadful mist' where 'no sun comes'. In the remainder of the poem there is a new recognition of the world around as an 'arena', one in which there is to be no 'glancing back' but instead a forward movement to the 'other side' where the 'wild smell' for which her heart yearns will replace the presently necessary 'athlete's incense'. The landscape seems to be taking on an increasingly Christian configuration. Perhaps the sway of the winter sun has already ended and been superseded by the 'Light that blinded Saul' (*The Dumbfounding*).[7]

The Dumbfounding contains further poems of inner search and debate, but they may be retrospective, and in any case they give the impression that the period of spiritual gestation has come to a close. 'The Two Selves' pictures two opposing aspects of the poet discussing the 'birds in the sky', which somehow stand for spiritual realities:

> And you *wait* for them here?
>
>> Oh no. It is more
>> like knowing the sound of the sea
>>   when you
>> live under the sea.

The response to the skeptical self reveals a maturing confidence. The 'Two Mayday Selves' (*D*, p. 11) are more mutually in harmony, yet the more hesitating one is urged to respond wholly to the new experience:

> The power of the blue and gold breadth
> of day is poured out, flooding, all
> over all.
> Come out. Crawl out of it. Feel

it. You
too.

It is the voice of a true finder speaking, one who can call for an end to talk and self-centred questioning, and in the simplest, most forthright language invite to participation in a new joy, a release. In 'Many As Two', reminiscent of Christina Rossetti's 'Uphill' or of Marvell's dialogue poems, the objections are now external to the new Christian, serving both to challenge and to define his life of discovery:

> 'Where there is the green thing
> life springs clean.'
>> *Yes. There is blessed life, in*
>> *bywaters; and in pondslime*
>> *but not for your drinking.*
> 'Where the heart's room
> deepens, and the thrum
> of the touched heartstrings reverberates—*Vroom*—
> there I am home.'
>> *Yes. And the flesh's doom*
>> *is—a finally welcome going out on a limb?*
>> (No thing abiding.)
> *No sign, no magic, no roadmap, no*
> *pre-tested foothold.* 'Only that you know
> there is the way, plain,
> and the home-going.'
>
>> *Outside the heartbreak home I know, I can own*
>> *no other.*
>> 'The brokenness. I know.
>> Alone.'
>> (Go with us, then?)

This is a remarkably subtle poem, in which the shifting indentation marks the development of the attitude of each speaker as the encounter proceeds. For our purposes it is significant that, though the finder, having known 'brokenness', can fully sympathize with that feeling, the two viewpoints expressed in the poem are really worlds apart—giving us a measure of the radical nature of the change that has occurred. The greenness of the new life means to the one the stagnation of 'pondslime', to the other a fresh and pure vitality. The 'way', clearly involving risk, may seem either a final madness or a 'plain' way home, depending on whether one is a seeker or a finder. Since one viewpoint includes and transcends the other, only a finder could write such a poem.

Having become fully taken up in the new life, Miss Avison can look back at the first moment of discovery, and attempt to picture the miracle of transformation. One such portrayal is given in 'Ps. 19', a personal interpretation of the statement, 'The fear of the Lord is clean, enduring for ever.' That fear (which in Proverbs 1 is called the 'beginning' of knowledge) is here defined as

> to love high
> and know longing for clear
> sunlight, to the last ribcorner
> and capillary—and wonder
> if, so known, a sighing-
> over-the-marshlands me
> might all evaporate, wisp away.

This is obviously the state of the searcher. The hyphenated epithet gives this fresh non-theological definition a personal touch, one which clearly recalls the seeking poet's fears that an encounter with ultimate reality might cramp the imaginative self. But this 'fear' paradoxically does include seeking as well as shrinking, and when 'sunward love' conquers, discovery comes: the love-fear proves to be

> —not boulderstone,
> baldness, slowly in fire consuming—but green
> with life, moss, cup-rock-water, cliff riven
> for a springing pine.

The whole poem hinges on the sun-metaphor for God, an image which does not change but is radically re-interpreted as the seeker becomes a finder, as the 'fire', being 'trusted', is revealed to be the life-giving 'enduring sun'. It is interesting to see that the now-understood seeking is defined in the early part of the poem with lucid precision, but that the language and syntax must be strained to express the greater reality of the finding.

Other poems describing the first discovery are 'For Tinkers Who Travel on Foot' and 'The Earth That Falls Away'. But an important question must now be raised. Having 'found', is one doomed to an inhuman fixity of position, perhaps a continual looking back to that first great experience, or, even worse, a pretence of sainthood in an attempt to live up to one's past light? The answer is that 'In the mathematics of God / there are percentages beyond one hundred'—the new creation is both 'whole' and a 'beginning'. In a poem of 'Marginalia' bringing out commonly unsuspected implications in Christ's teachings about the child and the kingdom of heaven, Miss Avison vividly describes the rhythm of vigour and weariness, the round of hopes, fears, and joys that makes each new day for the child (and for the Christian) a 'new life time'. The exciting, fresh details in this poem and in more than a score of others on 'secular' subjects (objects, people, scenes) show that the first 'finding' has made possible a multiplicity of further explorations and brought new light to their aid. As Malcolm Ross puts it, for the Christian, existence becomes a 'drama' in which no detail is without its 'wholly unique reality. No thing is insignificant.'[8]

Appropriately, then, in his review of *The Dumbfounding*, Smith comments on the 'purity' of Miss Avison's 'response to experience (*all experience*)'.[9] Yet for him it is the explicitly Christian poems that climax her achievement; and some of these, such as 'Person', are indeed stunning in their power. Authenticity is the keynote of these specifically Christian poems. They have the ring of truth that comes, in part, from the genuine search experience that preceded them, which in Amos Wilder's terms might be called the poet's 'baptism in the secular', her coming 'face to face with the reality of the first Adam'.[10] But there is also a 'recurrent' baptism, as the realism of the opening lines of 'Branches' indicates:

> The diseased elms are lashing
> in hollowing vaults of air.
> In movie-washroom-mirrors
> wan selves, echoing, stare.
>
> O Light that blinded Saul,
> blacked out Damascus noon,
> Toronto's whistling sunset has
> a pale, disheartened shine.

And the concluding stanzas of the poem deal directly with the problem of communicating a momentous 'finding'. Concerned to avoid the 'fly-by-night' approach of the superficially religious, the poet comes to a realization that genuine Christianity will spread when 'branches' of the Vine 'scatter to tell what the root / and where life is made.' It is only the human in touch with the divine that can 'show him [i.e., Christ] visible'. The gospel, as Wilder puts it, prevails 'by revelation, by bodying forth'.[11]

In surveying the contemporary scene, Kenneth Hamilton makes some relevant comments on religious search and discovery:

> It is not surprising that concentration upon the human condition should lead some artists to find religion a live option as they explore the landscape of the human self. The religious vision is one answer to the riddle of human existence; and it is an answer that declares itself right at the centre of man's descent into himself, when the resources of self-analysis are exhausted. Then comes the decision to accept—or not to accept—an understanding of the self and the world going beyond the bounds of the available and the verifiable. The religious believer says that not to believe would be a denial of the truth that has flashed upon his life, a truth establishing itself beyond his experience, yet confirming all other truths that he has discovered in his experience. The sceptic, choosing the opposite road, says that to believe is to take the easy way out. . . . The debate continues, and no impartial arbitration is possible. Yet, on whichever side he happens to stand, and wherever he has found his final loyalty, the artist helps us to see what is involved in making a decision.[12]

This able summary of an important 'religious' function of every serious modern artist also serves as a valuable commentary on the poems of Margaret Avison, who has seen things from both viewpoints, that of the seeker and that of the discoverer. Her poems trace the progression from one to the other, and make her final position clear.

But despite that conclusion, Miss Avison's poems, whether of search or of discovery, cannot be dismissed as 'propaganda'. Their rich sensitivity to all aspects of life, amounting to a wholesome 'secularity', their deep and incisive engagement in the world of thought and meaning, their full exploitation of all the modern resources of language and technique—all these mark them with the vitality which is the essence of true poetry. The poems of Christian discovery are fully contemporary and dynamic, deeply rooted in the experiential. By a union in the truly human, they manage to avoid the seeming dichotomy of Christianity and art that perturbed Auden.[18] In and through their value as poetry they have another value, a religious one which might well be appreciated by believers and others alike: they 'body forth' an answer to man's searchings that one may accept or reject, but not dismiss.

[No. 60, 1974]

[1] Margaret Avison, *Winter Sun* (London, 1960).

[2] A. J. M. Smith, 'Margaret Avison's New Book', *The Canadian Forum*, 46, 1966, 133.

[3] One must not, of course, read the poems as pure biography, but rather as what Blackmur calls 'life at the remove of form'—form implying a deliberate selectivity as well as the inevitable discrepancy between the poet's original intent and the finished poem, only the latter of which is available for inspection. Throughout my paper I take this distinction for granted, and simply refer to 'the poet' or 'Miss Avison' for the sake of convenience.

[4] Paul Claudel, *Poetic Art*, tr. Renee Spodheim (New York, 1948), p. 27.

[5] This type of verbal paradox, amounting to virtual self-contradiction, recurs in both Miss Avison and the later T. S. Eliot, and thus appears to be one of a number of marks of that poet's influence on her work. Other indications may be found in her allusiveness and use of symphonic 'movement' patterns (in the longer poems), and in her line rhythms and other metrical forms, including lyrical quatrains reminiscent, say, of those in the *Quartets*.

[6] It would be of biographical and perhaps of some interpretive interest to discover the relative date of composition of this poem. It might be taken as simply a hymn to spring, but its concluding images are remarkable anticipations of those in such poems of clearly Christian discovery as 'Ps. 19' (*D*, p. 24) and 'For Tinkers Who Travel on Foot' (*D.*, p. 36), the first of which is discussed later in this paper.

[7] Another poem in *Winter Sun* that might be a poem of Christian discovery is 'Birth Day' (p. 73), whose title could be taken as an allusion to rebirth.

[8] Malcolm Ross, 'The Writer as Christian', in Nathan A. Scott, Jr., ed., *The New Orpheus: Essays Toward a Christian Poetic* (New York, 1964), p. 86.

[9] Smith, 134.

[10] Amos N. Wilder, 'Art and Theological Meaning'. in Scott, p. 410.

[11] Wilder, p. 419.

[12] Kenneth Hamilton, *In Search of Contemporary Man* (Grand Rapids, 1967), p. 21.

[13] W. H. Auden, 'Postscript: Christianity and Art', in Scott, pp. 74-7.

Black and Secret Poet
Notes on Eli Mandel

John Ower

The pieces in Eli Mandel's four major collections (in *Trio*, 1954; *Fuseli Poems*, 1960; *Black and Secret Man*, 1964; *An Idiot Joy*, 1967) are as strange and as knotty as anything in Canadian poetry. Given the difficulty and singularity of his work, it seems wise first of all to place it in some sort of meaningful context. Three lines of analysis seem particularly useful in this connection. The first is that Mandel's ethnic background appears significant not only with regard to those poems containing specifically Jewish allusions, but may also serve as a major formative influence upon both the poet's vision and his style. Secondly, Mandel is a poet of spiritual upset and rebellion, and can be appreciated only in the atmosphere of crisis that gave birth to romanticism, existentialism, and contemporary anarchism. Thirdly, he is a myth-maker, and his work cannot be comprehended without some understanding of mythopoeia. In particular his poetry shows both the radical imaginative re-arrangement of reality and the plumbing of the unconscious mind which are characteristically interrelated facets of myth-making poetry. A discussion centred upon the three points just mentioned should help to account for the tonality of Mandel's work, as well as providing an opportunity to touch upon at least some of his more important themes and techniques.

In the first chapter of *Mimesis*, Erich Auerbach plays his own variation on Matthew Arnold's distinction between Hebraism and Hellenism as polar mentalities and major forces in Western civilization. That Mandel is himself aware of such a distinction in personal and artistic terms is shown in 'Charles Isaac Mandel':

> Those uplands of the suburban mind,
> sunlit, where dwell the lithe ironists,
> athletic as greeks, boy-lovers,
> mathematical in love as in science.
> Formalists. What have I to do with them?
> I gather the few relics of my father:
> his soiled Tallis, his Tefillin,
> the strict black leather of his dark faith.

His poetry in fact provides almost a text-book example of the vision and the literary 'style' which Auerbach finds in Old Testament literature. Auerbach observes that the Homeric preoccupation with a clearly articulated, uniformly illuminated sensory surface, in which everything is externalized and accounted for, is largely absent from the Biblical stories.[1] The empirical foreground yields precedence to spiritual and psychological matters running far beneath the surface, and only such aspects of a story as bear on these are narrated. These episodes derive their significance and coherence not from a 'horizontal' linkage in the phenomenal, but rather from a 'vertical' or symbolic connection to the secret purposes of God and to man's unexpressed responses. Both the impact and the difficulty of a poem like 'Black and Secret Man' arise from just such a 'Biblical' style:

> These are the pictures that I took: you see
> The garden here outside my home. You see
> The roots which hung my father, mother's
> Tangled hedge, this runnelled creeper vine.
> Here is the tree where in the summer hung
> The guest of summer, temple-haunting martlet.
> And here the tree with twenty mortal murders
> On its crown.

This sort of poetry, characterized like the Old Testament by 'certain parts brought into high relief, others left obscure, abruptness, suggestive influence of the unexpressed, "background" quality, multiplicity of meanings and need for interpretation',[2] is also characteristically 'modern'. However, Mandel's Jewish background may account at least in part for the sensibility underlying the method.

In his discussion of the Old Testament narratives, Auerbach also stresses the relative depth of their characterizations, and their concern with the developmental and problematic aspects of human existence.[3] Although these are again typical of modern literature, the almost obsessive self-exploration in Mandel's poetry, his preoccupation with evil and madness, and his search for a viable spiritual and psychological stance, could perhaps be classified as Hebraic. In particular, his concern with disintegration and degradation as a prelude to integrity follows the pattern of humiliation and exaltation in the careers of the Biblical heroes.[4] The macabre treatment of familial relationships in such poems as 'Joy of Conquest', 'Estevan Saskatchewan', 'Black and Secret Man', and 'Pictures in an Institution' recalls Auerbach's observation that in Jewish life the connection between 'the domestic and the spiritual, between the paternal blessings and the divine blessing, lead to daily life being permeated with the stuff of conflict, often with poison.'[5] This saturation of day-to-day existence with a profound and mysterious significance until it becomes supercharged with the 'sublime, tragic and problematic'[6] may also explain why in Mandel's poetry even the commonplace and the insignificant become charged with a strange and sometimes terrible *mana*.

All of the above comments can of course be summarized by saying that Mandel is a romantic. His, moreover, is a romanticism which is 'decadent' in Tindall's sense of a late efflorescence of a particular movement which pushes its implications to the limits of extremity or elaboration.[7] His first three volumes in particular can be seen as providing a Canadian counterpart to the late nineteenth and early twentieth-century writers in whom romanticism reaches its logical or illogical conclusions.

Romanticism, and late romanticism in particular, is intimately related to the spiritual crisis which has been brewing since the end of the eighteenth century, and it is not surprising that spiritual upset and rebellion should form two major ingredients in Mandel's poetry. Like those of many of the romantics and the existentialists, his troubles may centre in the fact that something has gone wrong either with God or with man's relationship to Him. In 'Day of Atonement: Standing', Mandel in a state of semi-rebellion confronts a 'fierce' God, and it is obvious that only drastic measures can mend the relationship. In *An Idiot Joy* there are murmurings that God, if not uncaring or absent, has at least 'failed to be unambiguous' in matters deeply concerning the poet. In this type of situation the old values based on religious faith, which traditionally substantiated and regulated almost every aspect of civilized life, inevitably become either dead or oppressive. As 'Hebraism' suggests negatively through its irony, this particular crisis will be felt with special acuteness by an individual from a background which was saturated with religion:

> The law is the law and is
> terribly Hebrew which is as you
> know mostly poems about cooking
> and meat to be cured in water and
> salt and children to be counted
> for pages of generation amid clean
> and also unclean women

If God is still present in this world of sterile regulation, it is in the form of Joyce's *deo boia*, and the law and order which He sanctions have a punitive rather than a saving force. The whole of the present dispensation in fact becomes demonic and destructive:

> When the echo of the last footstep dies
> and on the empty street you turn empty eyes,
>   what do you think that you will see?
>   A hangman and a hanging tree.

Such a vision quite naturally promotes an attitude of rebelliousness which can affect every aspect of the life of the afflicted individual. It is seen as morally imperative to break with the old covenant in all its manifestations in search of new values. In Mandel's poetry this drama of multiple rebellion is acted out particularly in *An Idiot Joy*. Thus in 'Psalm 24' modern Judaism is seen as being no longer an intimately lived experience like the religion of David, but rather a rabbinical bookishness which does violence to life and must therefore be cast off. 'The madness of our polity' rejects the present political and social order as the systematized sadism of bloodthirsty savages:

> On the prairies where I lived
> a-boy who put a needle in a gopher's eye
> knew more of civil law than all my friends,

The logical answer to such an establishment is the militant anarchism of 'The burning man' and 'Whence cometh our help?'.

In Mandel's poetry even the workaday world can become a

Kafkaesque nightmare in which the individual is imprisoned and destroyed by a demonic power-structure. In the first of the poems in *Trio*, an office building becomes a labyrinth in which the poet, after hours of bemused wandering, is finally confronted by the Minotaur of authority. 'Pictures in an Institution' similarly portrays the university campus in terms of an insane authoritarianism which can only provoke a violent reply. Finally it should be mentioned that Mandel's rebellion includes a psychological revolt against consciousness. If it is the reason and morality which we consciously accept, that have created the hangman's world, then it is only in the dark recesses of the Freudian or Jungian unconscious, however terrible these may seem initially, that we can possibly find salvation. This explains the poet's emphasis in *An Idiot Joy* upon the irrational as a force which is capable of sweeping away the old, dead order. Idiots and barbarians provide at least a 'kind of solution' to the problems of the modern world.

Mandel's poetry not only documents the various facets of existential rebellion, but also illustrates the danger inherent in cutting the umbilical cord of tradition. Urizen is expiring, but he is still alive enough to condemn to death, and the rebel, Atlas-like, assumes a terrible burden of guilt and anxiety. Thus in 'Thief Hanging in Baptist Halls' the poet's rejection of 'polite vegetation, deans, a presbyterian sun, / brick minds quaintly shaped in Gothic and glass' is accompanied by a feeling of humiliating public condemnation:

> I wish he would not shrug
> and smile weakly at me
> as if ashamed that he is hanging there,
> his dean's suit fallen off, his leg cocked
> as if to run
> or (too weak, too tired, too undone)
> to do what can be done
> about his nakedness.

Nor is this sense of reprobation unwarranted. *Black and Secret Man* was, its author tells us, 'written so that I could confront and recognize whatever is dark in human nature, and to discover how much of it is a reflection of self.' Such pieces as 'Secret Flower', 'The burning man' and 'The front lines' suggest that there is in fact as much evil to be exorcised from the rebel himself as there is in the world which he attacks. 'To a friend who sued the mayor and lost' stresses this point by means of Camus's paradox of the altruistic revolutionary falling to the same moral level as his opponents.

The existential rebel is not only burdened with his personal albatross of evil and guilt, but is ultimately threatened with the disintegration of both his psyche and his world-order. His revolt brings with it alienation and a lack of spiritual guidelines. A new self and a new world must somehow be forged out of emptiness and chaos in a terrible isolation. For Mandel, as we have said, the only hope seems to lie in a surrender to the black and turbulent forces of the unconscious in the hope that they carry within themselves the seeds of a new dispensation. The ever-present possibility of madness which this gamble involves is a significant theme in his work. In the early piece 'Orpheus', the act of poetic creation, which for Mandel is part and parcel of the revolt against consciousness, leads to the *sparagmos* of the personality. On the other hand, 'Crusoe' in *An Idiot Joy* suggests that the poet has written 'in order not to go mad'. That his art may indeed serve as a prophylaxis, releasing and objectifying his inner tensions, is suggested by the fact that many of his poems are permeated with what 'Manner of Suicide' terms 'the archaic symbolism of the psychotic'. Thus the macabre methods of self-extermination catalogued in that poem are really the grotesque projections of derangement. The poet evidently feels that there is a very real danger of suicide or insanity forestalling a spiritual rebirth.

However, there is in fact method behind much of the apparent madness of Mandel's imagery. Like Crawford, Jay Macpherson, and Reaney, he is a myth-making poet, and some grasp of the theory and practice of mythopoeia is essential to an understanding of his work. Historically speaking, Mandel's myth-making procliv-ity is another aspect of his romanticism, being traceable through such twentieth-century visionaries as Pound, Yeats, and Edith Sitwell to the climate of sensibility which produced the poetry of Shelley and Blake. It should, however, be noted that besides the influence of esoteric romanticism, the technique of the early poetry in particular shows a good deal of the more deliberate intellectual-ity of such modern 'metaphysicals' as T. S. Eliot and Robert Low-ell. This is especially true of the imagery, in which Mandel often achieves a powerful fusion of the romantic visionary metaphor with the metaphysical conceit. In some of the poems in *An Idiot Joy* there is a much freer association of images, but these pieces are closer to surrealism than to anything in English romanticism.

Speaking in rather crude generalities, we can say that romantic myth-making originates with a vision of the universe as being substantiated by a metaphysical principle by which it is rendered both one and alive. In the early poem 'Aspects in a Mirror' Mandel expresses this sense of the fundamental unity of the cosmos in terms of the Platonism which has contributed so much to the myth-making tradition:

> Delight me no longer with this glass,
> There are many things I should have done.
> All images grow dimmer, pass.
> The many are sustained in one.

Because of the ultimate oneness of the world, the distinctions made by empirical consciousness between different places, times, and material phenomena are in the last analysis meaningless. One mark of the myth-making poet is accordingly a radical vision which telescopes space and history and breaks down the logical compartments into which post-Aristotelian man has increasingly tended to divide his experience. Thus in the series of pieces which open his selection of *Trio*, Mandel the poet lost in the office building becomes the ancient Greek Theseus braving the labyrinth; an amateur aviator a combination of Daedalus and Icarus, a mining accident the dismemberment of Orpheus. Just as the myth-making poet plays tricks with place and time, so he violates at will such 'reasonable' distinctions as those normally drawn between man and nature, or between the animal, the vegetable, and the mineral:

> But parrots bring in sleep only the surly shape
> Of images of men turned into beasts
> Carrying their loads of shame upon their backs,
> That forest where the trees are shapes of girls
> And every stone an image of a face, and eyes
> Are in the flowers, and I could weep for all
> Those lost and stoned and silent faces.

Ultimately these lines suggest a poetic world in which, subject to the artist's intentions, anything is equatable with anything else. The poet's vision of faces in stone is especially characteristic of the mythopoeic sensibility. On the one hand, Mandel's image shows the proclivity of the myth-maker for representing everything in terms of life, and of human life in particular. On the other, it illustrates the characteristic belief that man can descend spiritually down the scale of being even as far as the inanimate. In 'Leda and the Swan' and 'Rapunzel' such downward transformations become part of a nightmare sexual fantasy, while in 'Entomology' the vicious sterility of a Urizenic society is expressed in images of insect-life. However, in 'The apology', a passage into the inanimate is associated with a process resembling the *samana* techniques for escaping the ego:

> I want the table to appreciate my
> delight in its leaves: I will stand on
> four legs and try hard to be wooden
> and brown with folding leaves
> I will fold and unfold my leaves
>   like a wooden butterfly
> and birthday cards can be put on me.

Both this passage and the one quoted immediately before it imply that not only are categories which carve up space, time, and matter in the last analysis unreal, but also that the dynamic unity of the universe finds expression in the metamorphosis of one form into another. In imagining himself a table, Mandel is participating in the activity of an 'esemplastic power' which drives matter through an endless succession of changes. The next logical step is for the myth-maker to see metamorphosis in terms of a series of interlocking cycles of organic growth and decay, evolution and atavism, which are manifested in every aspect of existence. That Mandel is at least aware of such a possibility is suggested in 'The Moon in all her phases':

> I'd say, in the old manner:
> she [the moon] imagines our existence,
> its changes, illusions

However, such a vision is yet to appear in his poetry in a systematically elaborated form.

It has been a standard assumption of romanticism that man is linked to the One which underlies the universe through his unconscious mind. With some apparent reinforcement from the psychology of Jung, this has obviously been adopted as a basic tenet of Mandel's poetic faith. Traditional symbols of the unconscious, including the cave, the labyrinthine building, and enveloping water, recur frequently in his work. His mythopoeia thus belongs to the world of archetypal symbolism which finds expression in dreams, hallucinations, and madness, in primitive myth and legend, in folk and fairy tales, and in the literary mode which Northrop Frye terms romance.[8] It shares with these diverse phenomena a logic of symbolic association very different from the processes of the conscious reason, and an emotional pitch more intense than that considered proper to mimetic fiction.

As Jung quite properly emphasizes, the archetypes of the unconscious are ambivalent,[9] and in linking himself to the *weltgeist* through the unconscious, the poet becomes possessed by a Dionysian energy which is at the same time good and evil, joyous and painful, beautiful and fearful, creative and destructive. From its very beginning romanticism was impelled to stress the negative side of the equation, and in its later phases a possession by and obsession with its demonic elements leads to the phenomenon of 'the romantic agony'. As the poem 'Orpheus' clearly shows, Mandel is very much a poet of the romantic agony. In order to gain the divine inspiration which is necessary for his art, the singer must venture into the black 'mine' of the unconscious. However, the 'daemonic, chthonic powers'[10] are terrible and destructive as well as creative, and the poet undergoes destruction at their hands:

> Who found his body and who found his head
> And who wiped god from off his eyes and face?

It is accordingly not surprising that mythopoeia should in Mandel's work be associated with the nightmare world of madness, perversion, evil, and violent crime. The poet is in fact 'a black and secret man of blood' and, as 'Manner of suicide' suggests, his act of creation is a form of self-destruction. In 'Thief Hanging in Baptist Halls', the artist is represented as both immolated and condemned, thus powerfully combining two motifs of the romantic agony which recur a number of times in Mandel's poetry.

However, although the world of mythopoeia becomes one of satanism, horror, and dissolution, it is paradoxically necessary for man's salvation. The poet, by submitting himself to the Dionysian through his unconscious, obtains the spiritual power to sweep away the sterile and demonic world of the hangman god. As is the case with the destruction wrought by the revolutionary, this negative process becomes a terrible but necessary first step in the recreation of a new order both externally and within. Through madness, perversion, and evil, the individual's old spiritually dead order of conscience and consciousness will be shattered. Moreover, as Joseph Campbell suggests with regard to the hero-quest, the pain and disintegration which must be undergone are really the negative face of ambivalent archetypes, which if boldly approached will show themselves to be propitious.[11] Through his very evil and agony, the poet returns to the radical innocence of 'an idiot joy' in which true creativity and a 'singular love' become possible. The imagination, in addition to being a power of vision, is thus one of recreation and redemption. The condemned and tormented artist is really analogous to the crucified Christ, whose act of sacrifice has regenerated both man and the world. Significantly enough, the poet's passion in 'Thief Hanging in Baptist Halls' is followed by a personal apocalypse:

> He dangles while the city bursts in green and steel,
> black flower in the mouth of my speech:
> The proud halls reel,
> gothic and steel melt in the spinning sun.

Similarly, in 'Manner of suicide', Mandel's contemplation of the most gruesome methods of self-destruction leads in the end to the revelation of 'a new heaven and a new earth' in which man is in the loving care of a beneficent Divinity. Such glimpses of illumination may perhaps foreshadow a more sustained visionary ecstasy such as we encounter in the poetry of Blake or Edith Sitwell.

Having attempted to place Mandel's poetry in context while touching upon some of his major themes and techniques, I will venture a brief appraisal of his work. On the credit side of the ledger can certainly be placed the toughness and power of his intellect. Some of his poems display a steadiness and clarity of insight into the depths of the self which is worthy of a trained analyst. The same keen-edged hardness characterizes his poetic technique at its best, and is particularly noticeable in the punch of some of his imagery. The following lines from 'Estevan Saskatchewan' illustrate the kick which Mandel's mind can deliver when it is in top poetic form:

> A small town bears the mark of Cain,
> Or the oldest brother with the dead king's wife

> In a foul relation as viewed by sons,
> Lies on the land, squat, producing
> Love's queer offspring only,
> Which issue drives the young
> To feign a summer madness, consort with skulls,
> While the farmer's chorus, a Greek harbinger,
> Forecasts by frost or rings about the moon
> How ill and black the seeds will grow.

This passage exemplifies another feature of Mandel's best poetry: an emotion which, like hot iron, glows and burns and yet is forged into hard, definite forms.

The forcefulness of thought and feeling in much of Mandel's verse is connected with the spiritual and moral accomplishment of a penetrating insight into the perversions of a sick soul in a sick world. This is only made possible by the poet's terrible honesty, which confronts the worst of which man is capable while carefully analysing and exposing his own involvement. Also to Mandel's credit is the spiritual vitality which can not only face degradation, but also find in it materials for creative self-expression and even 'an idiot joy':

> Lord, Lord, pollution everywhere
> But I breathe still
>   and breathless, sweet
> woodbine, colour of honey, touches my skin
> as if my unbelieving eyes made no difference at all

Finally, Mandel must be praised for the ironic detachment and wry humour which prove that he has maintained his sanity on the edge of the abyss:

> Notice: The library is closed to all who read
>   any student carrying a gun
>   registers first, exempt from fines,
>   is given thirteen books per month,
>   one course in science, one in math,
>   two options
>   campus police
>   will see to co-eds' underwear

Despite his evident virtues, Mandel seems to me to remain a promising rather than a mature or a major artist. One of the biggest deficiencies of at least the work before *An Idiot Joy* is the relative narrowness of its emotional range. This is to be connected with the fact that the besetting sin which the poet reveals to us is perhaps not the Oedipus complex or a desire for violence but rather an inordinate fixation of a too, too sensitive self upon the negative. However, a piece like 'Messages' shows that Mandel is capable of breaking out of his emotional straightjacket, and it is to be hoped that time will bring a more complete visionary conversion from the romantic agony to a divine comedy.

Mandel's poetry also seems to lack the all-embracing, precisely articulated world-picture and poetic structure which characterize the great visionaries. The backbone of the artistic stature of Dante, Milton, Blake, and Yeats is that all of them managed to order a wide range of experience around a spiritual centre, and also to develop a syntax of ideas and images. Something of this sort would provide Mandel with a basis for more ambitious poetic structures than his present brief pieces, or at least give a greater degree of coherence and direction to his future output.

There are also a number of technical flaws in the fabric of Mandel's poetry. In the earlier volumes, his intellect occasionally escapes from the control necessary for artistic success, and blemishes his work with preciosity, artificiality, or obscurity:

> What he was skulled in and built, the frame of,
> The grain and shelter of his house and place,
> Bone's trust of jointure and contract, all claims have
> Yielded in him who is separate and vagrant in flesh and place.

The typographical doodling of many of the poems in *An Idiot Joy*, although currently fashionable, also seems at times a bit contrived for comfort.

It is very much to Mandel's credit that his intellectual control prevents the melodramatic pitch which is proper to his world of romance from rising to the shrillness of Yeats's 'hysterical women'. However, in some of the poems in *An Idiot Joy* his voice does descend to the quaver of sentimentality. Such conceptions as 'dreaming beasts with huge unhurt eyes' and 'walnut-coloured men' who in 'far-off wind-swept voices / revolve their prayers as if they were wheels or stars' hover on the verge of whimsical pathos. The following passage has undoubtedly crossed the border-line:

> Tonight
> in the sky's filing-cabinet

> I discover my unwritten letters,
> xerox of the last mss
> by an unnamed, doubtless poor, scholar.

In his future poetry, Mandel should definitely eschew the Charlie-Chaplinesque.

Moreover, even at its best, his work seldom rises beyond a rhetorical utterance to the lyricism which is the mark of the fully integrated poetic sensibility. The technical toughness of the early volumes precludes the singing voice, and even the more flexible verse of *An Idiot Joy* is rarely lyrical. Only on a few occasions, as in 'The Speaking Earth', does he approach the fusion of intellect, emotion, and music which we find, for example, in Herbert's 'Virtue'. Perhaps Mandel should experiment more with the formal disciplines exemplified in the great lyric tradition of Spenser, Keats, and Tennyson.

By way of conclusion, it should be stressed that Mandel's poetry shows development as well as continuity. If nothing else, the pieces in *An Idiot Joy* display a gain in technical suavity. Mandel's further growth as an artist is only to be expected, and it will be interesting to see what lines it will take. In particular the future will tell whether he belongs to the company of what Frye calls unfolding artists, or whether he is a poet of metamorphic growth like Yeats. His work to date appears to be the expression of the metamorphic spiritual pattern of crisis and conversion. If this is indeed the case, his art may show some spectacular developments. As happened with Edith Sitwell, a relatively sudden onset of visionary ecstasy may be accompanied by an efflorescence of technique. Should this happen, Mandel may produce poetry which bears the same relationship to his present work as a butterfly to the chrysalis from which it painfully emerged.

[No. 42, 1969]

---

[1] Erich Auerback, *Mimesis* (Princeton, 1953), pp. 11-12.

[2] *Ibid.*, p. 23.

[3] *Ibid.*, pp. 17-20.

[4] *Ibid.*, p. 18.

[5] *Ibid.*, p. 22.

[6] *Ibid.*, p. 22.

[7] William York Tindall, *Forces in Modern British Literature* (New York, 1947), pp. 18-19.

[8] Northrop Frye, *Anatomy of Criticism* (Princeton, 1957), p. 33.

[9] C. G. Jung, 'Aion', *The Collected Works of C. G. Jung*, Vol. 9. Pt II (New York, 1959), pp. 68-9

[10] T. S. Eliot, 'The Dry Salvages', V. II, 40-1.

[11] Joseph Campbell, *The Hero with a Thousand Faces* (Cleveland, 1956), pp. 97-171.

Reaney Collected

Margaret Atwood

Watching poets' critical reputations is a lot like watching the stock market. Some poets make slow but steady gains and end up safe but dull, like Blue Chips. Others are more like shady gold mines: they're overvalued initially, then plunge to oblivion. More often it's a combination of the two, with each high period being followed by a low of sneers and dismissals and an ultimate recovery engineered by a later squad of critics who rescue the poet's reputation, from a safe distance.

This is especially likely to be true of a poet who, like James Reaney, has been associated with a trend, group, or movement which has either angered people or gone out of fashion. Judging from a sampling of recent critical commentary on his collected *Poems*,* Reaney's reputation is in its slump phase; which is a shame. Any poet who has created an original body of work, especially one of such uniqueness, power, peculiarity and, sometimes, unprecedented weirdness as Reaney's deserves better treatment. A critic might begin by attempting to actually *read* the poems, as opposed to reading into them various philosophies and literary theories which the poet is assumed to have. If you start this way, with the actual poems, one of your first reactions will almost certainly be that there is nothing else *like* them.

I'd never before read most of the uncollected single poems—my reading of Reaney had been limited to *The Red Heart*, *A Suit of Nettles*, *Twelve Letters To a Small Town*, and *The Dance of Death in London, Ontario* (as well as the plays and the short story 'The Bully'), so I was most intrigued by sections I, III and V of this

---

* James Reaney, *Poems*. Edited by Germaine Warkentin, New Press, (Toronto, 1973).

volume. I was especially struck by the early appearance of a number of Reaney images which crop up again and again, variously disguised, in his later work. The fascination with maps and diagrams ('Maps', 1945), the collections of objects ('The Antiquary', 1946), the sinister females, both mechanical ('Night Train', 1946) and biological ('Madame Moth', 1947), and that nightmare, 'The Orphanage', already present in 'Playbox', 1945—all foreshadow later and more fully realized appearances.

But what became clear to me during a chronological reading of this book is that most commentators—including Reaney himself, and his editor and critics—are somewhat off-target about the much-discussed influence of Frye on his work. I have long entertained a private vision of Frye reading through Reaney while muttering 'What have I wrought?' or 'This is not what I meant, at all,' and this collection confirms it. Reaney is to Frye as a Salem, Mass. seventeenth-century tombstone is to an Italian Renaissance angel: Reaney and the tombstone may have been 'influenced', but they are primitives (though later in time) and their models are sophisticates. The influence of Frye, however, was probably a catalyst for Reaney rather than a new ingredient; let me do a little deductive speculation.

The world presented to us in the early poems, up to and including *The Red Heart* (1949), does not 'work' for the poet on any level. The people in them are bored and trivial, like 'Mrs Wentworth', or they are actual or potential orphans, loveless, lost, or disinherited, like the speaker in 'Playbox' or the one in 'Whither do you wander?':

> . . . I never find
> What I should like to find;
> For instance, a father and mother
> Who loved me dearly . . .
> Instead I must forever run
> Down lanes of leafless trees
> Beneath a Chinese-faced sun;
> Must forsaken and forlorn go
> Unwanted and stepmotherishly haunted
> Beneath the moon as white as snow.

The reverse side of the melancholy state of being an orphan—hate for and disgust at the rest of the world and the desire for revenge—

is explored in two other orphan poems, 'The English Orphan's Monologue' and 'The Orphanage', but in these the orphans are not touching and wistful children; they are repulsive, 'With plain white/And cretinous faces', or filled with elemental destructiveness. Within a larger social context, the speakers are stifled by their society, like the speaker in 'The Canadian', who longs to escape from a parlour haunted by his 'grim Grandfather' and the Fathers of Confederation to 'hot lands' and 'heathen folks' (a theme treated more succinctly later in 'The Upper Canadian'). In these 'social' poems, Reaney does not analyse, he dramatizes; and, like a dramatist, he counterpoints. Thus to the smothered longing of the provincial in the 'Canadian' poems he opposes the sneering of a cosmopolite who has escaped the Fathers of Confederation, is reading Tristram Shandy and Anais Nin, and who says to the 'proletariat':

> Your pinched white and gray faces
> Peer in
> Like small white tracts held off at a
>   distance.
> Well . . . is it not all very beautiful?
> As you stand hungry in the rain
> Just look to what heights you too may
>   attain.
> ('The Ivory Steeple')

If this poem had been written by anyone else but Reaney, everyone would have called it savage socialist satire; in fact it's a good deal more savage and socialist than much that passes by that name.

In these early poems the objects—and the poems bulge with objects—create the effect of a kind of rummage sale, partly because the objects are lacking in all but personal significance:

> . . . my spotted ring
> And the wool blanket hemmed in red . . .
> Also the corduroy suit
> And the scarf with the purple bars . . . ('Play-box')

> The Cup had the outlines of a cup
> In a lantern-slide
> And it was filled with Congou tea
> What did it mean this cup of tea?
>   ('Faces and the Drama in a Cup of Tea')

The speaker can rarely make 'sense' of them by relating them to anything else; all he can do is record them, and the effect is a still-life, captured and rendered immobile, like the pictures Miss ffrench takes in 'Kodak':

> They have their camera.
> No one sits in its gloomy parlour
> Of pleated walls.
> No wind stirs or ghost stalks . . .
> And all my garden stands suddenly
>   imprisoned
> Within her pleated den.

In the early poems on 'love'—and there are quite a few of them—the love is either unconsummated, as in 'Platonic Love', or it turns into sex, which is as inextricably linked with death as it is in the poetry of Al Purdy. This is sex observed through a child's eyes, foreign and monstrous. At times Reaney manages a kind of queasy humour, as in 'Grand Bend', which begins:

> It is the rutting season
> At Grand Bend
> And the young men and the women
> Explode in each others' arms
> While no chaperones attend.

More often it is simple horror, mixed with revulsion, as in 'The Orphanage':

> They that lie pasted together
> In ditches by the railroad tracks
> And seethe in round-shouldered cars
> With the lusty belches of a Canadian
>   spring.
> Young men with permanent waves
> Crawl over ghastly women
> Whose cheeks are fat as buttocks . . .

'So love does often lead a filthy way to death' one poem ends, and another concludes, 'It has always been that lust / Has always rhymed with dust.'

Reaney's early world, then, is an unredeemed one, populated

with orphans and spiritual exiles, littered with couples engaged in joyless, revolting, and dangerous copulation, and crammed with objects devoid of significance. In it, babies are doomed as soon as conceived (as in 'Dark Lagoon'), the 'real world' is the one described at the end of 'The School Globe', filled with 'blood, pus, horror, stepmothers and lies', and the only escape is the temporary and unsatisfactory one of nostalgic daydreaming. If you believed you lived in such a world, you'd surely find the negative overwhelming. Anyone familiar with the techniques of brainwashing knows that all you have to do to convert almost anyone to almost anything is subject him to a nearly intolerable pressure, then offer him a way out. The intolerable pressures rendered with such verbal richness in the earlier poems are those of the traditional Christian version of this earth, but with Christ (and escape to Heaven) removed; sin with no possibility of redemption, a fallen world with no divine counterpart.

Frye's literary theories—this is a guess—would surely have offered Reaney his discredited childhood religion in a different, more sophisticated, acceptable form: the Bible might not be *literally* true, but under the aegis of Frye it could be seen as metaphorically, psychically true. Frye's 'influence', then, is not a matter of the critic's hardedged mind cutting out the poet's soul in its own shapes, like cookie dough: 'influence', for good poets, is surely in any case just a matter of taking what you need or, in reality, what you already have.

Frye made a difference (and again I'm guessing) not so much to Reaney's choice of materials, or even to his choice of forms, but to the kinds of resolutions made available to him. Horror remains and evil is still a presence, but a way past the world, the flesh, and the devil is now possible. The redemptive agents are all invisible, internal: they are the imagination, the memory, verbal magic (Reaney has several poems about language, and many references to the magic tongue) and—I'm thinking here of the short story 'The Bully'—dream. These elements are so important in Reaney's work because the hideousness of existence can be redeemed *by them alone*: it is the individual's inner vision, not the external social order, that must change if anything is to be salvaged.

It is this arrangement of priorities that surely accounts not only for some of Reaney's themes, but also for some of his characteristic structures, in the plays as well as the poems. The pattern I'm thinking of is that of the sudden conversion—a Protestant rather than a Catholic pattern. If you think of the Divine Comedy with the Purgatorio left out, you'll see what I mean: we get the hellishness of the 'earthly' situation and the quick turnabout followed by a transcendent vision, but we are never told how you get to the vision—what process you undergo, what brings it about. No indulgences sold here; it's Faith, not Works, and you just somehow have to 'see'. There are several Reaney plays (*The Sun and the Moon, The Killdeer*) in which the evil witch figure is defeated simply by being perceived as a fraud; but in the lyric poetry, this structure can best be illustrated by that unsettling poem, 'The Sparrow'. It's a poem about grubby lechery in the most unappealing places— underpass, the episcopal church - symbolized by obscene chalk drawings, and the fourth verse starts like this:

> Dirty, diseased, impish, unsettling, rapist
> Illegitimate, urban, southless, itching,
> Satyromaniac, of butcher string the harpist,
> The sparrows and their gods are everything.

Then comes the turn:

> I like to hear their lack of tune
> On a very cold winter snowy afternoon.
> They must be listened to and worshipped
>   each—
> The shocking deities: ding dung is sacred
> So is filthiness, obscenity . . .

And the last stanza makes the point: *everything*, not just beauty, is in the eye of the beholder:

> Christ and Gautama and Emily Brontë were
> Born in the midst of angelic whir
> In a dripping concrete den under,
> Under the alimentary trains: it is we
> Who see the angels as brown lechery
> And the sacred pair—Venus and Adonis
> As automatons coupled as a train is.
>   And so step down my chalky reader,
>   Why keep our festival here
>   In this crotch?

Ding dung chirp chirp:
A sparrow sings if you but have an ear.

In Reaney's work, the Songs of Innocence come *after* the Songs of Experience; in fact, you can take a number of figures or images from the earlier poems and follow them through the *corpus*, watching how the Lost Child gets found (most notably in *Night-Blooming Cereus*), how the sinister Orphan gets changed into the harmless comic-strip Little Orphan Annie, how the baby doomed from before birth is allowed more latitude (though he can be the Christ Child as parody dwarf, he can also be the real Christ Child or magic baby; see 'A Sequence in Four Keys'), and how the collection of random objects is permitted (or perhaps forced) to have universal significance (see, for instance, the pebble, the dewdrop, the piece of string and the straw, in 'Gifts').

The problems I have with Reaney's work are both theoretical (I can't see certain pieces of evil, for instance Hitler and the Vietnam War, as angelic visitations or even unreal, no matter how hard I try; and I don't think that's a flaw in my vision) and practical—that is, some of the poems work admirably for me and others don't get off the ground at all. Reaney's best poems come from a fusion of 'personal' and 'mythic' or 'universal'; when they lean too far towards either side, you get obscurity or straight nostalgia at one end or bloodless abstraction at the other. And at times, reading his work, I feel the stirrings of that old Romantic distinction between the Fancy and the Imagination, though I try hard to suppress it; I even hear a voice murmuring 'Whimsy', and it murmurs loudest when I come across a concrete image linked arbitrarily and with violence to a 'universal' meaning. If you can see a world in a grain of sand, well, good; but you shouldn't stick one on just because you think it ought to be there.

But his is a Collected rather than a Selected; it isn't supposed to be Reaney's best poems, it's all of his poems, and I can't think of any poet who produces uniformly splendid work. It's by his best, however, that a writer should ultimately be judged; and Reaney's best has an unmistakable quality, both stylistic and thematic, and a strength that is present only when a poet is touching on something fundamental. Certain of Reaney's poems do admirably what a number of his others attempt less successfully: they articulate the primitive forms of the human imagination, they flesh out the soul, they dramatize—like Blake's 'Mental Traveller'—the stances of the self in relation to the universe. That sounds fairly heavy; what I mean is that Reaney gets down to the basics—love, hate, terror, joy —and gives them a shape that evokes them for the reader. This is conjuring, it's magic and spells rather than meditation, description or ruminating; Coleridge rather than Wordsworth, MacEwen rather than Souster. The trouble with being a magic poet is that when you fail, you fail more obviously than the meditative or descriptive poet: the rabbit simply refuses to emerge from the hat. But you take greater risks, and Reaney takes every risk in the bag, including a number of technical ones that few others would even consider attempting.

[*No. 57, 1973*]

The Masks of D. G. Jones

E. D. Blodgett

'pour se reconnaître, il faut se traduire'

Public silence surrounding the work of D. G. Jones in Canada is inexorable but not inexplicable. His three books of poetry have emerged and disappeared apparently without complaint against the more strident and ephemeral appeals of the poetry of the past decade in this country. Beside the meteoric flash of such writers as Leonard Cohen and, now, Margaret Atwood, Jones' subtle brilliance seems a pale fire indeed. This is because Jones is a poet who is penetrating with care and delicate concern many of Canada's more troubling aesthetic preoccupations. He is a poet of courage whose surfacing is always deceptive and often misleading in a country where the search for self and heritage can be so exhausting that most poets would prefer to settle for any mode of irony that would both expose the mysterious folly of self-discovery and, also, prevent whatever fulfilment of exploration might be possible.

This is the poetry of an imagination that was early formed, and such changes as occur are those of a style deepened only by tragic events[1]. It should be remarked, nevertheless, how the centre of Jones' circles of radiation is placed in his first book. As a poet who seems only minimally ready for statement, he enunciated an almost consuming passion in his first poem in *Frost on the Sun*[2] entitled 'John Marin'. Jones' passion is for art, form, and the artist's ambiguous relation to the world present to the eye. Every volume of his poetry has, in fact, begun with meditations on this problem. *The Sun Is Axeman*[3] opens reflecting upon Anne Hébert; *Phrases from Orpheus*[4] moves confidently into the same kind of aesthetic dimension. By the third book, however, the self is no longer a spectator of a simple other; there the spatial order of his early work yields to an interplay, suggested in the course of the second book, of kinds of perceptual events where

> The cries of children come on the wind
> And are gone. The wild bees come,
> And the clouds.
>
> And the mind is not
> A place at all,
> But a harmony of now,
>
> The necessary angel, slapping
> Flies in its own sweat.

The transmutation of 'place', which was so much a part of design for the poet to whom Jones here almost to his undoing boldly alludes, is where the ambiguity of speech and its mode of visual revelation focus in his poetry. But Jones, unlike Stevens, never teaches explicity, never *tells* it 'As it is, in the intricate evasions of as'. The Canadian poet's persona is every part, no part, a picture and absence; as he remarked once, 'In order to recognize yourself, you have to be translated.'[5] He is Hamlet's voice and his father's ghost. He would be present to disappear, as he indicated in his first book:

> I would eliminate this bombast, this
> Detail of type, and leave an image,
> And a space—in which the birds or trees
> Find all their palpable relations with the earth.
> ('A Problem of Space')

Conjoined, finally, to a love for art and the world seen as theatre, is a need for masks, either tragic or Edenic, whose role is to reflect upon how the place of tragedy—a disharmony of then—is at once present, illusory, and quick with death.

If it is true that an exceedingly refined notion of art resides at the centre of Jones' consciousness, it is the sense of the visual relations of things and their deceptions that shades both the imagery and form of the poems. In its approximation to visual art, his poetry in fact illuminates imagery which is by its nature and in its effect illusory and deceptive. Similar to any image cast upon a screen, the 'place' where it reflects is a blank, a reminder and menace of absence. The mechanics of beaming light is complicated *a fortiori* by the poet's ability to blend images. Jones' arrival at such aesthetic positions does not seem to be through an interest in film but rather via an obsession with photographs and painters—not only Marin, but also Klee, Chagall, the Hour books of the Duke of Berry, Cézanne, Matisse, Hokusai, and Chinese art in general. Such an interest may be attributed to the fact that the poet is himself an amateur artist, and that he had once considered becoming an architect. These interests are more likely only aspects of an intensely visual imagination, and a peculiar bent for the way things come and go before the eye. The eye, as he suggests in 'Phrases from Orpheus', is a kind of cosmic organ of nutrition:

> We are fed
>
> in the eye of God
>
> in solitary, albeit blind
> and intimate

Eye, as he notes elsewhere, is the reflector of all things:

> The universe spins in a golden eye
> And summer shrinks in four black claws.
>
> ('The Osprey')

As he exhorts in 'The River: North of Guelph':

> O thin stream
> if you must be the image of my mind
> let me be that glass through which the light
> shines—O mind,
> be nothing, be
> that translucent glass.
>
> A crow, grown tired of cawing,
> lights
> on a dead branch;
> he folds his wings; the sun
> gleams black.
> A fallen leaf
> drifts and catches on a twig.
>
> A tin
> funnel,
> pitched into the middle of the stream,
> catches the light

and sends it back.

The poem stops almost thoughtlessly short of the Emersonian order of identities, for the final desire is dialectical and like a game of ball played with light against the modulating dark of things. Hence, while he may observe that 'the general / Identification / Leads us to love',[6] the sense of the phrase seems to derive its meaning from the following:

> I am always your lover: walls
>
>> and the fences of time,
>> or the night, but discover
>> the world has been joined
>
>> indivisible, everywhere, ever.
>> ('Nocturne: in the Way of a Love Song')

While walls, as the same poem makes clear, are 'merely façades', their face is sufficient to blur into ambiguity and prevent all things from being one; and like certain styles of painting, they prevent finalities such as vanishing points. In a stanza redolent of epanaleptic elegy, the poet suggests how much is possible:

> I am the light where you find shadows,
> I am the night in which you shine.
> To your extension I am time.
>> ('A Place for "P"')

Of shorter poems that demonstrate succinctly what I have been saying, I would choose 'Antibes: Variations on a Theme' from the second book, from which I cite the concluding six stanzas:

> 'Night Fishing at Antibes'
> (Picasso: August, 1939)
> Introduces
>
> The town and castle of Antibes
> In violet tones.
> In the exhausted harbour, two
>
> Grotesque youths, spearing
> Fish in the lamplight,
> Register a degeneration.

Even the girls, standing
On the antique quai, one
Eating an ice-cream cone suggest

Necrosis. They watch
Under fallen stars, while the town
Corrupts in silence.

Antibes: there are
Places whose very emptiness
Mirrors our betrayal.

It has been remarked that this is a kind of nineteenth-century travel poem. Among its few faults, this need not be numbered. Its faults are more technical: an occasional failure of cadence, an unnecessary use of 'very' in the next to last line. Its virtues, emerging like flotsam in many of the stanza's final lines, should suggest that little is being described in this poem, but much is thrust delicately into our purview and then removed. The poem has no background other than the repetition of the word 'Antibes'. The speaker is a demonstrator; his role is to thin out the three- or four-dimensional world to a screen where action is naught, where, 'under fallen stars', gods are aligned with 'trivial flesh', creation becomes 'repro- duction', and where all process is a silent corruption. The strength of the poem is not the apparent idea, but the skill with which emptiness becomes a mirror against the reader's eye. The action of the poem has nothing to do with either the speaker or the figures he indicates. The action depends upon a random superimposition of accidentally related images. But the modulation of imagery relent- lessly urges upon us the fact that fantasy, memory, noon, night, Nicolas de Staël's suicide, an older painting of Picasso—that all these show us how the world becomes picture steadily emptying itself of centre and depth: time, deceptions of memory, fallen gods, necrosis become positions and azimuths of the visual world.

As a paradox working against the persuasive order of the poem's stanzas, we are urged to believe in the momentary and exclusive validity of every point of reference. In an article on David Milne, Northrop Frye speaks of a similar effect in Oriental and medieval painting:

> . . . it is absurd to say that Oriental or medieval painting is flat . . . or that it has no perspective. The perspective is there all right, but it is a

convex perspective which rolls up on the observer instead of running away from him. In some Oriental pictures the observer's eye seems to be at the circumference of the picture, so that it opens inward into the mind. Perspective in this kind of painting is not a mechanical handling of distance, but a proportioning of visual interest, which makes a man look smaller when further away because he is then pictorially less important.[7]

To proportion visual interest is precisely Jones' role in the poem. Against the depth-creating properties of line, colour, and form, the poet juxtaposes time, plays with the irony of language, remembers the images of other men and, without any suggestion of continuity, allows Antibes to die at noon, at evening, and at night, while somebody eats ice-cream. And where is Cap d'Antibes if not a projected fantasy?

My reference to the work of Milne is neither casual nor fortuitous. Jones himself wrote a poem on Milne with the evocative title 'A Garland of Milne'. Turn after turn of the poem summons up images of the painter's haunting canvases and exhibits a brief and allusive anthology. In many ways, Jones' Milne is an archetypal Canadian, the man who made a garden of the bush, for whom

> All space came out in flowers
> miraculous, erupting from a void or mouth.

But what is admired in Milne can also be admired in Jones, for whom the form of a poem, particularly a longer one, is a spatial composition in which the tonalities of margins, masks, and fragmentary implosions create an interplay of voices whose perspectives mix 'background' and 'foreground' which, for the unwary, seems inhuman.[8] The persona of these poems may indeed have no precise outline, but the effort to project a shape, to cast a 'profile in the birdless air',[9] to shadow forth the labyrinth of the human spirit in the formal design of the poem, is what distinguishes Jones from the unexamined romanticism of his contemporaries. The persona, finally, is a creation of a poem's design.

What always characterizes Jones' levelled manner of speech is its reflective pitch. It is at once a meditation and an argument; it surrounds the world witnessed over the shoulders of both Narcissus and Li Po, the Chinese and the classical ('more practical and more /

Frequented"[10]) pool of the mind playing one reply against another. Sometimes the poet's attitude emerges dry and pure, as in the image chosen as the title for his recent study of themes and images in Canadian literature, *Butterfly on Rock*. But the larger poems brood almost bizarrely over the water illusions of Narcissus' pool, a place of expected dissolution in expansion, and unforeseen restoration into depth:

> So neither swim nor float. Relax.
> The void is not so bleak.
>
> Conclude: desire is but an ache,
> An absence. It creates
> A dream of limits
>
> And it grows in gravity as that takes shape.
> ('I Thought There Were Limits')

Thus limit as a screen returns as an accepted illusion turning upon the grave. Such limits are wall-façades: they are interstitial, and so conjoin while seeming to divide. While the butterfly is not rock, he illuminates inertia and is defined by being there.

Of façades, the simplest is the mask. But the pathos of masks, as the poet asserts in the form of most of his poems, is their totally amorphous capability: they droop from branches like Dali's dead time-pieces. So in a poem dedicated to Michèle Lalonde:[11]

> Here you know nothing.
> You are a rag, blown by the wind,
>
> A negligée of sunlight on some twigs.
> Here the Beast
>
> Lifts you like a broken bush—
> Old nests
>
> Tumbling from your hair. The Beast
> Snuffs your flesh,
>
> Your limbs, smelling of summer . . .
> Like a dead child's
>
> Broken to the wind . . . like tears

> Dried in his hands.
>
> ('Les Masques de l'âme')

Mask is modulation—it is in the same order of phenomena as a visual proportion. Hence their adoption by Jones is neither classical nor archetypal in Northrop Frye's sense. They are less disturbing than the mask borne at the conclusion of *The Story of O*, but they are equally attuned to the mortal and transitory. The woman is often Eve and often Persephone; and the speaker, when not Orpheus, Orestes, Odysseus, Phosphor, can assume even the guise of Michael the archangel in a curious peripheral allusion to the dissolution of the poet's first marriage ('To Eve In Bitterness'). The paradox of Jones' use of the mask is such that, while it evokes some of the playfulness of Cocteau and Giraudoux posing past against present (the foreground and background of time), he seems to have abandoned the stability that past can provide in the mask. The past seems totally over in Jones, a blurred background. Yeats would recreate past; Jones' touch seems to make it more remote. To that extent the past belongs to the visual presence of time:

> The osprey disappears, dissolves,
> As suddenly returns, his wing
> Banked at another angle on the wind. And so
>   all things
>
> Deliquesce, arrange, and rearrange in field.
>
> ('Mr Wilson, The World')

As I have suggested, to find in these poems, even when no mask is employed, a unified voice similar to a unified vision, is not necessary. Jones' strategy is field composition. In the first section of 'Soliloquy to Absent Friends' the speaker's voice comes only from the vast solitudes of northern winters:

> Micheline,
> the winds dissolve our towns; the streets
> where once we played, bound each to each, even
> in solitude to others yet unknown
>   twist like mirrors in the twisting wind
>   and are dissolved.
> Micheline,
> the world is a leafless wood; we stare

abruptly upon tundra and the sky—
        soul's frontiers where we meet,
          knowing ourselves only
      capacities for loneliness,
      solitudes wherein the barrens sound.

The second section addresses Quixote and cites W. C. Williams'
poem on the red wheel barrow. The third evokes Quixote again,
now announcing that

                Quixote, only your hands,
    their unproductive gestures on the air, *welcome*
    or *goodbye*, root us in the vast
    silence, the abyss where elsewise all things drift,
    a rain of fragments falling into death.

As a kind of gathering and fourth act, the next section is a surprising and intricately structured panel description of the month of
February in the *Très riches heures* of the Duke of Berry. Everything
is there, the magpies who 'drop sounds like barley in the muted
yard', haystack, wood, axeman and drover, village and cold that
'has cast a greenish glow / On the dissolving hills'. Even in late
medieval France, dissolution stood upon the margins, but within
the frame there is 'No distance, no abyss'. Here art plays the role of
the monitory mask and screen, reminding us of what we have lost.
The fact that it is ancient art transformed to word only underscores
the elegiac character of the image. It is a poignant intrusion of the
Ptolemaic order upon a world where 'abyss is infinite'. Its only
consolation is the scant cheer of a pictorial presence:

    And so bound round is the abyss,
    By winter void, by battle and by labour and by love,
    By homely comfort that will warm the thighs,
    That in the Duke of Berry's *Book of Hours*
    You and I, and old Quixote, Micheline,
    And men and women whom we never knew,
    And others whom we shall never know,
    May find one bed together against cold.

But no one can live in or by an illuminated book, and the poet's
advice is only sufficient for that poem. We may, in fact, consider
the didactic hortations of the last section ('Let us be bare, / Let us

be poor') as simply a shift of mood to suggest a variation of proportion. It is for Jones a new resolution of the dilemma of 'Antibes:
Variations on a Theme'. Within the whole order of shifts
employed to seize and release evasions of as, a parainesis, a poised
margin, the appeal to art and Quixote and Williams, all these are
aspects of an attitude towards life that Jones admires in Archibald
Lampman. He observes that 'at the centre of [Lampman's] poetry
we find a celebration of the abundant well of universal energy and
of its embodiment or epiphany in the manifold variety of life'.[12]
Jones, with more technical variety, aims at such successive epiphanies of visual variation.

Of the longer poems, the most achieved is the title poem from
Phrases from Orpheus, whose stature and originality arise at once
against the kind of technical tradition in which Jones participates
and the modern treatment of the Orpheus story as it has developed
in Europe.[13] In this poem the poet plays off in a disturbing manner
Eliot's 'voices' of soliloquy and direct address. It is disturbing, for
he adopts, among others, the mask and mythological hints of
Orpheus; he then speaks across the mask in another voice, more
modern, approaching probably his own, and this voice speaks to its
own, and not the mate of Orpheus, Euridice. Weaving through
these voices is heard the voice of literary allusion; and that voice
speaks contrapuntally against a kind of voice of no time and no
body, which can be considered a parody of what Eliot calls the
impersonal voice. This final voice gives shape to the modern drive
to make the world an image and then to seize it as image. It is the
voice of illusion, despair, and loss *made visual*. Taken together, the
four dimensions of the poem turn with varied response and intensity upon the several descents that the ancient myth evokes, and as
the poem proceeds, its profoundly self-reflective character reminds
us that Orpheus' need as a singer was intimately involved with the
loss of the substantive world. He falls into the pool of Narcissus.
Jones stamps his understanding of the fluid tangent of word and
thing by an almost terrified response to the visual dissolution of
things in time, such as one observes—and there are a number of
poems that contain this mystery—in the punctuation of the 'present' through an old photograph. Hence, Jones puts on the mask of
Orpheus not to return the reader to a mythic past where there will
be 'no distance [and] no abyss', but rather to open into the shared

abyss because it is more courageous, as he suggests, to embrace mortality than to embrace the image which is beautiful only. The poem becomes Jones' most sustained effort to probe his consuming passion for art and the dark it aims to lighten.

This poem, to an extraordinary degree, employs margins to define masks, and the technique exemplifies in verse the proportioned play of visual interest. Part of the speaker's loss (in his first voice) is his brother's death, and the visit to the morgue runs through a remembered sentence from de Maupassant while the speaker broods on the problem of language at death:

> et la bête saignante, le sang sur les plumes,
> le sang sur mes mains, me crispent le coeur à
> le faire défaillir
>   It
>   is
>   silence
>   when the great
>   trays
>   are
>
>   pulled out
>
>   speaks
>
>   the cold
>   cadavre gives up
>   the word
>
>   as if
>
>   love
>
>   speech
>
>   were but a hollow cup
>   drinking fills

Language, of course, participates in the normal curve of the Orphic story: it is a katabasis of recessive backgrounds. It should also be observed that, going beyond Eliot, Jones has split his voice to play off the problem of the gnomic (and, hence, suggestively Orphic) against the blankness of death. It is a technique characteristic of the whole. Its function is to point the central attitude that the gnomic must partake of an awareness of death. To seek the substance of gnomic realities dissociated from mortality is to court a kind of total dissolution. Such, I take it, is the point of one reminiscence that arrives and departs in the poem without echo except for its suggestion of desperate illusion:

> I remember a girl like a blonde
> wolf eyes
> straight from the forest and made up a
>
> lioness she wanted
>
> nothing but music and
> the elegant sadness of
>
> *garde-moi la dernière danse*
>
> there by the highway (her
> mother could pitch logs, drive
> cattle or deliver a calf) the young men
>
> didn't exist
>
> a Tartar, in love
> with rumours of the Byzantine Court
> wanting
>
> nothing
> but what she could not have

Here the abyss is infinite: she strikes into the poem like a vision choked with visions. Her centre is nowhere. As Antony perceives himself dying, she is a shapeless apparition. The necessary centre is grave; it combines gravity and shadow. As the first voice asks later, briefly adopting the mask of Orpheus but clearly suggesting the modern world of photography and image-making:

> Is that flesh
> hangs in the darkness?

I have passed
those lovers withered,
crucified

upon the beam of sight

The distinction that emerges, assisted by the unusual word-play, is
that the House of Hades is not the *camera oscura* we would imagine it
to be. To win the assurance of mortality, which is the assurance of
what we are, the apparent tricks of the visual world must be faced
and endured, as if an Antonioni movie were really a form of
infernal purgatory, 'upon the beam of sight'. The descent continues:

Without
death honour is

perilous

a bright plaque

and beautiful

in Plato's vision

Descend
in the dark house

and not unlike

the
promiscuity of gods

embrace
the cold clay, the dirty
plaster

Disorder after death
appals

My love is not among them

My
love is in your midst

>   bitten by the snake
>   she is not
>
>   there in Hell
>
>   a shy
>   animal in grass
>
>   nor yet
>   exposed and like the glare
>   rock
>
>   but dark
>
>   her captured flesh (her flowers
>   are moonflowers
>
>   more the negative
>   of that
>
>   posed photograph
>   and tan
>   girl in sunlight

The gradations of descent, measured by recessive margins, step first into an allusion to John Crowe Ransom's 'The Equilibrists' from which the italicized words are displaced. The allusion fits: Ransom's world is the pure world where lovers tease like ideal photographs—

> And rigid as two painful stars, and twirled
> About the clustered night their prison world,
> They burned with fierce love always to come near,
> But honor beat them back and kept them clear.

The place that Jones evokes is equally prison but of several superimposed dimensions deliberately unfocused, as opposed to 'clear'. The epigraph to the Canadian poem—'each in his prison / We think of the key'[14]—points directly to this fact; and so also the poem's shape and central metaphor bear upon the closure of prison and death. But if our existence is a *huis clos*, some prisons are better for us than others, hence the dialectic employed between illusion and mortality. At the core of death the new life is possible. In that regard, Jones is paradoxically Dantesque, despite his efforts in *Butterfly* to persuade us otherwise. The dialogue beginning 'My / love is in . . .' is emblematic of the central argument: love is only where death is, not posed and tempting as 'a shy animal' (which refers to the imaged girl at the beginning of the poem). Incapable of being Platonic, she does not participate in 'the promiscuity of the gods', an image strongly suggestive of the third stanza of 'Antibes'. The necrosis of Antibes, one might add, is made to sustain precarious and limited existence.

Most modern poetry runs the risk of becoming merely cosmopolitan. This poem runs not only that risk, but also that of being rooted in a sensibility that is normally taken for granted between the contending views of British and American writing. Canadians have made a virtue of remaining parochial within the blown universe. This poem's particular risk is that it assumes that the Orpheus myth, contrary to the usual assumption, is not a pattern for Gnostic modes of salvation. It is enough simply to hang on through death's winter that 'descends like a glacier into the soul'.[15] By suggesting that literary allusion and image-making are metaphors for sterility, a kind of life without the definition of death, Jones is then able to persuade us that the Orpheus story, a major monument of our literary tradition, participates in illusion as well. Thus the myth subserves the poet's central preoccupation with visual art whose eye-play is the place of our awareness of mortality.[16] Pure perception against a screen of non-death would be otherwise senseless. By so envisioning the myth as a dramatization of illusion and death, he strips the myth of its general character as a pattern or order. The myth's ambiguity is displayed everywhere in the poem's ambiguity. It projects deception as the only place where the self can be identified as an event capable of death. Along with other major modern views of the pattern, 'Phrases from Orpheus' constitutes an important revision. Jones' burden is not that there is immortality in song, despite the ironies of language, but that survival is a visual craft.[17] But such a burden is fundamental to his art, apparent from the poem that opens *Frost on the Sun*, and traceable through all the kinds of *trompe-l'oeil* that his poems light upon.

A complete appraisal of the work of D. G. Jones cannot overlook the art of his short poems. It is these poems that distil the kinds of technique I have pointed to. They are not simply lyrical; they press carefully against their form at the edge of evanescence. These poems, to modify slightly the subject of 'On a Picture of Your House', often seem to be

> no place. And I confess
> what I protect is your
> capacity for loss,
>
> your freedom to be no one, look
> so naked from that window
> you are lost in light.

So to protect art, by allowing it the freedom to disappear and to return as Jones' notion of the poet does, is, on a small scale, to suggest the amorphous character of the artist in consonance with his art. From the outset, from *Frost on the Sun*, Jones has sought a voice and a persona that without becoming cosmic would dramatize the problem of the world's conflicting claims. In 'Phrases from Orpheus' a kind of resolution occurs in which the persona plays against other voices. The risk of the persona has less to do with language and silence than with the visual and non-visual presence of background and foreground. Absence in Jones is not silence but disappearance. Hence, as he remarks in 'For Françoise Adnet', 'Time is space, it glows'. The longer poems seek such a spatialization of event; the best of the shorter poems employ such a technique by superimposing imagery in a manner suggestive of theatre. Sometimes the movement is syllogistic:

> The grey hills, like whales,
> Journey in the winter sea;
>
> I hardly know if I'm alive,
> Or shall ever love again—
> Unless I journey with the whales
> To where the hills rise up: green.
>
> ('Winter Hills')

The strength of the poem is probably thematic: the arena from colourless to green can be called the landscape of Jones' persona. In 'Phrases' it is a similar dialectic from the image as illusion to death as substance that draws the speaker apart. A more exquisite care for the demand of form is manifest in 'Washed Up' from his last book:

> The rock
> rising from water,
>
> cedars
> twisting from rock,
>
> clouds
> and a single birch—
>
> Nausicaa
> playing in the wind.

The technique is painterly; and Nausicaa, a kind of mask for the speaker's Odysseus, has nothing of a Homeric past, but is a psychological dimension of the Laurentian Shield. And Nausicaa, 'playing in the wind', is a desire as evanescent as the act of becoming green. The figure is merely a mask; she belongs to wind; her role is to provide visual ambiguity, for Odysseus was not made for that child.

Some objects lose substance by being seen too much. Or, to put it another way, a frequency of modified images suggests the same kind of ambiguity as several voices emerging from different levels of awareness. So 'Devil's Paint Brush'—

> After the rain
> They are rust upon the field,
>
> They are suns
> Burning in a spider's space,
>
> They are
> Nipples by Matisse—One
>
> White daisy
> Is a virgin or a saint,
> A vestal in a host of flames.
>
> Musk is their smell,
> Like sunlight on a girl's face.

The paradox of the poem is that all the things the flower becomes are 'flat', brilliantly coloured and totally non-tactile. They are not nipples but 'Nipples by Matisse'. These things are as painful visually as a Nausicaa of wind, and they are things whose deceptiveness belongs to the vision of mortality.

To seize mortality in the form of art—it can only fail as an endeavour. Had Orpheus been a painter, many things would have been 'lost in light' and dark. Jones seems haunted by this: if art cannot possess anything by illusion, what can? 'Where do they go?' he asks of snow buntings. And he enjoins:

> You must think of the birds
>
> And make them as you will:
> Wood or stone or broken clay
> With a brown glaze.
>
> You must lie down in the dark
> In the naked fields.
> You must think of the birds
>
> And make them as you will.

In a poem entitled merely 13/3/72 he speaks of the effort to make art mortal so as to overcome death:

> Je tourne vers toi
> à travers l'effritement des âges
> pour n'être que ta pierre fine
>
> pour n'être enfin
> que ta chair[18]

Jones is rarely so spare: art is simply fine stone; mortality, thy flesh, with all the ambiguity that demands. Loss is broadly spatialized into a crumbling field. As in 'Phrases', the action of actualization is dialectical, for the speaker moves 'à travers' as if to foil absence by becoming its foreground, by becoming finally, the act of art, and so dramatizing an illusion played against the eye of death, 'pour "naître" enfin'.

I would avoid any conclusion that would call Jones a romantic. I would say rather that I have been endeavouring to sketch aspects of a Canadian, of a classical Canadian, poetry. James Reaney has remarked that

the Canadian poet has to stay in the country and at the same time act
as if he weren't in it. It looks as if I'm saying that the Canadian poet
has to be some sort of poltergeist.[19]

I see Doug Jones so, shuffling in his Northern American attic,
brooding upon Anchises and another Lavinia. But it is a past that
has become untimed and makes the present difficult to perceive. It
is an ambiguity peculiar to Canada, and Jones has observed it as
well in public papers in which the American that explodes from
Whitman to Ginsberg is welcomed as a continental possession, but
the Pentagon is condemned as simply 'European'. Jones' response
to the predicament is natively elusive, but it is as centrally Canadian as the work of Lampman to whom I have referred, and to
Lampman's contemporary, Charles G. D. Roberts, who provides
an image that captures the harshly beautiful sense of 'butterfly on
rock'. While Layton's butterfly is precariously near its own death,
the butterfly at the end of 'The Sentry of the Sedge Flats' illuminates the pitiless character of death. It is a brilliant image cast upon
a mortal ground through which illusion endures:

> . . . a splendid butterfly, all glowing orange and maroon, came and
> settled on the back of the dead heron, and waved its radiant wings in
> the tranquil light.[20]

From such situations, Jones' poetry and the best of Canadian literature arise, full of sidelong glances forth into the world and back
into itself.

[No. 60, 1974]

---

[1] See the long poem, 'Sequence of Night', *Tamarack Review*, 50, 1969, 104-26 which endeav-
ours to illuminate the familial aspects of such tragedy.

[2] (Toronto, 1957).

[3] (Toronto, 1961).

[4] (Toronto, 1967).

[5] Compare Anne Hébert's letter to Frank Scott in *Dialogue sur la traduction* (Montréal, 1970), pp.
47-8. I am grateful to Barbara Belyea for drawing my attention to this and other kinds of
similarities that exist between 'Le tombeau des rois' and 'Phrases from Orpheus'.

[6] De Profundis Conjugii Vox Et Responsum' from *Phrases from Orpheus*.

[7] 'David Milne: An Appreciation', *Here and Now* 2, 1948. rep. *The Bush Garden* (Toronto,
1971), p. 204.

[8] See David Helwig 'Poetry East, West and Centre', *Queen's Quarterly*, 75, 1968. 533.

[9] 'A Danger of Birds', *The Canadian Forum*, June 1972, 15.

[10] 'Li Revived' from *Frost on the Sun*.

[11] A useful introduction for the English reader to her work may be found in *Ellipse*, 3, 1970, 4-41, ed. chiefly by D. G. Jones.

[12] *Butterfly on Rock* (Toronto, 1970), p. 99.

[13] See Walter A. Strauss, *Descent and Return—The Orphic Theme in Modern Literature* (Cambridge, 1971) for an extended discussion of the myth's European development from Novalis.

[14] An inversion of T. S. Eliot, 'The Wasteland', 413.

[15] 'Soliloquy to Absent Friends'.

[16] Compare George Bowering's suggestive and penetrating article, 'Etre chez soi dans le monde', *Ellipse*, 13, 1973, 81-103.

[17] Strauss remarks, p. 249, that song is the basis of the myth, and that the poet's role is one of unifying the cosmos, but nowhere does he elaborate upon the fact that Orpheus lost Eurydice because of looking.

[18] *Ellipse*, 13, 1973, 2.

[19] 'The Canadian Poet's Predicament', *University of Toronto Quarterly* 26, 1956-7, 284-95, rep. in *Masks of Poetry*, ed. A. J. M. Smith (Toronto, 1962), p. 120.

[20] *Neighbours Unknown* (London, Melbourne and Toronto, 1911), p. 63.

Leonard Cohen
Black Romantic

Sandra Djwa

Writing on 'The Problem of a Canadian Literature', E. K. Brown pokes fun at the genteel conservatism that characterizes Canadian writing:

> Imagination boggles at the vista of a Canadian Whitman or a Canadian Dos Passos. The prevailing literary standards demand a high degree of moral and social orthodoxy; and popular writers accept these standards without even . . . rueful complaint.[1]

If Brown considers a Whitman or a Dos Passos improbable, a Canadian Gênet, a Canadian Burroughs, or a Günter Grass is clearly beyond expectation. Yet it is in precisely this tradition—that of the contemporary Black Romantics, as we might call them—that Leonard Cohen appears to belong.

Cohen's poetry reads like an index to the history of European romanticism; from the epigraph to *Let Us Compare Mythologies* (1956) through *The Spice-Box of Earth* (1961) to the 'lady' of 'garbage flowers' in *Flowers for Hitler* (1964), his progress is from Keats and Lawrence through Baudelaire to Gênet. In brief, this is a movement from a qualified acceptance of the romantic ideal as it is embodied in art ('For ever wilt thou love and she be fair') to the decadent romanticism of a *fin de siècle* aesthetic in which the ugly replaces the beautiful as the inspiration for art.

Reading through Cohen's work we become aware of an unsatisfied search for an absolute. In his world there are no fixed values, spiritual or sensual, that stand beyond the transitory moment, and the moment itself, experience made myth, blends imperceptibly with other moments and other mythologies, so that in the shifting the values change, leaving only the value of experience made art:

> Those days were just the twilight
> And soon the poems and the songs
> Were only associations
> Edged with bitterness
> Focussed into pain
> By paintings in a minor key
> Remembered on warm nights
> When he made love to strangers
> And he would struggle through old words
> Unable to forget he once created new ones
> And fumble at their breasts with broken hands.

Cohen's dominant theme, the relationship between experience and art, and more specifically the suggestion that the value of experience is to be found in the art or 'beauty' distilled from it, is a familiar motif of the late romantics. It first appears in Cohen's work as an epigraph to *Mythologies* taken from 'The Bear' by William Faulkner:

> 'She cannot fade though thou hast not had thy bliss',
> McCaslin said: 'For ever wilt thou love and she be fair'.
> 'He's talking about a girl', he said.
> 'He had to talk about something', McCaslin said.

This preface to a poet's first book suggests an amused recognition of a certain attitude to experience; the rationale is that of love for art's sake. But if this attitude is familiar, the irrational neo-gothic world from which the poet takes this stance is not at all familiar, at least in Canadian poetry. Particularly in his two later books, *Flowers for Hitler* and *Beautiful Losers* (1966), Cohen would seem to be closest to the European tradition of Baudelaire, Sartre, and Gênet, and to their American affiliates Henry Miller and William Burroughs.

In contrast to the later European tradition from Baudelaire to Gênet, Canadian writers have not wandered very far from first-generation romanticism. Strongly influenced by Wordsworthian natural piety and reinforced by the Calvinist urge towards moral uplift, the native line in English-Canadian poetry might be characterized by the straightforward statement and explicit morality of a D. C. Scott, an E. J. Pratt, or an Earle Birney. Despite Lampman's flirtation with the Symbolists and Marjorie Pickthall's coy apprenticeship to Swinburne, imagistic technique was not fully recognized as such in Canadian poetry until the thirties, and the Decadent sensibility, with its attendant themes of masochistic death, self flagellation, and religious inversion, is reflected only faintly in Carman's work of the nineties, recurs briefly in the thirties with Leo Kennedy's *The Shrouding*, and does not appear again until just recently in the late fifties. Notably, this Decadent sensibility is most explicit in the works of the younger writers Leonard Cohen, Daryl Hine, and Mordecai Richler, all of whom have come into contact with the European tradition.

Consequently Cohen does have some grounds for asserting, as he does on the back cover of *Flowers for Hitler*, that his 'sounds' are new in Canada and possibly subject to critical misinterpretation. Admittedly he does stress the same religious, sexual, and social protest as do Klein, Layton, and Dudek, and he does take the same missionary delight in the poetic vocation of the Montreal Group *pour épater le bourgeois*. But Cohen's technique is considerably more complex than that of Layton or Dudek, and the vision and sensibility which he expresses are sufficiently different from those of Klein to suggest that he has moved into a different tradition. In this connection we might compare the world view of Klein's *Hitleriad* (1944) with that of Cohen's *Flowers for Hitler* (1964). Along with the structure and style of Pope's *Dunciad*, Klein's *Hitleriad* is invoking the rational Neo-Classical world where human folly can be effectively chastised by the wit of a righteous indignation:

> Let anger take me in its grasp; let hate,
> Hatred of evil prompt me, and dictate.

Cohen, on the other hand, insists upon the relativity of evil; Hitler is 'ordinary', Eichmann 'medium'. In this perspective, irrational evil is accepted as a normal part of the human make-up which can even come to have a certain attractiveness:

> It happens to everyone. For those with eyes who know in their hearts that terror is mutual, then this hard community has a beauty of its own.

This reference to the strange 'beauty' which can spring from a community of evil and suffering invokes Baudelaire's *Fleurs du mal*. And it is Baudelaire's flowers of evil grafted with those of Gênet which Cohen uses to provide the structural myth of *Flowers for Hitler*. In this book the moments of beauty which the poet attempts to create, like those of his protagonist Kerensky, 'when poems grew like butterflies on the garbage of his life', are moments which cannot come into being unless evil is first admitted. Like his mentor, the T. S. Eliot of *The Waste Land*, and for that matter like Klein also, Cohen wants to bring a guilty world into recognition of itself: 'I wait / for each one of you to confess.' But unlike Klein, and again following Eliot, the confession that Cohen demands is one which accepts personal responsibility for evil as the natural corollary of being human. Having accepted this awareness of evil, as does the protagonist of 'The New Leader', the individual is then released from the negative virtue of 'threading history's crushing daisy-chain with beauty after beauty', and face to face with the ugliness of self:

> Drunk at last, he hugged himself, his stomach clean, cold and drunk, the sky clean but only for him, free to shiver, free to hate, free to begin.

This would seem to be a basically post-World-War-II position: the romantic voyaging 'I', bereft of religious belief and Hegel's cosmic rationalism ('the sky clean'), sets out to discover his world. And as in Sartre's *Nausea* or Heller's *Catch-22*, this involves the attempt to come to terms with existence itself. Faced with a world which he sees as irrational, evil, and grotesque, an evil and an ugliness which he shares because he is human, with only a momentary hope of vision and that perhaps delusive, the modern anti-hero accepts evil as part of existence and immerses himself within it, both in terms of the external world and through the journey into self.

This immersion in destruction, often accomplished through a combination of alcohol, drugs, and sex, would seem to be metaphysical in nature in that it is an attempt to find a new answer to the human predicament by going down instead of up. In this sense it might be considered the modern romantic myth. Where Wordsworth and Coleridge attempt the transcendental leap, Baudelaire, Rimbaud, Huysmans, and the modern Gênet, Sartre, and Burroughs all spend a season in hell. Experience is the distinguishing mode of the Byronic hero, the later Victorian Decadents and their twentieth-century descendants, the Black Romantics. For the past twenty years the subject of the modern romantic has been increasingly the fascination of evil and its relationship to the process of destructive metamorphosis. Cyril Connolly, in a recent attempt to define 'modernism', finds its essence in this quatrain by Baudelaire:

> Only when we drink poison are we well—
> We want, this fire so burns our brain tissue,
> To drown in the abyss—heaven or hell
> Who cares? Through the unknown we'll find the new.[2]

As this excerpt makes clear, the value of the abyss is not only the pleasure of new sensation but the possibility of a new revelation beyond the experience itself. The danger inherent in this credo would seem to be the temptation it offers to mistake catalogued sensation for new revelation.

In Cohen's work this possibility of a new revelation is specifically associated with the myth of descent culminating in the creation of art. In his first book of poetry, *Let Us Compare Mythologies*, the structural myth is that of the death of the poet-god Orpheus and the possibility of his resurrection in art. Like Eliot's *Waste Land* the book moves through cycles of winter death followed by spring rebirth, and the poet-victim as a part of this cycle moves between the extremes of innocent and destructive love. In terms of the controlling Orpheus myth, the figure of the beloved woman suggests Eurydice while the madwoman evokes the Bacchanals. In the poem 'Letter', the poet-victim, aware of his impending death, addresses the madwoman directly: 'How you murdered your family / means nothing to me / as your mouth moves across my body'. The poems of this cycle would seem to make a strong case for submission to a destructive love which, unlike the romantic escapism of such poems as 'On Certain Incredible Nights', can lead to a new beauty and a new order. Consequently the poet embraces the 'real', sacrifice goes on ('Hallowe'en Poem'), and the poet's brain exposed, 'the final clever thrill of summer lads all dead with love', becomes a 'drum' to be 'scratched with poetry by Kafka's machine'. The rationale for this disintegrative experience is explicit in the poem 'Story'. Only by allowing the madwoman full sway is it possible for the poet as victim to find his place in art: 'to understand one's part in a legend'.

It is this myth of art which seems to provide the basic structure in Cohen's work. In his first book the myth of descent is presented primarily as the desolation of Eliot's *Waste Land*. In *The Spice-Box of Earth* this longing for the old lost ideals is re-worked in terms of a neo-Hassidic myth. No longer able to accept a despotic God, the poet as priest is forced beyond Genesis into a desolation which is 'unheroic, unbiblical'. Lawrence Breavman, the poet as lover, finds himself in the same position in Cohen's next book, *The Favourite Game*. Breavman's alienation grows throughout the novel until he is finally stricken with panic and loneliness; it is then that he realizes that a new experience awaits:

> He stumbled and collapsed, tasting the ground. He lay very still while his clothes soaked. Something very important was going to happen in this arena. He was very sure of that. Not in gold, not in light, but in this mud something necessary and inevitable would take place. He had to stay to watch it unfold.

The experience that waits for Breavman is a recognition of the evil and irrationality symbolized by Baudelaire's mud-flowers. In *Flowers for Hitler* this recognition is presented as a disintegrative experience which is both frightening and pleasurable. This descent into evil is savoured in much the same way as the young Breavman enjoys his adolescent satanism ('Fuck God'), yet the very process of daring the abyss is a propulsion into an irrational, frightening world. Similarly, the narrator-historian of *Beautiful Losers* is forced through the motions of Sartre's nausea in a grimy sub-basement room that gradually fills up with his own excrement.

In Cohen, as with Baudelaire and Sartre, the value of this disintegrative process is given as the creation of art. 'Elegy', the first poem in *Let Us Compare Mythologies*, expresses this myth of descent in the death of the poet-god Orpheus:

> He is descending through cliffs
> Of slow green water
> And the hovering coloured fish
> Kiss his snow-bruised body
> And build their secret nests
> In his fluttering winding sheet.

From the disintegrating body of the dead god comes art; the 'secret nests' of 'hovering' fish. In a later poem, 'These Heroics', the poet explains that it is because he cannot be 'fish' or 'bird' that he makes dreams and poetry from love. The association of poet and bird is common to Horace, Baudelaire, and Rilke, and in each case the bird symbolizes the poet's aspiration. Cohen's addition of a 'fish' to this complex with primary associations of disintegration, points up his belief that the creative process is one which moves between aspiration and disintegration. Associated with the poetic, sexual, and religious aspiration which forms one pole of Cohen's system is the dove, the beloved, and Catherine Tekakwitha; clustered about the other pole, the process of disintegration, is the fish, the Black Mass, the Bacchanals, 'F' and Edith. Through art—the 'nests' of 'Elegy', the 'kite' of *Spice-Box*, the 'butterflies' of *Flowers for Hitler* —the poet attempts to reconcile the two. For example, the exiled poet-priest of *Spice-Box* finds that neither religious belief nor physical love can fill up the void between 'a ruined house of bondage and a holy promised land'. This reconciliation of the spirit and the flesh is only to be found in the fairy-tale land of art:

> Out of the land of heaven
> Down comes the warm Sabbath sun
> Into the spice-box of earth

or in the artifact itself; the spice-box, one of the symbols of the Jewish Havdallah service marking the Sabbath's end, becomes a metaphor for the human form divine.

A similar conclusion is reached in Cohen's later books; Breavman learns that although love is a 'creation', the favourite game is not love alone but the flesh made art:

> When everyone had been flung . . . into the fresh snow, the beautiful part of the game began. You stood up carefully, taking great care not to disturb the impression you had made. Now the comparisons.
> Of course you would have done your best to land in some crazy position, arms and legs sticking out. Then we walked away, leaving a lovely field of blossom-like shapes with footprint stems.

In *Flowers for Hitler*, Cohen takes the blackness of the human capacity for evil and from it attempts to extract the flowers of art. In this perspective the poet emerges as recorder: 'neither / father nor child/ but one who spins / on an eternal unimportant loom / patterns of war and grass / which do not last the night.' Similarly all the four main characters of *Beautiful Losers* find themselves to be both artist and pattern. Through the experience of failure, the narrator, his

Indian wife Edith, his guide and lover 'F' (cf. Pynchon's 'V'), and the Iroquois saint, Catherine Tekakwitha, are each precipitated on a journey into self which results in the recreation of existence:

> Not the pioneer is the American dream . . . . The dream is to be immigrant sailing into the misty aerials of New York, the dream is to be Jesuit in the cities of the Iroquois, for we do not wish to destroy the past and its baggy failures, we only wish the miracles to demonstrate that the past was joyously prophetic, and that possibility occurs to us most plainly on this cargo deck of wide lapels, our kerchief sacks filled with obsolete machine guns from the last war but which will astound and conquer the Indians.

Because it is Cohen's thesis that the experience of failure is indispensable for the creation of art, the book becomes a case study of the *fleur du mal* 'beauty' of such losers. Through a pop-art catalogue of sensation, the narrator proceeds to the superior 'magic' represented by Catherine Tekakwitha (1656-1680). Tekakwitha functions primarily as an artist of religion, her name is defined as meaning 'she who, advancing, arranges the shadows neatly'. As the narrator further explains, a saint is associated with the 'energy' of love: 'contact with this energy results in a kind of balance in the chaos of existence'. Through her influence as it is manifested directly and through the other two characters, the narrator-historian passes through nausea (like his prototype, Sartre's Roquentin) to the point that it is suggested that the novel is produced from his experience.

Despite the contrivance of Cohen's central myth, *Spice-Box* and *The Favourite Game* are impressive, well-written early books, and perhaps largely because of the glimpses they offer of realized experience. *Flowers for Hitler* and *Beautiful Losers* are less rewarding, not only because they are more dominantly written to formula, but also because of the increasingly self-conscious attitude of the poet as persona in relation to the codification of his central myth. What I miss in Cohen's later books is the sense that the writer is attempting a subjective re-interpretation of evil or failure as the case might be. Instead, Cohen's successive books offer variations on a theme within other men's myths. This technique has the advantage of structural neatness, and there are few Canadian readers who have not expressed delight at Cohen's technical virtuosity, but it also has the serious disadvantage of sacrificing organic growth and original discovery to a pre-determined formula. Little can happen in *Flowers for Hitler* or *Beautiful Losers* because Cohen has already determined what will happen even before the experience takes place. Furthermore, because he is committed to a view of life and art which is essentially that of religious aspiration followed by sexual inversion, Cohen is further limited in his presentation of experience and his delineation of character. Experience and characters can only come from the Yellow Books of the 1880s and 90s. The case study of the young hero and his *saison en enfer*, the division of the romantic *femme fatale* into her opposite but complementary aspects of innocent and destroyer (cf. Catherine and Edith), are familiar features of Decadent literature as is the presentation of the satanic, often homosexual, friend and alter-ego ('F').

The limitations of this vision would seem to be the limitations of Decadent literature in general; it substitutes a narrowed, bizarre area of human experience at the expense of the ordinary human average, and it negates the dignity of ordinary human encounter to a hierarchy of art. Because this vision, although limited, is of primary importance to the author, his characters are subordinated to it. As types, they depend on increasing doses of sensationalism to be effective. In this connection it is possible to trace the increasing sensationalism associated with the figure of the friend as he is presented from *The Favourite Game* to *Beautiful Losers*. Like the mentor of Oscar Wilde's *Portrait of Dorian Gray*, 'F' is memorable for his epigrams rather than for a sense of character in depth. Part of the difficulty involved in Cohen's perception of character would seem to be related to the fact that his characters are conceived as part of an internal myth. Cohen, for example, is both poet-writer and persona and the two often merge. This can sometimes be effective as in the poem 'You Have The Lovers' from *Spice-Box* where the poet-lover and poet-spectator are universalized but more often the trio of two lovers and a spectator leads to sensationalism or the plain voyeurism of the sun-bathing sequence in *Beautiful Losers*.

The sensibility which reports the sensationalism of the disintegrative experience is quite different in kind from that which we usually associate with Canadian poetry. Faced with an absurd world, Cohen is no longer able to call on Klein's humane rationalism for the redress of evil. Instead there is some attempt to exorcise evil by filtering it through the comic mode. This Black Humour is apparent in Cohen's description of Nazi concentration camp atrocities:

> Peekaboo Miss Human Soap
> Pretend it never happened
> . . .
> I say let sleeping ashes lie.

Here the brutal is introduced as a witty aside and the particular *frisson nouveau* of the poem seems to arise from the juxtaposition of the erotic, infantile world of Bathing Beauties, 'peekaboo' and 'let's pretend', with the horror of real concentration camps where soap is made from human fat and ashes. At first glance Cohen appears to be having a nasty laugh at the expense of Jewish suffering. Alfred Purdy, in fact, describes the subject of *Flowers for Hitler* as little more than the after-dinner talk of 'a good conversationalist who had to say something'.[3] But on closer inspection it might be suggested that this is an attempt to come to terms with a painful experience. Through the medium of Black Humour it is possible to see the selection of a Miss Human Soap as the fun and games of an absurd world. And because Cohen has presented horror as an absurdity, there is a possibility of moving on to a new affirmation in a way that is not open to Klein in his *Hitleriad*. But at the same time (and it is this which makes Purdy's comments relevant) the dichotomy between the epigraph to *Flowers for Hitler*, which is an excerpt from Primo Levi warning against the disintegration of personality, and the sensationalism of the book itself, leads us to question the integrity of Cohen's vision—a question which does not arise in connection with the Black Humour of Selby's *Last Exit to Brooklyn* or Grass's *The Tin Drum*.

Coming to terms with this view of experience is as tricky as the attempt to decide whether or not pop-art is a contradiction in terms. Yet it can be said that the qualities which make Cohen's work fairly easy to describe—myth as literary structure, central persona, a consistent view of life and art—are also those qualities which mitigate against further development in his later work. In general I find Cohen's poetry often too derivative to be impressive, and the mythic technique, once the key has been supplied, too simple to be suggestive in the largest sense. Cohen does play the game very well; his mythologies are clever, often witty, sometimes very moving; yet even at its best, Cohen's favourite game is still

Eliot's or Baudelaire's or Sartre's. But Cohen is attempting to write of contemporary themes in a contemporary way. His concern with alienation, eroticism, and madness, together with the experimental techniques of *Flowers for Hitler* and *Beautiful Losers*, unlike the dominantly early nineteenth-century romanticism of the Montreal Group, are the concerns of post-World-War-Two writing. For Cohen, as for Heller, Burroughs, Grass, and Selby, the old rules of religious rationality and romantic idealism exist to be questioned. The last twenty years has seen the codification of a new group of writers whose focus is on the disintegrative vision, and it is in their footsteps that Cohen is following. Because this new vision, like that of the Decadents, is an inversion of traditional romantic 'myth' and morality, and because it is often presented with the irreverent wit of the new Black Humourists, we might be justified in calling this attitude to experience, Black Romantic.

Within the world of the contemporary Black Romantic, the disintegrative experience is presented not only through the journey into self but also through the form of the work. Both, in turn, are microcosms of the reductionist cycle of the larger world. The form of *Beautiful Losers*, with its disjointed inner monologues interspersed with snippets of history and clippings from comic books, is substantially the 'cut-up' technique of William Burroughs alternating with one of the stylistic tricks from Sartre's *Nausea* which might be distinguished by the fact that Every Word Begins With A Capital. Both techniques suggest the merging of values which cannot occur without a breakdown in the structure of the world which they represent. In *Beautiful Losers*, as in Céline's *Journey To The End Of Night*, it is the universe itself which is breaking down, proceeding gradually but inevitably through the process of entropy. Cohen illustrates this process and then attempts to reverse it when the once glorious 'F' disintegrates into a smelly old man but then escapes from the novel page (and, incidentally, the human predicament) by metamorphosing himself into a movie of Ray Charles. This is a flippant example, but it is another reminder that the Black Romantic justifies his presentation of disintegration by insisting that the breakdown of the old 'false' categories leaves the way open for both reader and author to create new order. In Cohen's work this justification is more impressive in theory than in practice. Techniques such as Cohen's 'pure list' or Burrough's 'cut-up' are successful only when there is some direction suggested for the movement beyond recorded disintegration, and it is this larger revelation which is most absent from extended passages of *Beautiful Losers*.

For these reasons I suspect that Leonard Cohen is more important in Canadian writing for the contemporary movement which he represents than for the intrinsic merit of his work to date. The world of the Black Romantic may not be a particularly pleasant one, but its awareness of the darker side of human consciousness is a helpful counterbalance to a literary tradition that professes an ignorance of the human animal as complete as any of the Pollyanna Glad Books. As early as 1928 we can find A. J. M. Smith insisting: 'the Canadian writer must put up a fight for freedom in the choice and treatment of his subject'. Suggesting that desperate conditions require desperate remedies, he concludes: 'our condition will not improve until we have been thoroughly shocked by the appearance in our midst of a work of art that is both successful and obscene.'[4] *Beautiful Losers*, as successful pop-art, may just provide the function Smith has in mind. At the same time, I am sorry to see Cohen join Layton in the role of public educator, because if he does have a future as a serious writer—if he wants one—it is back in the writing of *The Favourite Game* before Cohen, persona, solidified.

[No. 34, 1967]

[1] E. K. Brown, 'The Problem of A Canadian Poetry', *Masks of Fiction* (Toronto, 1961).
[2] Cyril Connolly, *The Modern Movement* (London, 1966).
[3] Alfred Purdy, 'Leonard Cohen: A Personal Look', *Canadian Literature* 23, 1965.
[4] A. J. M. Smith, 'Wanted, Canadian Criticism', *The Canadian Forum* 91, 1928.

Power Politics in Bluebeard's Castle

Gloria Onley

Is it possible for men and women to stop mythologizing, manipulating, and attacking one another?

Margaret Atwood, 1971

If the 'argument' of Sidney's *Astrophel and Stella* is 'Cruel Chastity', the argument of Atwood's *Power Politics* is cruel sexuality. The cover design[1] pictures a knight in armour from whose extended arm and gauntletted hand depends, like a game trophy, the body of a woman, torso swathed in mummylike bandages, head down, hair trailing on the ground at the knight's feet. This inversion of the traditional posture of *homo erectus*—a deliberate echoing of The Hanged Man of the Tarot pack—is repeated in the novel *Surfacing* with David's sadistic upending of his wife, '"twatface"' Anna. In *Power Politics*, as in Atwood's two novels, the unrequited love of courtly myth gives way to its equally frustrating modern form, a hedonistic, yet somehow mechanical union. The woman in *Power Politics* feels that her being is lacerated and her capacity for vision destroyed by subjection to a sadomasochistic sexual love:

> you fit into me
> like a hook into an eye
> a fish hook
> an open eye

Atwood's ironic inversion of courtly love connects her art with the revelations of McLuhan, Millett, Roszak, and Chesler about the social mythology of Western culture. Romantic obsession with lover or husband is presumed to provide the woman with her most satisfying form of existence. 'To a man, love and life are things apart. To a woman, love is life itself', preaches The Sensuous Woman, echoing Byron.[2] The compulsively exact male/female polarity of 'doing' and 'being' implied by Atwood's sardonic conversion of garment fastener into deadly weapon expresses the conviction of the female prisoner of the machismo love structure that romantic love, in its modern version, is a devastating mode of existence. 'Have to face it I'm / finally an addict', the 'hooked' woman in Power Politics concludes. In 'an air stale with aphorisms', a unique relationship that is sustaining yet liberating and joyous does not develop and, through a painful succession of claustrophobic encounters, Atwood suggests that maybe her female persona is looking for something that just doesn't exist.

Recent studies of the situation of women in our patriarchal society have established that the essential female traits are considered to be passivity, masochism, and narcissism.[3] Atwood's 'fish hook . . . open eye' image perfectly condenses this cultural definition of 'normal' female personality and emotional capacity and hurls it at the complacent romantic sensibility. Hence the poet Robert Read writes of 'Atwood as acupuncture'; her manipulations anaesthetize his persona so that she may gulp his heart down her 'icy throat' (The Canadian Forum, Dec., 1972, 9). But Atwood is also aware of the basic victor/victim patterning she explores in Survival (1972), her thematic guide[4] to Canadian literature, as a vicious circle. The woman in Power Politics can proclaim with an ironic self-awareness that verges on compassion: 'Night seeps into us / through the accidents we have / inflicted on each other / Next time we commit / love, we ought to / choose in advance what to kill.'

To Atwood, the love-aggression complex is an historical-personal fact. The cover of Power Politics expresses the predicament of women in the sexist society:

> My love for you is the love
> of one statue for another: tensed
>
> and static. General, you enlist
> my body in your heroic
> struggle to become real:
> though you promise bronze rescues

you hold me by the left ankle
so that my head brushes the ground,
my eyes are blinded . . .

There are hordes of me now, alike
and paralyzed . . .

The theme of *Power Politics* is role-engulfment: 'You refuse to
own / yourself, you permit / others to do it for you . . . ' The self is
lost to the social role of romantic lover, warrior, wife, superman:
fulfilment means incarnation within the archetype: ' . . . through
your own split head / you rise up glowing; / the ceiling opens / a
voice sings Love Is A Many / Splendoured Thing / you hang suspended above the city / in blue tights and a red cape, / your eyes
flashing in unison'. Self-emergence is as difficult as pacifism in a
world of war: 'If you deny these uniforms / and choose to repossess
/ yourself, your future / will be less dignified, more painful, death
will be sooner . . . ' Beyond the mask of social role lies the paradox
of Western culture: a postulated uniqueness of self that may not
exist, or perhaps cannot be known, if it does exist:

You drift down the street
in the rain, your face
dissolving, changing shape, the colours
running together

My walls absorb
you, breathe you forth
again, you resume
yourself, I do not recognize you

You rest on the bed
watching me watching
you, we will never know
each other any better
than we do now.

The antithesis of the mask is the 'face corroded by truth, / crippled,
persistent', asking 'like the wind, again and again and wordlessly, /
for the one forbidden thing: / love without mirrors and not for /
my reasons but your own'. Poised on the brink of a metaphysical

negation of individuality, the disillusioned female lover is possessed by a harsh nostalgia. At the same time there is a continuation of a previous movement in Atwood's poetry towards accepting the visitation of archetypal presences as a substitute for authentic interknowledge of the selves, as in 'your jewelled reptilian / eye in darkness next to / mine' or 'you descend on me like age / you descend on me like earth'. But the implicit quest is always for some alternative to the sadistic penetration and destruction of the 'fish hook—open eye' relationship, for some 'reality' behind the engulfing political role, and for some communion with that 'reality'. *Power Politics* confronts us with an entropic modern world in which a formerly solar masculinity now operates as a suction pump to exhaust and destroy the environment:[5]

> You are the sun
> in reverse, all energy
> flows into you and is
> abolished; you refuse
> houses, you smell of
> catastrophe, I see you
> blind and one-handed, flashing
> in the dark, trees breaking
> under your feet, you demand,
> you demand
>
> I lie mutilated beside
> you; beneath us there are
> sirens, fires, the people run
> squealing, the city
> is crushed and gutted,
> the ends of your fingers bleed
> from 1000 murders

The imagery in Atwood's novels also expresses mechanization and destruction, but there the woman's helpless suffering or retaliation changes into an urgent desire for liberation.[6] In *The Edible Woman*, where social intercourse proceeds by means of 'finely adjusted veneers', and the dominant aesthetic is conformity to the consumer ideal ('I love you especially in that red dress') images express role-engulfment as an omnipresent fate shared by everyone from the protagonist, Marian, a reluctant market researcher, to the 'office virgins'. To Marian, her fiancé's very clothes 'smugly [assert] so much silent authority', she fears they would be warm, if touched. Dickens' caricatures and Bergson's essay on mechanization as a principle of comedy seem to underlie Atwood's satirical description of character and behaviour. Despite the humour, sex-role mechanization is associated with death, until Marian finally sees Peter as a 'dark homicidal maniac with a lethal weapon'. A conditioned product of his consumer society, Peter is preoccupied with establishing, perpetuating, and worshipping himself within the glossy confines of the urban male image: a *Playboy* bachelor-hood followed in due time by a *House and Garden* marriage. The 'lethal weapon' with which he tracks and attempts to capture Marian is, of course, a camera; escaping from its focusing eye, Marian runs away from aggressive consumption and towards selfhood, rejecting the role of 'soapwife' in a never-ending soap opera.

Deciding to remain an individual involved in a variety of human relationships, Marian defeats the shaping power of the sexist consumer society. Making a surrogate self out of cake and then eating it in a comic parody of ritual cannibalism, she both destroys a false image and reabsorbs her culturally split-off female self. This form of magic, a self-assertive process of encoding and eliminating what she is *not*, looks forward to the ritual destruction of false images of the self at the end of *Surfacing*; it is a comic anticipation of the magic more seriously practised by the schizoid personality to restore its connection with the world.

Marian's fiancé refuses to eat her cake body; unable to liberate himself from consumerhood by comic communion, he rejects even the possibility of self-knowledge. Peter's social world is luxurious, totally artificial, self-consciously sensual; the mirrored spaces of his apartment lobby epitomize the glittering surfaces of urban reality: the world of technological hedonism founded on industrial technology. The 'high electric vibration of this glittering space', is the concept of the ego as consumer—the grossly inflated ego extending itself in voluptuous narcissism through its glittering 'made-up' surfaces: images of chrome and glass, arranged interiors, iced cakes, elaborate hairdos, face-makeup, sequinned dresses, ritualized, mechanized social behaviour. It is in reaction to this world of surfaces that Marian slowly becomes unable to eat anything at all. Psychoanalytically, the ego of the cultural being in a state of fixation at the level of oral aggression, an infantile state of consciousness in which 'the good' is the consumable or edible, including other people. Marian's consumption of the 'edible woman' is a transformation ritual to get her outside of this one-dimensional social nexus, in which the potential self is condemned to collective narcissism as an alternative to genuine interaction with others.

In *Power Politics*, sexual love is imaged several times as a shattering of the ego that seems to be epitomized in the collision between mirrors of 'They travel by air': 'your / body with head / attached and my head with / body attached coincide briefly / ... we hurtle towards each other / at the speed of sound, everything roars / we collide sightlessly and / fall, the pieces of us / mixed as disaster / and hit the pavement of this room / in a blur of silver fragments'. In the semantic universe of technological man, what ought to be separate modes of existence somehow mirror each other through the shaping effect of myth. Hence velocity and violence enter into personal relationships. The woman cries to her lover, 'I lie mutilated beside / you ... How can I stop you? / Why did I create you?' Men and women are political prisoners of the sexist society, trapped as victors/victims in their own reflections of the world and of each other. Only in orgasm ('a kick in the head ... sharp jewels / hit and my / hair splinters') or in fantasied death do the mirrors shatter.[7]

A persistent strain in Atwood's imagery, appearing in the poetry as well as in *Surfacing*, is the head as disconnected from, or floating above, the body.

> But face it, we have been
> improved, our heads float
> several inches above our necks
> moored to us by
> rubber tubes and filled with
> clever bubbles, ...   (*Power Politics*)

Often the imagery describes the body as a mechanism remotely controlled by the head; sometimes the neck is sealed over; always the intellectual part of the psyche is felt to be a fragment, dissociated from the whole. The 'head' of Atwood's schizoid persona is the 'Head' described in Michael McClure's 'Revolt' (reprinted in Roszak's *Sources*), the Head that 'quickly ... fills with preconception and becomes locked in a vision of the outer world and itself. ... The Head [that] finally may act by self-image of itself, by a set and unchanging vision that ignores the demands of its Body'.[8] We

think of Anna in *Surfacing*, locked into her *Playboy* centrefold stereotype, her soul trapped in a gold compact, her capacity for love
locked into a sadomasochistic pattern. The narrator describes her:

> Rump on a packsack, harem cushion, pink on the cheeks and black
> discreetly around the eyes, as red as blood as black as ebony, a
> seamed and folded imitation of a magazine picture that is itself an
> imitation of a woman who is also an imitation, the original nowhere,
> hairless lobed angel in the same heaven where God is a circle, captive
> princess in someone's head. She is locked in, she isn't allowed to eat
> or shit or cry or give birth, nothing goes in, nothing comes out. She
> takes her clothes off or puts them on, paper doll wardrobe, she copu-
> lates under strobe lights with the man's torso while his brain watches
> from its glassed-in control cubicle at the other end of the room, her
> face twists into poses of exultation and total abandonment . . .

Anna conforms; therefore, she is. The narrator inhabits her own
cartesian hell. Locked into a sex role herself by the conspiracy of
her friends, pursued by 'geometrical sex' as 'an abstract principle',
her past 'marriage' and 'baby' a fantasy rationalization or restruc-
turing of the personal history she cannot live with, she is clearly
intended to be a representative schizoid personality: 'I realized I
didn't feel much of anything, I hadn't for a long time. . . . At some
point my neck must have closed over, pond freezing or a wound,
shutting me into my head; since then everything had been glancing
off me, it was like being in a vase . . . '

During the course of her search for her father, a biologist living
in isolation near the Quebec-Ontario border who has mysteriously
disappeared, she becomes painfully aware of 'what circuits are closing' in her friends' heads and in her own. Responsible for the
group's survival in the wilderness setting, she finds the mandatory
sexual 'liberation' of her lover and friends depressing and alienating. For her, it depersonalizes them into cartoon figures or rock
drawings, linear caricatures of humanity. 'Shadowing' her along
the trail to where she is pragmatically contemplating, not the
'names' but the 'forms' and 'uses' of the various plants and fungi,
Anna's husband David imposes his one-dimensional, linear, or
'phallic' thrust on nature:

> [The Death's Angel] sprang up from the earth, pure joy, pure
> death, burning, white like snow.

... 'Hi, watcha doin'?' he said ...

... it was like trying to listen to two separate conversations, each interrupting the other. 'A mushroom,' I said. That wouldn't be enough, he would want a specific term ... 'Amanita.'

'Neat,' he said, but he wasn't interested. I willed him to go away but he didn't; after a while he put his hand on my knee. . . . His smile was like a benevolent uncle's; under his forehead there was a plan. . . .

'How about it?' he said. 'You wanted me to follow you.' . . . He reached his arm around me, invading . . . I twisted away and stood up . . . 'You're interfering.' I wiped at my arm where he had touched it.

He didn't understand what I meant, he smiled even harder. 'Don't get uptight,' he said, 'I won't tell Joe. It'll be great, it's good for you, keeps you healthy.' Then he went 'Yuk, yuk,' like Goofy.

Through the perceptions of her narrator, Atwood records again the pathology of a sexual relationship in which the male asserts his masculinity by inflicting physical or psychological pain:

... then [Anna's] voice began ... a desperate beggar's whine, *please, please* ... She was praying to herself, it was as if David wasn't there at all. *Jesus jesus oh yes please jesus.* Then something different, not a word but pure pain, clear as water, an animal's at the moment the trap closes.

It's like death, I thought ...

'He's got this little set of rules. If I break one of them I get punished, except he keeps changing them, so I'm never sure. He's crazy, there's something missing in him, you know what I mean? He likes to make me cry because he can't do it himself . . . '

Echoing Laing's description of the depersonalized alienated personality—'Bodies halfdead: genitals dissociated from genitals'—the narrator conceives a mental ideogram for David's kind of love: 'it would be enough for him if our genitals could be detached like two kitchen appliances and copulate in mid-air, that would complete his equation.' Her sudden vision of David as 'an imposter, a pastiche', relates him to the 'creeping Americanism' that she feels is moving up into Canada, destroying the landscape, the animals, and the people. 'He didn't even know what language to use, he's forgotten his own, he had to copy. Second-hand American was spreading over him in patches . . . He was infested, garbled . . . it would take such time to heal, unearth him, scrape down to where he was true.' At her worst moment of alienation, she sees those around her as evolving, 'half-way to machine, the left-over flesh atrophied and diseased'.

The cultural link between depersonalized sex and modern technology is suggested by George Steiner in *In Bluebeard's Castle: Notes Towards a Redefinition of Culture*.[10] Steiner comments on the significance of the 'maniacal monotony' of de Sade:

> . . . that automatism, that crazed repetitiveness, . . . directs us to a novel and particular image, or rather silhouette, of the human person. It is in Sade . . . that we find the first methodical industrialization of the human body . . . Each part of the body is seen only as a part and replaceable by 'spares.' In . . . Sadian sexual assaults, we have a brilliantly exact *figura* of the division of labour on the factory floor.

Throughout *Surfacing*, as in Sadian fantasy, sex is linked with mechanization, coercion, and death:

> . . . I didn't want him in me, sacrilege, he was one of the killers . . . he hadn't seen, he didn't know about himself, his own capacity for death.
>
> 'Don't,' I said, he was lowering himself down on me, 'I don't want you to.'
>
> 'What's wrong with you?' he said, angry; then he was pinning me, hands manacles, teeth against my lips, censoring me, he was shoving against me, his body insistent as one side of an argument.

Anna's compulsive need to conform to male expectations makes it impossible for her, despite a degree of self-knowledge, to view other women as friends ('she resented me because I hadn't given in [to David], it commented on her'), and fills her with unconscious self-loathing. As Anna's relationships with others seem to fall almost totally within a general sadomasochistic tendency, and as her love for David seems to be a kind of death, so detective stories are her 'theology'.

To repulse David's attack, the narrator is able to use magically her awareness of his golem quality:

> His wrist watch glittered, glass and silver: perhaps it was his dial,

the key that wound him, the switch. There must be a phrase, a vocabulary that would work, 'I'm sorry.' I said, 'but you don't turn me on.'

'You,' he said, searching for words, not controlled any more, 'tight-ass bitch.'

Obviously, David is projecting. In David, and to a lesser extent in Joe, Atwood creates a parody of the mighty hunter:

> [They] appeared . . . one at either end of a thinnish log. They were proud, they'd caught something. The log was notched in many places as though they'd attacked it . . . David wanted some footage . . . for *Random Samples* . . . In the end they stuck the axe in the log, after several tries, and took turns shooting each other standing beside it, arms folded and one foot on it as if it was a lion or a rhinoceros.

Their film, a development from the camera imagery of *The Edible Woman*, is an aimless stockpiling of randomly chosen images—a linear, mechanical imitation of natural flux that is the equivalent in art of their other male activities. Just as ineffectual hacking at the log is rationalized as male strength, so a total lack of vision becomes creative spontaneity when David decides that the film 'might be even better if it was out of focus or over-exposed, it would introduce the element of chance, it would be organic.' In both novels, Atwood satirizes a general tendency to rationalize—or transcendentalize—conformity to unsatisfactory behaviour patterns.

In connection with their posturing for the film, the narrator senses again the vicious yet pathetic narcissism of David and of her lover, Joe: 'He didn't love me, it was an idea of himself he loved and he wanted someone to join him, anyone would do . . . ' Fear and hatred of the repressed 'female' element of personality erupts in David's conversation:

> 'None of that Women's Lib,' David said, his eyes lidding, 'or you'll be out in the street. I won't have one in the house, they're preaching random castration, they get off on that, they're roving the streets in savage bands armed with garden shears.'

To Atwood's intuitively psychoanalytical consciousness of human nature, engulfment in the sexual role, as she satirically exposes it in *Surfacing*, means that the ego of the cultural personality tends to become fixated at the stage of analsadism, condemned to the hellish circle of self-definition through violence, in which each man kills the thing he loves, in one way or another.

The end of Chapter 18 brings the sexual politics of *Surfacing* to a ritual climax of judgement and rejection by the peer group:

> 'She hates men,' David said lightly. 'Either that or she wants to be one. Right?'
> A ring of eyes, tribunal; in a minute they would join hands and dance around me, and after the rope and the pyre, cure for heresy . . .
> 'Aren't you going to answer,' Anna said, taunting.
> 'No,' I said.
> Anna said, 'God she really is inhuman,' and they both laughed a little, sorrowfully.

Rejecting her assigned sex role, Atwood's protagonist becomes the modern equivalent of the heretic or witch—the mentally ill or 'inhuman' person, the deviant by means of whose existence 'normal' values are asserted and maintained. At this point, the expulsion / escape of the unfeminine wilderness guide begins. Skulking animal-like beyond the clearing until her friends have abandoned her (as she wishes), she approaches and returns from the verge of total madness.

Alone in the house her father built, she reflects: 'Logic is a wall, I built it, on the other side is terror.' Starting to groom herself, she feels a 'surge of fear', knows the brush is 'forbidden', knows why:

> I must stop being in the mirror. I look for the last time at my distorted glass face: . . . reflection intruding between my eyes and vision. Not to see myself but to see. I reverse the mirror so it's towards the wall, it no longer traps me, Anna's soul closed in the gold compact, that and not the camera is what I should have broken.

She then destroys all the 'artifacts' of her past life: among other symbols, her childhood drawings, 'the rabbits and their archaic eggs'; the 'confining photographs' of her family heritage; her own false art, the 'bungled princesses, the Golden Phoenix awkward and dead as a mummified parrot'. Her ritual destruction of all falsely defining images of her self and others, her temporary rejection of all linear structures (house, fence, even garden), her reversion to primitive survival by eating roots and mushrooms, leads her to an hallucinatory identification with the matrix of nature, in which the artificial structures of language and culture dissolve for a moment, and she becomes a microcosm of the biosphere:

> The forest leaps upward, enormous, the way it was before they cut it, columns of sunlight frozen; the boulders float, melt, everything is made of water, even the rocks. In one of the languages there are no nouns, only verbs held for a longer moment.
>
> The animals have no need for speech, why talk when you are a word.
>
> I lean against a tree, I am a tree leaning. I break out again into the bright sun and crumple, head against the ground.
>
> I am not an animal or a tree, I am the thing in which the trees and animals move and grow, I am a place.

As Atwood notes in the Introduction to *Survival*, Northrop Frye suggests that in Canada 'Who am I?' at least partly equals 'Where is here?' Here, in *Surfacing*, is the liberated naked consciousness, its doors of perception symbolically cleansed; the 'place' is the Canadian wilderness, which becomes the new body or rediscovered original body of the psychosomatic human. The radiant plurality of the organismic realm into which the narrator descends is epitomized in the image of the frog: 'A frog is there, leopard frog with green spots and gold-rimmed eyes, ancestor. It includes me, it shines, nothing moves but its throat breathing.' The fairy-tale theme of metamorphosis is present: the narrator transforms herself from a schizoid personality into a basic human creature by going down into forest, swamp, and water, into a primitive Edenic reality where frogs, no longer revolting or worthless, become fellow creatures of the biosphere—breathing, shining kinfolk of the human. The basic metaphor of descent and surfacing is itself a transformation of Atwood's inherited romantic image of death by drowning. The last part of the novel is thus a paradigm of descent into and ascent from the fluid ego boundary state of schizophrenia.[11] But it is a carefully controlled, artistically simulated descent, of therapeutic purpose and value within the psychoanalytic dimension of the novel. The ego core (or inner self) of the narrator always retains its integrity, except for a fleeting moment during the peak experience of hallucinatory oneness with nature where Atwood seems to be synthesizing a primitive state of mind analogous to Lévy-Brühl's 'participation mystique'. Like Laing, Atwood seems to believe that schizophrenia is a form of psychic anarchy: a usually involuntary attempt by the self to free itself from a repressive social reality structure. John Ayre quite rightly terms her a 'psychic iconoclast'.[12]

In *Surfacing* and *The Edible Woman*, it is as if Atwood had inferred from the glittering surfaces of our social images the Freudian theory of personality as narcissistic, accomplishing self-definition through various forms of aggression, ranging from overt coercion to the subtle forms of unconscious 'induction' revealed by Laing. At the end of *Surfacing*, when the wilderness guide returns to the cabin where she had at the beginning of her descent into madness turned the mirror to the wall, symbolically rejecting the feminine image represented by Anna's gold compact, she turns the mirror around again and regards herself as she has become:

> ... in [the mirror] there's a creature neither animal nor human, furless, only a dirty blanket, shoulders huddled over into a crouch, eyes staring blue as ice from the deep sockets; the lips move by themselves. This was the stereotype, straws in the hair, talking nonsense or not talking at all. To have someone to speak to and words that can be understood: their definition of sanity.
>
> That is the real danger now, the hospital or the zoo, where we are put, species and individual, when we can no longer cope. They would never believe it's only a natural woman, state of nature, they think of that as a tanned body on a beach with washed hair waving like scarves; not this, face dirt-caked and streaked, skin grimed and scabby, hair like a frayed bathmat stuck with leaves and twigs. A new kind of centrefold.

Beneath this ironic transformation of Narcissus' mirror lies Szasz's concept of the 'mentally ill' person as political prisoner of the social reality structure of his society, as enforced by institutional psychiatry, Laing's 'mind police'. A fusion of many literary forms, Menippean satire, diary, wilderness venture, even the Canadian animal story, *Surfacing* is the classic human animal story: the wilderness guide as social deviant becomes a scapegoat, driven out of the technological society for her sexist peers so that they may define themselves by their rejection of her.

By the end of the psychological quest, it is clear why, as Atwood stated earlier in *The Circle Game*, 'Talking is difficult' and why in *Surfacing* 'language is everything you do'. The difficulty in human relations, metaphored in *Surfacing* as exile from the biosphere, is metaphysically related to the exploitative use of language to impose psychological power structures. The need for communion in *Power Politics* is paralleled by the realization that language tends to warp in the hand from tool to weapon: 'The things we say are / true; it is our crooked / aims, our choices / turn them criminal,' and there is a corresponding recognition of the value of silence: 'Your body is not a word, / it does not lie or speak truth either. / It is only here or not here.'

In 'Hesitations outside the door', Bluebeard's castle is the place where 'you twist all possible / dimensions into your own'; it is the house 'we both live in / but neither of us owns.' As the self defines itself in relation to others, so Bluebeard cannot be himself without a victim/wife. Each induces the other to participate in the structuring of the myth. There is a surrealistic sense in which language itself, because it is habitually and unconsciously used to erect and impose false structures, is Bluebeard's castle. The 'wife' cries to 'Bluebeard': 'Don't let me do this to you, / you are not those other people, / you are yourself / Take off the signatures, the false / bodies, this love / which does not fit you / This is not a house, there are no doors, / get out while it is / open, while you still can . . .' To use language at all is to risk participation in its induction structure; to define is to risk committing or inciting violence in the name of love.

Why this should be so is suggested by George Steiner in his analysis of the current barbarisms of Western culture: there is a sense in which the grammars themselves 'condescend or enslave'.

> Indo-European syntax is an active mirroring of systems of order, of hierarchic dependence, of active and passive stance . . . The sinews of Western speech closely enacted . . . the power relations of the Western social order. Gender differentiations, temporal cuts, the rules governing prefix and suffix formations, the synapses and anatomy of a grammar—these are the *figura*, at once ostensive and deeply internalized, of the commerce between the sexes, between master and subject . . .

For Atwood, the basis of the victor/victim patterning she sees in human relations in *Survival* and reflects in the male/female relations of her own literary structures is also psycholinguistic—that is, inherent in the monotheistic, patriarchal social reality structure of Western culture, within which man habitually defines himself by aggression and which has reached a pinnacle of alienation in sexist, technological society, the 'America' of the alienated self. The narrator of *Surfacing* remembers her brother's childhood obsession, with 'wars, aeroplanes and tanks and the helmeted explorers', and realizes that his sadistic treatment of his experimental animals and his military interests are intimately related to his adult habit of imposing moral categories upon nature:

> Below me in the water there's a leech, the good kind with red dots on the back, undulating along like a streamer held at one end and shaken. The bad kind is mottled grey and yellow. It was my brother who made up these moral distinctions, at some point he became obsessed with them, he must have picked them up from the war. There had to be a good kind and a bad kind of everything.

In Atwood's poem 'Hesitations outside the door', Bluebeard in his castle is both the suffering Christ, the emergent masochistic half of the sadomasochistic Judeo-Christian tradition, and the culturally defined sadistic male, participating with his wife in the melancholy inevitable fusion of Eros and Thanatos:

> What do you want from me
> you who walk towards me over the long floor
>
> your arms outstretched, your heart
> luminous through the ribs
>
> around your head a crown
> of shining blood
>
> This is your castle, this is your metal door,
> these are your stairs, your
>
> bones, you twist all possible
> dimensions into your own.

The myth is a destructive one: it defines love as sacrifice and suffering, and consummation as death. As in *Surfacing*, the sadistic male uses women mechanically as keys to self-definition by aggression:

> In your pockets the thin women
> hang on their hooks, dismembered

> Around my neck I wear
> the head of the beloved, pressed
> in the metal retina like a picked flower.

If men possess and use women as keys, women have been conditioned to worship men as icons (the Victorian locket, the religious medal). These interlocking attitudes have had the effect of fragmenting and destroying for Atwood's persona the perhaps mythical but longed-for natural order ('women . . . dismembered': 'the head of the beloved . . . like a picked flower'). The concept of ownership or romantic 'possession' resulting in exploitation by the man and idealization and obedience by the woman is found throughout *Power Politics* in many of its versions and inversions of the basic prisoner or victim-of-love theme. In 'After the agony in the guest / bedroom', the would-be lover, resting in the woman's arms in a parody of the *pietà*, 'wine mist rising / around him, an almost / visible halo', asks 'do you love me' and is answered by cruciform manipulation:

> I answer you:
> I stretch your arms out
> one to either side,
> your head slumps forward.

followed by a further relocation and another kind of purgation:

> Later I take you home
> in a taxi, and you
> are sick in the bathtub.

Atwood's delineation of the lovers' agonizingly compulsive tendency to relate primarily through suffering, brutally exposes the sadomasochistic nexus of the monotheistic, patriarchal society. The woman of *Power Politics* brings to her love relationships the advantage of intellectual enlightenment, but her analytical approach serves only to invert the power structure:

> I approach this love
> like a biologist
> pulling on my rubber
> gloves & white labcoat
>
> You flee from it

like an escaped political
prisoner, and no wonder...

Please die I said
so I can write about it

She is aware of her own propensity towards sadistic sublimation.

In Atwood's exploration of sexual politics within the patriarchal value structure, orgasm becomes 'a kick in the head,
orange / and brutal, sharp jewels hit and my / hair splinters', a
redemption by death of the self: 'no / threads left holding / me,
I flake apart / layer by / layer down / quietly to the bone.'
There is great ambivalence. The desired ego-transcendence, with
its suggestion of a joyous return to a mythic primitive state of
consciousness where the 'skull unfolds to an astounded flower', is
also dangerous, for 'learning / speech again takes / days and
longer / each time / too much of / this is fatal.' In Atwood's
poetry, the psychological basis and the value in human relationships of the individualism of Western man is very much in question: partly by reference to her sense of self-definition by violence explored in the transactional social worlds of the two novels, where individualism becomes a potent carrier of death; and
partly by reference to a presumed primitive, non-linear, and
pluralistic state of being which functions as a mythic reference in
most of her poetry from the earliest work on, emerging in *Surfacing* as a utopian alternative to alienation. In the love poems the
tension between individuality and isolation, on the one hand, and
loss of identity and sexual fulfilment on the other, is extreme and
cannot be resolved. Imagistically it is an anguished oscillation
within the *either/or* psycholinguistic structures of Western man,[13]
the existentialist trap the wilderness guide describes as the 'walls'
of 'logic'. An oscillation between the polarities of civilized /
primitive, individual / generic, male / female (in terms of Atwood's camera imagery, focused / unfocused), in which reciproc-
ity of being, psychosomatic wholeness, and a sense of genuine
communion, as *integrated qualities of experience*, remain mythic
states forever beyond reach. The channels of communication and
action are patriarchal almost beyond redemption. ' . . . you rise
above me / smooth, chill, stone- / white... you descend on me
like age / you descend on me like earth'. In her earlier poem,
'Dream: Bluejay or Archeopteryx', there is an attempt to invert

the hierarchic structure: 'in the water / under my shadow / there was an outline, man / surfacing, his body sheathed / in feathers, his teeth / glinting like nails, fierce god / head crested with blue flame'. (*Procedures for Underground*)

Atwood suggests that the end of sexual politics might come only with the end of civilization, as in 'The accident has occurred... we are alone in... / the frozen snow', when problems of physical survival would replace problems of psychic survival. Images of desert, ocean, and tundra are attractive in that they presume a settler-like equality of the sexes, working together, an absolute need for compassion; but repellent in that they are places of isolation from humanity where the known forms of self-definition and of personality, however unsatisfactory, are absent. The isolation and limitation of romantic love is mirrored everywhere in the landscape of Atwood's poetry; the couple marooned on the island, stranded in the car, or in the house in a snowstorm, surviving the holocaust, and, finally, buried together. The couple-structure of love is opposed by the community of the dance, 'the circle / forming, breaking, each / one of them the whole / rhythm... transformed / for this moment...' (*Procedures for Underground*); by the circle or flux of playing children; and by the dissolving of the ego-structure into sleep or into landscape as celebrated in 'Fragments: Beach'. 'In the afternoon the sun / expands, we enter / its hot perimeter... light is a sound / it roars / it fills us / we swell with it / are strenuous, vast / rocks / hurl our voices / we / are abolished... the sleepers / lose their hold on shore, are drawn / out on a gigantic tide / we also make the slow deep / circle / until / the sea returns us / leaves us / absolved, washed / shells on the morning beach.' (*Procedures for Underground*)

Throughout her work Atwood speaks of other languages: 'multilingual water' and 'the jays, flowing from tree to tree, voices semaphoring, tribal' of *Surfacing*. In *Procedures for Underground* she tells of learning 'that the earliest language / was not our syntax of chained pebbles / but liquid'. *Surfacing* abounds with examples of oral aggression or the sadistic use of language for self-definition. Linguistic channels of communication are felt to be analytic, dissecting, futile, impelling the narrator to break out of her received mental categories by psychic anarchy. To the alienated self, linear, logical thought structures operate like knives on the body of love. The narrator remembers her abortion in imagery that is a paranoid echoing of Sadian mechanization: 'Nobody must find out or they will do that to me again, strap me to the death machine, emptiness machine, legs in the metal framework, secret knives.' Imagining her future child, her 'lost child surfacing within her', by reference to her utopian organismic realm, as 'covered with shining fur, a god', she decides, 'I will never teach it any words.'

The anguished lack of communion between the lovers in *Power Politics* is, for Atwood, the inability of the alienated self to break through the thought structures of Western culture. In Atwood's story 'Polarities' (*The Tamarack Review*, No. 58, 1971), overt demands for what the American poet Gary Snyder calls 'inter-birth'—self-fulfilment through participation in a web of inter-relationships—are regarded as symptoms of madness. The protagonist Louise, who is isolated, even from her intellectual peers, by her deviance from the typical feminine role, tries to create a sense of wholeness by manipulating her friends into a literal acting-out of the title of Atwood's earlier book of poems, *The Circle Game*. Louise has a vision of the city as a topographical image of human relations: 'The city is polarized north and south; the river splits it in two; the poles are the gas plant and the power plant.... We have to keep the poles in our brains lined up with the poles of the city, that's what Blake's poetry is all about.' Her disorientation from conventional reality causes her friends to take her to the hospital where she is put into a chemical straitjacket.

Later her colleague Morrison wants to rescue her, but is finally disgusted by his ability to achieve masculine self-definition only in response to drug-induced tellurian femaleness: 'He saw that it was only the hopeless, mad Louise he wanted, . . . the one devoid of any purpose or defence. . . a defeated formless creature on which he could inflict himself like shovel on earth, axe on forest, use without being used, know without being known.' Morrison realizes that Louise's description of him is essentially accurate: 'Morrison refuses to admit his body is part of his mind.' He has a sudden perception of human warmth as the only answer to 'futile work and sterile love', and of the impossibility of achieving it through mechanical means, either technological ('the grace of the power plant and the gas plant') or magical ('the circle game'). The eyes 'yellowish-grey', 'alert, neutral' of the wolves in the pen at the game farm where he has gone after leaving the hospital, foreshadow the wolf's eyes of the hallucinatory image of the father in *Surfacing*. Without human communion, Morrison realizes, leaning against the wolf pen, 'dizzy with cold', there is only 'the barren tundra and the blank solid rivers, and beyond, so far that the endless night had already descended, the frozen sea.' Morrison's spatial co-ordinates accurately symbolize his psychic predicament.

Louise attempts to create a body of love by substituting the 'paleologic' of children and primitive peoples[14] for the unsatisfactory social syllogisms of the patriarchal reality structure. Mapping the repressive social polarities onto the landscape, she practises a form of primitive magic to overcome the collective insanity of communal isolation in 'apartments'. To read Atwood's description of insanity by social definition and of psychic iconoclasm in 'Polarities' and *Surfacing* in conjunction with contemporary works which analyse the social construction of reality is to realize that what Atwood calls 'mythologizing' is usually a conscious or unconscious enforcement of the sexual 'polarities' inherent in the myths of romantic love, nuclear marriage, the machismo male, and the 'feminine' woman. As an intelligent woman and a poet, Atwood indicates that we must somehow escape from this alienating cultural definition of personality and human relations. In *Surfacing* the schizoid personality's magic ritual accomplishes her mental escape from role-engulfment into the personal eclecticism or search for new forms spoken of by Steiner.

> I . . . step into the water and lie down. When every part of me is wet I take off my clothes, peeling them away from my flesh like wallpaper . . .
>
> My back is on the sand, my head rests against the rock, innocent as plankton; my hair spreads out, moving and fluid in the water. The earth rotates, holding my body down to it as it holds the moon; the sun pounds in the sky, red flames and rays pulsing from it, searing away the wrong form that encases me, dry rain soaking through me, warming the blood egg I carry. I dip my head beneath the water, washing my eyes . . .
>
> When I am clean I come up out of the lake, leaving my false body floated on the surface . . .

In *Survival* Atwood distinguishes between Nature's order, 'labyrinthine, complex, curved', and the order of Western European

Man, 'squares, straight lines, oblongs'. The Canadian settlers having a strong preconception of order as inherent in the universe, build their 'straight-line constructions, but kill something vital in the process . . . often Nature in the form of a woman.' In Atwood's poem 'Progressive Insanities of a Pioneer', the settler who fails to impose order on nature has his head invaded by 'the Nature which he has identified as chaos, refusing to recognize that it has its own kind of order'. The interplay between images of fence / garden, vegetable / weeds in *Surfacing*, and the narrator's voluntary exclusion from the fenced-in garden as part of her magic ritual, are an obvious development from this earlier exploration. Atwood also comments that the pioneer's final state of insanity may be a progressive development from an implicit earlier state, since 'suppression of everything "curved" may itself be a form of madness.'

In *Surfacing* the final hallucinatory vision is of the father, the scientist, the man who has both imposed intellectual order on nature and, presumably, taught his daughter the skills of survival in the wilderness. At first she projects on to the father, whose back is to her, her own realization of the limitations imposed by linear structures:

> He has realized he was an intruder; the cabin, the fences, the fires and paths were violations; now his own fence excludes him, as logic excludes love. He wants it ended, the borders abolished, he wants the forest to flow back into the places his mind cleared: reparation.

But then she progresses through her 'insanity' to a further stage of enlightenment:

> He turns towards me and it's not my father. It is what my father saw, the thing you meet when you've stayed here too long alone . . . it gazes at me for a time with its yellow eyes, wolf's eyes, depthless but lambent. . . . Reflectors. It does not approve of me or disapprove of me, it tells me it has nothing to tell me, only the fact of itself.
>
> Then its head swings away with an awkward, almost crippled motion: I do not interest it. I am part of the landscape, I could be anything, a tree, a deer skeleton, a rock.
>
> I see now that although it isn't my father it is what my father has become.

The dissolution of all mental structures returns man completely to nature: *he* becomes *it*. By first experiencing a dissolving of the ego into landscape and then objectifying in the human figure with wolf's eyes the consequences of maintaining this 'participation' as a state of consciousness, the narrator is able to visualize the furthest limits to which the dissolution of mental structures can be pushed without the permanent merging with the landscape that occurs in insanity, when the ego appears to dissolve into a totally schizophrenic state from which there is no returning.

Thus the father becomes a 'protecting spirit' embodying both the vital anarchic impulse of the self, the husk-dissolving creative spirit, and the essential conservative element. As in the suspended animation of the final hallucination, the fish jumping, turning into a primitive artifact or rock-drawing in mid-air, hanging there suspended, 'flesh turned to icon', then softening and dropping back into the water, an 'ordinary fish' again, there is a sense of all life as a temporary configuration of psychic energy, part of a greater flux of what earlier poets like Pratt thought of as cosmic energy structuring itself in personality and through work.[15] For Atwood, despite the apparent oscillation between ideal and real[13] implied by the image of the fish leaping, integrity of form resides primarily in the natural structure, not in the imposed social form or myth; thus being has a biological rather than a transcendental authority.

The narrator of *Surfacing* returns to sanity with the realization that she can refuse to participate in the destructive 'mythologizing' of her society: 'This above all, to refuse to be a victim.... The word games, the winning and losing games are finished; at the moment there are no others but they will have to be invented, withdrawing is no longer possible and the alternative is death.' Arising renewed from the non-evaluative plurality of nature, the wilderness guide comprehends that reality is, as William James said, a 'multi-dimensional continuum'. For the first time she understands and has compassion for the subjective dimensions of others. She realizes 'the effort it must have taken [her father] to sustain his illusions of reason and benevolent order', and how her mother's 'meticulous records' of the weather 'allowed her to omit... the pain and isolation.' Her perception of her lover is altered: 'he isn't an American, I can see that now... he is only half-formed, and for that reason I can trust him.' She has escaped her former sense of total closure, thus achieving a liberated self and a basis for action within the world.

Atwood's sense of 'participation mystique' as an alternative to alienation plays its numinous part in a personal dialectic of myths, restoring to sanity the wilderness guide of *Surfacing*. However authentic or inauthentic her concept of the primitive may be outside of the world of her alienated women, it manifests the search for new forms of reality spoken of by Steiner. The last chapter of *Surfacing* makes essentially the same statement as Birney's lines: 'No one bound Prometheus / Himself he chained', but makes it within the new context of awareness supplied by such fields as cultural anthropology, the sociology of knowledge, and environmental studies. Interdisciplinary insights are leading us quickly towards what Atwood might term an ecology of human energy, a bioethic to replace what Steiner calls 'the black-mail of transcendence'.[16] Atwood's poems and stories are not resigned and 'graceful' sublimations of what is usually referred to as the human condition. Rather they are frighteningly precise image structures, iconoclastic keys to getting mentally outside of Bluebeard's Castle.

[No. 60, 1974]

---

[1] By William Kimber for the Anansi edition. Kimber's design appears again on the jacket of the first American edition, Harper & Row, 1973.

[2] 'J', *The Sensuous Woman* (New York, 1969).

[2] Phyllis Chesler documents *Woman and Madness* (New York, 1972) by reference to these studies.

[4] In my review article '*Surfacing* in the Interests of *Survival*'(*West Coast Review*, January, 1973) I suggest that *Survival* is really an ethical treatise presented as a thematic guide to Canadian literature. The present article, accepted for publication in March 1973, is a development from this previous consideration of Atwood's work in relation to the psychology of R. D. Laing.

[5] Atwood's vampire story, 'The Grave of The Famous Poet', *72: New Canadian Stories*, ed. David Helwig and Joan Harcourt (Oberon Press, Canada, 1972), should be read in conjunction with *Power Politics*. As in *Power Politics*, the lovers form a closed system, a deadly dyadic field characterized by violence and exhaustion. See references to Atwood in my review article, "Breaking Through Patriarchal Nets to The Peaceable Kingdom", *West Coast Review*, January, 1974.

[6] The movement from bondage to liberation is not a chronological development of theme. *The Edible Woman* was written in 1965 (letter, Atwood to Onley, Dec. 30, 1972).

[7] The mirror is one of Atwood's favourite images. See 'Tricks with Mirrors' in *Aphra*, Fall 1972. "Mirrors/are the perfect lovers,/ . . . throw me on the bed/reflecting side up,/fall into me,/it will be your own/mouth you hit, firm and glassy/ . . . You are suspended in me,/ beautiful and frozen, I/preserve you, in me you are safe./ . . . I wanted to stop this,/ . . . this life of vision only, split/and remote, a lucid impasse./I confess: this is not a mirror,/it is a d o o r/I am trapped behind/I wanted you to see me here,/say the releasing word,, whatever/

that may be, open the wall./Instead you stand in front of me/combing your hair.' Compare *Surfacing*, pp. 175 and 190.

8 (New York, 1972).

9 For the narrator of *Surfacing*, 'American' signifies not a national identity but a mode of existence. See Chapter 15.

10 (New Haven, 1971).

11 Compare R. D. Laing's description of Julie in *The Divided Self*, Chapter II.

12 *Saturday Night* (November, 1972), 26. 'Atwood plays the role of psychic iconoclast, pulling the categories of existence apart and presenting a broken, confused reality that her readers must often back into order for themselves . . . she demands uncomfortable mental confrontations that most people would obviously prefer to avoid.'

13 According to the cultural anthropologist Melville J. Herskovitz, the tendency to dichotomize experience by using thought structures based on polarities is characteristic of Euroamerican culture. *Cultural Relativism: Perspectives in Cultural Pluralism* (New York, 1972), 238-9.

14 Before his death Lévy-Brühl came to realize that there is in fact no difference between primitive mentality and our own. As Herskovitz comments, all human beings think 'prelogically' at times (*op. cit.*, 28-9). Louise is not thinking and acting in terms of objectively provable causation, hence to the Euroamerican mind she appears to have regressed to a childish or 'primitive' mode of thought. Much of our thinking and behaviour is similarly dased on questionable premises, but if there is a consensus of opinion that the premises are valid, then the behaviour is held to be reasonable or 'sane'.

15 Sandra Djwa, 'E. J. Pratt and Evolutionary Thought: Towards an Eschatology', *Dalhousie Review* Autumn, 1972), 417.

16 Weyland Drew, in 'Wilderness and Limitation' (*The Canadian Forum*, February, 1973), suggests that the real strength of the ecological movement lies in its association with the Romantic and libertarian traditions—'traditions which have respected the subconscious and the primitive' (18). His observation that 'the only context in which Canadian nationalism can be acceptable is in the service of the ecological movement . . . as a responsibility to the land' seems to apply to the wilderness guide's dread of 'creeping Americanism' in *Surfacing*, and to her pragmatic yet mystical relationship to the Canadian wilderness.

MacEwen's Muse

Margaret Atwood

Now you comprehend your first and final lover in the dark receding planets of his eyes, and this is the hour when you know moreover that the god you have loved always will descend and lie with you in paradise.

— MacEwen, 'The Hour of the Singer' (unpublished, 1969)

In reading Gwendolyn MacEwen's poetry it is a temptation to become preoccupied with the original and brilliant verbal surfaces she creates, at the expense of the depths beneath them. But it is occasionally instructive to give at least passing attention to what poets themselves say about their work, and MacEwen has been insisting for some time that it is 'the thing beyond the poem',[1] the 'raw material'[2] of literature, that above all concerns her. There is, of course, more than one thing beyond the poems, but there is one figure whose existence is hinted at throughout her work and who acts as a key to much of it. This is the Muse, often invoked and described but never named; and in MacEwen's poetry the Muse, the inspirer of language and the formative power in Nature, is male. Ignore him or misinterpret him and her 'muse' poems may be mistaken for 'religious'[3] ones or reduced to veiled sexuality. Acknowledge him, and he will perform one of the functions MacEwen ascribes to him: the creation of order out of chaos.

The twentieth-century authority on the poetic Muse is, of course, Robert Graves. In his *White Goddess*,[4] he asserts that the Muse is always female, and if it isn't it should be. Poets who have the bad luck to be women should write either as priestesses of the Goddess, singing her praises or uttering her oracles, or as the Goddess herself. That some female poets have recalcitrantly invoked a

Muse of the opposite sex would be viewed by Graves as new-woman perversity; but then, he labours under the same difficulty as does Freud when he tries to discuss female psychology and Jung when he deals with the *animus* archetype: he's a man. There are several male Muses about, even in Canadian poetry;[5] often when the reader comes across an unnamed 'you', he would be better employed searching for the Muse than for someone with a birth certificate and a known address. But no one has invoked the male Muse with such frequency and devotion as has Gwendolyn MacEwen.

MacEwen is a poet whose interests and central images have been present from the time of her early publications, though her ability to elaborate them, clarify them, transform them and approach them from different angles has developed over the years. Thus her first small pamphlet, *Selah* (1961), contains two images which are later viewed more specifically as incarnations of the Muse: the God-figure and the winged man. The God of the first poem is spoken of as having 'fathered' the hills and as being 'the guardian / of the substance of light',[6] but he is remote; he encloses the individual human life but remains unknown by it ('we ... do not even ... hint You'). This distant God reappears in MacEwen's later work as the 'almost anonymous' God of 'The Two Themes of the Dance'[7] and the electrical First Cause of 'Tesla'.[8] Although he is the ultimate source of all power, including the power of language (as early as 'Selah' he is spoken of as one who 'writes', and 'sound and light' flow from his 'tongue' in 'Tesla'), he cannot be conversed with. This may explain the rareness of his appearances: MacEwen much prefers a Muse who may be addressed or who may provide the other voice in a dialogue.

The image of the winged man does not begin as an incarnation of the Muse. In 'Icarus' (*Selah*), the parallel developed is that between Daedalus and Icarus, and the Muse, addressed as 'you', and the poet, with the wings—instruments of flight—being quite explicitly the poet's pen, and the flight of Icarus, ending in destruction, being the writing of a poem which is later burnt. Here the Muse stands in the relation of quasi-father to the poet,[9] as is usually the case when MacEwen employs the words 'legacy', 'heritage', and 'inherit'.[10] But having once used the Icarus image, MacEwen takes it through a whole series of transformations. Always the man-bird is a creature halfway between human being and supernatural power. When he is ascending, he is a human being aspiring towards godhead;[11] when he is descending, he is the divine Muse in the act of becoming incarnate.

In the first 'Icarus' poem, in which Icarus becomes a 'combustion of brief feathers', the idea of burning is connected with the winged man, and it reappears almost every time the figure itself does. For the god-man the first is divine; for the man-god it is either destructive or regenerative, the fire that precedes a phoenix-like rebirth. The man who flies but dies is readily available for sexual metaphor, as witness 'Black and White' and 'The Phoenix'.[12] In the first poem the Muse is descending, becoming incarnate; in the second he is an individual man becoming Muse ('beyond you, the image rising from the shoulders / is greater than you . . . '). In *A Breakfast for Barbarians* the flaming birdman makes an ironic appearance as a 'motorcycle Icarus', 'without wings, but burning anyway', a profane version of the divine Muse who 'cannot distinguish between sex and nicotine'.[13] Instead of the Muse's descent into the flesh or even Icarus' descent into the sea, the poet imagines a splashdown into Niagara Falls. But the flying Muse is back again full-fledged in *The Shadow Maker*. In the book's first poem, 'The Red Bird You Wait For',[14] he appears, now more bird than man, as poetic inspiration itself, the Muse in its Holy Ghost form which rises phoenix-like from its own ashes only to descend once more 'uninvited':

> Its shape is a cast-off velvet cape,
> Its eyes are the eyes of your most forbidden lover
> And its claws, I tell you its claws are gloved in fire.

That the image of the descending Muse caught in mid-flight is far from exhausted for MacEwen is made evident in the recent unpublished poem, 'The Hour of the Singer'.

Having become incarnate, the Muse may both disguise and reveal himself in many forms. There are a number of poems in *The Rising Fire* and *A Breakfast for Barbarians* which praise men in action: the athletes, the escape artist, the surgeon who is 'an Indian, and beautiful, and holy',[15] the several magicians, are all men but more than men, possessed at the sacramental instant by a power greater than their own, the power of their craft, skill or performance.[16] In these poems the poet places herself at a distance; she watches the act but does not participate directly. Instead she transforms the act into a metaphor for the poetic process; in 'The Magician', for instance, the magician's 'fingers' genius / wave out what my poems have said'.[17] This kind of male figure is thus both Muse or inspirer and one who is himself inspired. Though these figures are partial masks assumed temporarily by the Muse, they are never total revelations.[18]

All of the above figures are taken from 'real' life: some of the poems in which they appear are dedicated to actual people, others (such as 'The Athletes', set in an explicitly Canadian park) are located in a world which may be identified, more or less, with the objective external one. But there are two other forms of the Muse which belong to his own proper realm, that of the imagination. These are the king and the singer-dancer, the Muse at his most static as sacramental object and at his most dynamic as sacramental creator-actor. Song and dance, princes and kings are used as images in the early pamphlets, and 'The Two Themes of the Dance' and 'The Absolute Dance'[19] are tentative explorations of the relationships among dance, poetry, and the divinity of the Muse; but not until *A Breakfast for Barbarians* are Muse, dance, and kingship synthesized.

The poems most important in this respect[20] are 'Black Alchemy', 'Finally Left in the Landscape', 'Subliminal', and 'The Aristocracies'. 'Black Alchemy' and 'Finally Left in the Landscape' complement each other. In the first, the emergence of the elemental Muse from formless water and his taking shape as 'the prince of laughter' 'cancels the cosmos': the world disintegrates, turns fluid, to be recreated by his word which is a dance:

> . . . in his dance
> worlds expire like tides, in his flaming
> dance the nameless cosmos
> must await its naming.[21]

But in 'Finally Left in the Landscape', it is the Muse, not the world, which has disappeared. Here the poet invokes the 'dancer' who is also a 'deity'. He is both present and absent: the poet seeks him, but finds only possible fragments of him. Her task is to gather him together (*vide* Isis and Osiris), to seek him as a whole, and her poetry is part of the attempt to recreate him; though her 'lines can only / plagiarize his dance',[22] since, though absent, he remains the originator of both language and world.

'Subliminal' and 'The Aristocracies' deal with the relationship between Muse and poet, and with their mutual involvement in time. In 'Subliminal', the poet, having achieved a state of mind in which 'there is no time . . . but co-presents, a static recurrence',[23] is able to hold the Muse still for an instant in order to contemplate him: ' . . . in that substratum I hold, / unfold you at random.' He is seen as both dynamic and static: ' . . . you do not move / but are always moving.' But such a state cannot persist: both must re-enter the world of time, in which movement forward is the only possibility:

> I rise to see you planted
> in an earth outside me,
> moving through time
> through the terms of it,
> moving through time again
> along its shattered latitudes.

'The Aristocracies' is placed at the end of *A Breakfast for Barbarians*, and pulls together a number of its motifs. The figure addressed is the Muse, incarnate as lover but also as a 'natural' king; the tension in the poem is created as the poet's vision moves from the Muse as man to the Muse as a supernatural power ('The body of God and the body of you / dance through the same diagonal instant / of my vision . . . '[24]), a movement which both traps the human element in the man, turning him into a 'crowned and captive dancer', and makes him eternal:

> You must dance forever beneath this heavy crown
> in an aristocratic landscape, a bas-relief of living bone.
> And I will altogether cease to speak
> as you do a brilliant arabesque within the bas-relief,
> your body bent like the first letter
> of an unknown, flawless alphabet.

The Muse exists both inside and outside time, and like the letters on a page he is static yet in movement. Bodies as alphabets occur earlier in *A Breakfast for Barbarians*, and, again, word-thing meta-phors date back to *Selah*; the importance of this body-letter lies in the fact that it is the first letter and the alphabet to which it belongs is unknown. The Muse is always *about* to be interpreted: he can never be completely deciphered.

Two attributes of MacEwen's Muse worth noting are his prefer-ence for a certain sort of landscape and the cyclical nature of his appearances. Before *The Shadow Maker*, the Muse's landscape tends to be identified with actual, reachable landscapes: those of the south and east rather than those of the north and west, exotic Palestinian, Arabian or Greek locales as opposed to bleak Canadian ones. The landscape of the Muse is also the landscape of the imag-ination, and there is often a sense of the grim 'altogether Kanadian' reality of metal cities, snow, breakfasts of 'unsacred bacon'[25] and the mechanical clock-time present pulling against a different kind of reality, that of the ornate, hierarchical landscapes and the ancient stone city-scapes of the Middle East, or of the bell-time or blood-time[26] of a more organic past. In *The Shadow Maker*, the poet is clearer about the relationship between self and Muse. Here she takes 'the roads that lead inward . . . the roads that lead down-ward',[27] and although the south-eastern landscapes are still present,[28] the Muse's most authentic landscape is identified more positively with the inner landscape of dream and fantasy. 'Song for a Stranger' has Muse and poet meeting in a mutual dream to 'plot / the birth of a more accurate world' in a setting of 'pavilions' and 'pools'.[29] In the two songs from the 'Fifth Earth', the meeting takes place in a kind of science-fiction otherworld. Towards the end of *The Shadow Maker*, the Muse is seen more as a potential force than as an actual or incarnate being: the 'chosen abyss' of the title poem[30] has replaced the 'chosen landscape'[31] of *A Breakfast for Bar-barians*.

The encounter between Muse and poet is an increasingly dominant theme in MacEwen's poetry. Through their meeting each actual-izes the other, and together they are able to enter the Muse's landscape, he as a returning exile, she more often as an alien dis-coverer or explorer rather than a native. Together, also, they form the divine or cosmic couple which is a recurring image in the poetry. This couple may be either the original (and rather vegeta-ble) Adam-Eve, the 'man and woman naked and green with rain'[32]

of 'Eden, Eden' (who reappear, for instance, in the pastoral, innocent, season-linked couple of 'We Are Sitting on a High Green
Hill'[33]); or it may be an earth-sky couple like that in 'Seeds and
Stars'.[34] It is interesting to juxtapose the early 'couple' poem, 'Tia-
mut',[35] in which the female figure is 'Chaos', 'the earth . . . sans
form'[36] and the male figure is the shaper, the divider, the former of
Cosmos, with the later poem 'The Name of the Place', in a sense
its other half. In the later poem, the god and goddess responsible
for the divided world momentarily glimpse a regained unity: 'All
things are plotting to make us whole / All things conspire to make
us one.'[37] There is a strong pull in MacEwen's poetry towards
completion, synthesis: if the divine couple could ever permanently
join, the universe which has emanated from their division would
be drawn back into them and all things would indeed be truly one,
a sky-earth, flesh-spirit, spirit-flesh landscape which would also be
the homeless 'adam'[38] returned from exile[39] and a dance containing
its own 'extremity'.[40] Time and space would be abolished.

But the union of Muse and poet is limited by the flesh, and even
when it takes place in dream or fantasy it is bound by the strictures
of time and, in poetry, by the length of the poem. Hence the
emphasis on the cyclical nature of the Muse's appearances. Again,
the wheel or cycle is an image used frequently by MacEwen. The
revolving wheel is an organizing symbol in *Julian the Magician*, and
in 'The Ferris Wheel'[41] it is made a 'wheel of lyric' connected with
the writing of poetry as well as with the movement of life around
the 'still middle, the / point of absolute inquiry'. Wheel, circle, and
still centre occur as images again in 'The Cyclist in Aphelion'.[42]
But the moving wheel becomes the shape of time itself in three
poet-Muse poems in *A Breakfast for Barbarians*: 'She',[43] which draws
on Rider Haggard's tale of the reincarnations of a pair of lovers;
'Green with Sleep',[44] in which the 'great unspeakable wheel',
which is both diurnal time and the mythical time of recurrences,
renews the lovers; and 'Cartaphilus',[45] in which the two lovers
encounter each other repeatedly: 'Whoever you love it is me
beneath you / over and over. . . . ' In *The Shadow Maker* the wheel
image is connected not only with the poet's own circular movement,[46] but also with the circularity of time and the recurrences of
the Muse. 'First Song from the Fifth Earth' is even more positive
than is 'Cartaphilus' about the underlying identity of all the incarnations of the Muse: 'I say all worlds, all times, all loves are

one. . . . '[47] 'The Return', in addition to illustrating the theme of recurrence, is one of the clearest 'Muse' poems MacEwen has written, and is worth quoting in its entirety:

> I gave you many names and masks
> And longed for you in a hundred forms
> And I was warned the masks would fall
> And the forms would lose their fame
> And I would be left with an empty name
>
> (For that was the way the world went,
> For that was the way it had to be,
> To grow, and in growing lose you utterly)
>
> But grown, I inherit you, and you
> Renew your first and final form in me,
> And though some masks have fallen
> And many names have vanished back into my pen
> Your face bears the birth-marks I recognize in time,
> You stand before me now, unchanged
>
> (For this is the way it has to be;
> To perceive you is an act of faith
> Though it is you who have inherited me)[48]

Who has created whom? Is the male Muse as Marduk shaping the female chaos of the poet into an order of defining her by contrast (as in 'The Shadow Maker'), or is the poet putting the Muse together out of words, as she sometimes suspects?[49] Is the Muse outside the poet, or is he inside, a fragment of the self? Does he exist outside time, or can he be apprehended only through time and through the senses? These are questions the poems ask; the answers to them are never final, since another turn of the wheel may invalidate all answers. The poet wrestles with the angel, but to win finally, to learn the true name of the angel, would be to stop the wheel, an event which she fears.[50] The last poem in *The Shadow Maker*, 'The Wings', is a series of questions; in it the Muse, despite his many names, languages, and landscapes, is again nameless. He has created, destroyed, and restored innumerable worlds and several phases of the poet herself, and through the poet's invocation is about to begin the process again.

'I want to construct a myth,' Gwendolyn MacEwen has written, and she has indeed constructed one. MacEwen is not a poet interested in turning her life into myth; rather, she is concerned with translating her myth into life, and into the poetry which is a part of it. The informing myth, developed gradually but with increasing clarity in her poetry, is that of the Muse, author and inspirer of language and therefore of the ordered verbal cosmos, the poet's universe. In MacEwen's myth the Muse exists externally beyond sense, but descends periodically as winged man, becomes incarnate for a time as magician, priest-king, lover or all of these, then dies or disappears, only to be replaced by another version of himself. Though the process is cyclical, he never reappears in exactly the same form. Each time he brings with him a different landscape and language, and consequently a different set of inspirations, though beneath these guises he keeps the same attributes. He is a dancer and a singer; his dance and his song are the Word made flesh, and both contain and create order and reality. The poet's function is to dedicate her life to the search for the Muse,[52] and the poetry itself is both a record of the search and an attempt to reproduce or describe those portions of the song-dance which she has been able to witness. The Muse is both 'good' and 'evil', both gentle and violent, both creative and destructive; like language itself, he subsumes all opposites. Since he is infinite, the number of his incarnations is potentially infinite also. Though the final poem in *The Shadow Maker* may look like a last word, each of MacEwen's previous collections has an ending which is really a beginning: the 'growing' of *The Rising Fire*, the 'unknown' alphabet of *A Breakfast for Barbarians*. Here the final word is 'floods'—chaos comes anew, a chaos which invites the creation of a fresh cosmos. There is little doubt that the Muse will rise again from his ashes in yet another form.[53]

[No. 45, 1970]

---

[1] 'The Double Horse', *The Rising Fire* (Hereafter referred to as TRF), p. 18.
[2] Introduction, *Breakfast for Barbarians*. (Hereafter referred to as BB).
[3] A. Schroeder in *The Vancouver Province*, July 25, 1969.
[4] With which Miss MacEwen is familiar: see 'Thou Jacob', *BB*, p. 27.
[5] Where however the Muse, male or female, is more typically a place rather than a person. But see e.g. Jay Macpherson's Angel and some of the male figures in Dorothy Livesay's *Plainsongs*.
[6] 'Selah', *Selah*.
[7] *TRF*, p. 41.
[8] *BB*, p. 19.

⁹ Compare Graves, for whom the Muse is, among other things, a Mother.

¹⁰ Compare e.g. 'The Return', *The Shadow Maker* (hereafter referred to as *SM*), p. 81. Nor is it strange to find the 'boy' as parallel for the poet; this is elsewhere the case in MacEwen's poetry: see e.g. 'Dream Three: The Child', SM, p. 56.

¹¹ Compare the astronauts of 'The Cosmic Brothers' (*TRF*) and 'The Astronauts' (*BB*); compare also the poet as a child, attempting to fly with the help of the magic word SHAZAM, as humorously recounted in 'Fragments of a Childhood' (*Alphabet*, No. 15, December 1968, 10).

¹² *TRF*, pp. 19, 57.

¹³ 'Poem Improvised Around a First Line', *BB*, p. 16.

¹⁴ *SM*, p. 2.

¹⁵ 'Appendectomy', *BB*, p. 42.

¹⁶ Compare also Julian in *Julian the Magician*

¹⁷*BB*, p. 36.

¹⁸ MacEwen's interest in Christ is connected with his role as divine priest-king-physician incarnate; he is not the original or archetypal Muse, but another of the Muse's earthy incarnations.

¹⁹ *TRF*, pp. 41, 43.

²⁰ Though see also 'Thou Jacob', the 'Arcanum' series, and the cosmic dance at the electron level in 'Tesla'.

²¹ *BB*, p. 40.

²² *BB*, p. 52.

²³ *BB*, p. 31.

²⁴ *BB*, p. 53.

²⁵ 'The Last Breakfast', *BB*, p. 35.

²⁶ See for instance 'The Drunken Clock', the last poem in the pamphlet of that name.

²⁷ 'The Wings', *SM*, p. 82.

²⁸ As in, for instance, such poems as 'One Arab Flute' and 'The Fortress of Saladin'.

²⁹ *SM*, p. 53.

³⁰ The Shadow Maker', *SM*, p. 80.

³¹ 'Finally Left in the Landscape', *BB*, p. 52.

³² *The Drunken Clock*.

³³ *SM*, p. 58.

³⁴ *SM*, p. 71.

³⁵ *TRF*, p. 5.

³⁶ Compare other women-as-earth images: e.g. in the verse play *Terror and Erebus*, in 'Poet vs. The Land' (*Selah*), and in 'The Discovery' (*SM*, p. 31.)

³⁷ *SM*, p. 16.

³⁸ 'The Catalogues of Memory', *TRF*, p. 66.

³⁹ Compare also 'The Caravan'; *BB*, p. 51.

⁴⁰ 'The Absolute Dance', *TRF*, p. 43.

⁴¹ *TRF*, p. 49.

⁴² *BB*, p. 7.

⁴³ *BB*, p. 9.

⁴⁴ *BB*, p. 28.

⁴⁵ *BB*, p. 46.

⁴⁶ See 'Dream Three: The Child' *SM* p. 56.

⁴⁷ *SM*, p. 68.

⁴⁸ *SM*, p. 84.

⁴⁹ See e.g. 'The Face', *BB*, p. 9.

⁵⁰ See e.g. 'Fragments of a Childhood', in which the pronouncing of the 'Final Formula' would stop everything.

⁵¹ *BB*, Introduction.

⁵² Compare again Graves, though for MacEwen the Muse is less Nature than creating Word, or Logos.

⁵³ See, for instance, the recent poem 'Credo' (*Quarry*, Vol. 19, No. I, Fall 1969, 5), in which the poet says, 'no one can tell me that / the Dancer in my blood is / dead . . .'

Two Authors in Search of a Character
bp Nichol and Michael Ondaatje

Stephen Scobie

It was surely coincidence enough that two of Canada's finest young poets should both, in one year, produce books on the notably non-Canadian legend of Billy the Kid, without the further coincidence that both should win Governor-General's Awards. Of course, bp Nichol's award was for four books, of which *The True Eventual Story of Billy the Kid* is the shortest, and perhaps the slightest; this point has had to be made in response to the controversy over giving such an award to 'fifteen paragraphs of bad pornography'. If Nichol's book is 'bad pornography', that is only because it is good art; and although it is, at least superficially, a very much slighter book than Michael Ondaatje's *The Collected Works of Billy the Kid*, it is not wholly absurd to examine them in the same light. The reasons why these authors should choose this subject—rather than some roughly equivalent Canadian figure, such as Louis Riel, or even Paul Rose—are to a great degree personal. It is quite possible that bp wrote his book just for fun, because Michael was writing his.[1] More relevantly, Ondaatje's book is a natural outgrowth from his love of Hollywood (and Italian) Westerns: among his favourite films are Sergio Leone's mythic *Once Upon a Time in the West*, and Arthur Penn's contribution to the legend of Billy the Kid, *The Left Handed Gun*. (Ondaatje's book is subtitled 'Left Handed Poems'.) But in addition to these personal reasons, the figure of Billy the Kid is particularly relevant to certain central concerns in the work of these poets, and, especially in Ondaatje's case, their treatment of him becomes a major contribution to the development of their work. The purpose of this article, then, is to examine the two books and their widely different approaches to the legend of Billy the Kid, and to see how these approaches illuminate the characteristic concerns and obsessions of the two poets.

It should perhaps be stressed at the outset that this kind of approach is in a way a distortion of Nichol's book. *The True Eventual Story of Billy the Kid* is primarily a joke, a clever and light-hearted skit, as opposed to the intense seriousness of Ondaatje's approach. Nichol's jokes are, however, on potentially serious subjects. To work out all the thematic implications which his fifteen paragraphs barely suggest may seem like building mountains out of molehills; and, though I believe the foundations are there for such an enterprise, the elaboration should not obscure the fact that the most characteristic virtues of Nichol's book are its wit, its economy, and its refusal to take itself too seriously.

Nichol's title stands in a long tradition of books claiming to tell the 'truth' about Billy: *The True Life of Billy the Kid* by Don Jenardo (1881); *The Authentic Life of Billy, the Kid* by Pat Garrett (ghost-written by Ash Upson) (1882); *Billy the Kid, the True Story of a Western 'Bad Man'* by Emerson Hough (1901); *The Saga of Billy the Kid* by Walter Noble Burns (1926); *The Real Billy the Kid* by Miguel Otero (1936); *The Authentic Death of Hendry Jones* by Charles Neider (1956); *The True Story of Billy the Kid* by William Lee Hamlin (1959) etc. The point about all these 'true' and 'authentic' biographies is that very few of them are. The historical facts about Billy have been buried under a vast accretion of legend.

The legend itself has changed and developed over the years. For the first twenty years or so after Billy's death, writers strove to outdo each other in creating ever more extravagant pictures of his villainy; he became a devil incarnate, a paragon of evil. Then, about the beginning of this century, the trend reversed; Billy became sentimentalised into a poor misunderstood kid, excuses and justifications were found for his killings, he was transformed into a folk-hero of the Robin Hood variety. In 1930 the first of Hollywood's film versions of Billy the Kid starred the former All-American football star, Johnny Mack Brown; thirty years later, Penn's film starred Paul Newman.

The major work in this posthumous 'rehabilitation' of Billy's reputation is Walter Noble Burns' *The Saga of Billy the Kid*, which Ondaatje acknowledges as his major source. Burns' book is of highly questionable historical accuracy, and is filled with writing in the style of the following:

Fate set a stage. Out of nowhere into the drama stepped this unknown boy. Opposite him played Death. It was a drama of Death and the Boy. Death dogged his trail relentlessly. It was for ever clutching at him with skeleton hands. It lay in ambush for him. It edged him to the gallows' stairs. By bullets, conflagration, stratagems, every lethal trick, it sought to compass his destruction. But the boy was not to be trapped. He escaped by apparent miracles; he was saved as if by necromancy. He laughed at Death. Death was a joke. He waved Death a jaunty good-bye and was off to new adventures. But again the inexorable circle closed. Now life seemed sweet. It beckoned to love and happiness. A golden vista opened before him. He set his foot upon the sunlit road. Perhaps for a moment the boy dreamed this drama was destined to a happy ending. But no. Fate prompted from the wings. The moment of climax was at hand. The boy had his hour. It was Death's turn. And so the curtain.

Although Ondaatje's literary abilities are far above Burns', several of the legendary accretions which Burns perpetuated show up again in Ondaatje's book. For instance, Ondaaje follows Burns in setting the shooting of Tom O'Folliard by Pat Garrett on Christmas night. This was one of many emotional touches added by Burns to reflect against Garrett's character (for, as Billy changed from villain to hero, Garrett necessarily swung in the opposite direction) and to develop the theme of Billy's betrayal. In actual fact, the shooting took place on December 18th. Further, Ondaatje's account of Azariah F. Wild's participation in this event is pure invention; both Burns and Garrett himself mention Wild only once in passing, and not in connection with this incident.

This kind of consideration is important, of course, only to the very limited extent to which Ondaatje's book is concerned with giving an accurate historical view of the Kid. Clearly this is not his intention, though some passages (such as the death of Charlie Bowdre) do appear to be quite accurate, and the general tone of many of the descriptions, the wealth of detail and the intensity of the images' realization, must appear very convincing to the unwary reader. Like many writers, Ondaatje alters the facts of Billy's death (as, hilariously, does Nichol); one of the standard tricks of writers sentimentalizing Billy was to pretend that someone else (in one version, his own father!) had been shot by mistake and that Billy, complete with Mexican sweetheart, rode off into the sunset. Penn's film has Billy committing virtual suicide by pretending to go for his gun when he is in fact unarmed; after Garrett's shot, Billy staggers forward holding out his empty hand to the killer.

But Ondaatje's and Nichol's alterations and manipulations of historical fact are not due, as is the case with many previous writers of 'true' and 'authentic' histories, to ignorance or to the desire to 'justify' Billy; rather they fit in with the most recent developments of the legend of Billy the Kid, which move away from the simple pendulum of what Kent Ladd Steckmesser calls 'The Satanic Billy' and 'The Saintly Billy' towards much more complex uses of the total *idea* of Billy the Kid, fact and fiction, as a mythological character. This examination of the mythology of Billy the Kid is apparent in such works as Samuel R. Delany's splendid SF novel *The Einstein Intersection*, in which he appears as 'Bonny William' or 'Kid Death', and Michael McClure's play *The Beard*, in which, somewhere in eternity, he conducts a brilliant, repetitive, and obscene dialogue with Jean Harlow.

This, incidentally, may be one reason why both Ondaatje and Nichol treated a 'non-Canadian' subject: few Canadian outlaw-heroes have been as widely and as thoroughly mythologized as Billy the Kid, though the process is perhaps taking place with Riel. Anyway, 'non-Canadian' is a red herring: mythology may be national in origin, but the significance of a figure as completely metamorphosed as Billy the Kid is totally international.

To return, then, to Nichol's title: 'this' he assures us 'is the true eventual story of billy the kid.' The first page of Nichol's book is a demonstration of the absolute relativity of any definition of 'truth' in a case like this.

> It is not the story as he told it for he did not tell it to me. he told it to others who wrote it down, but not correctly. there is no true eventual story but this one. had he told it to me i would have written a different one. i could not write the true one had he told it to me.

Compare this with Pat Garrett's 'Authentic Life', which opens with the claim that 'I have listened, at camp-fires, on the trail, on the prairies and at many different plazas, to his disconnected relations of events of his early and more recent life.' Garrett continues to list a number of people who knew Billy and whom he has personally interviewed or written to; he can therefore 'safely guarantee that the reader will find in my little book a true and concise relation of the principal interesting events therein, without exaggeration or excusation.' The whole is intended 'to correct the thousand false statements which have appeared in the public newspapers and in yellow-covered, cheap novels.' Burns at one point disingenuously admits:

> The foregoing tales may be regarded, as you please, as the apocryphal cantos of the saga of Billy the Kid. They are not thoroughly authenticated, though possibly they are, in the main, true. Most of them are perhaps too ugly to have been inventions. If you are skeptical, your doubt may be tempered by the fact that they have at least always gone with the legend and have such authority as long-established currency may confer.

Nichol's paragraph may be read as a commentary on these and all similar claims. The 'true' and 'eventual' story cannot be told by any eye-witness; the more 'reliable' their claims are, the less they are to be trusted. If Billy himself had told the story to Nichol, 'i would have written a different one.' The paragraph is a dismissal of any possibility of objective truth in reporting; it insists that any observer changes what he sees as soon as he attempts to express it. Language does not report reality: it creates reality. From this, two conclusions might emerge: first, that even if Billy himself were to tell his own story, he could not tell it truly; and second, that the only 'true' story is the one which rejects any attempt at historicity and aims instead at the 'truth' of a work of art; 'eventually all other stories will appear untrue beside this one.' Of course there is a tongue-in-cheek element here: Nichol is fully enjoying his outrageous claim that his fifteen-paragraph joke is going to replace all other versions of the story, including, presumably, that being written by his friend Michael Ondaatje. But beneath the joke is the deadly seriousness of the artist who can dismiss everything outside his own creation, claiming it alone as an absolute. And these views of language and art are surely at the very centre of Nichol's aesthetic, his proclamation of 'the language revolution'. What matters, then, is not so much the factual record—how many men Billy actually killed or in what year he was actually born—as the legendary image that he lived 21 years and killed 21 men. (For what it's worth, it appears more probable that he lived about 24 and killed about 7.) The 'eventual' story of Billy the Kid is beyond history.

The 'historical' view is even more explicitly rejected in Nichol's second Chapter. The first paragraph reads:

> history says that billy the kid was a coward. the true eventual story is
> that billy the kid is dead or he'd probably shoot history in the balls.
> history always stands back calling people cowards or failures.

It should be remembered that the mythical image of Billy as out-
law-hero is a Romantic idea, as the figure of the Outsider is, from
Goethe's Werner on, the central Romantic image; and that Nichol
himself (as Ondaatje acknowledged in a recent interview) is a
Romantic. This condemnation of history—as an impersonal process
which coldly 'stands back' from its subjects and thus judges rather
than sympathizes—is also a Romantic view. History may even be
seen as the 'official' view of an Establishment which has to reject
all rebels and outlaws as 'cowards or failures'. It is only at a safe
distance in time that a figure like Louis Riel can be 'officially'
viewed as a hero. The task of the rebel, then, is not to stand back,
but to get in there and 'shoot history in the balls'. But Nichol's
Billy, being dead, can't do this. In fact, as becomes clearer,
Nichol's Billy is the ultimate loser.

What, then, is beyond history? It is legend, or myth. This is the
level at which Ondaatje's book operates, but not Nichol's: and this
is one of the fundamental differences between them. For Nichol's,
legend is as much a liar as history:

> legend says that billy the kid was a hero who liked to screw. the true
> eventual story is that were billy the kid alive he'd probably take
> legend out for a drink, match off in the bathroom, then blow him
> full of holes. legend always has a bigger dick than history and history
> has a bigger dick than billy had.

This view sees legend as more potent (literally as well as metaphorically) than history, but equally dangerous. And the danger lies
precisely in its power, its stability, its vividness, its energy—all the
qualities, in fact, of Ondaatje's book. But Nichol's Billy is at the
bottom of the power structure, he always has the shortest dick. His
status is that of the ultimate loser, and he is always ephemeral:

> rumour has it that billy the kid never died. rumour is billy the kid.
> he never gets anywhere, being too short-lived.

This underlies the difference in length between the two books. It
is not simply that Nichol's is a small joke tossed off in fifteen para-

graphs: the shortness, the casualness of the book are intrinsic to its view of Billy. The difference between Ondaatje's 100 pages and Nichol's 5 is the difference between legend and rumour. Ondaatje's book *fixes* a certain view of the Kid into an intense, fully realized image; but for Nichol, the 'eventual' truth is beyond even this, and his image of Billy is insubstantial, flickering, changing, dying. Ondaatje creates a myth; Nichol tells a joke.

Ondaatje's mythmaking is a careful process, built up by various means, and he indicates in several ways the degree to which he is presenting a legendary or poetic image of the Kid. There is, for instance, the concern with photographs. The book opens with an account of photography at the time of Billy's life, indicating the difficulty (which is also Ondaatje's) of taking a sharp image of a moving object. Huffman, the photographer, claims to have succeeded: 'spokes well defined—some blur on top of wheel but sharp in the main.' In the same way, Ondaatje has fixed an image of Nichol's evanescent rumour. The very fine cover, by Roger Silvester, uses an image by the early experimental photographer Muybridge, who made studies of the motions of people and animals through multiple exposures: again, there are possible analogies to Ondaatje's methods. But what the photograph shows is not always accurate: Paulita Maxwell claims that a photograph of Billy doesn't do him justice—surely an ironic phrase. Indeed, it was the reversed image of one famous photograph of Billy which led to the mistaken idea that he was left-handed. All contemporary authorities, including Garrett, remember Billy as right-handed; but his left-handedness fits in better with the legendary image of the outsider. Burns mentions Billy's being left-handed, but doesn't make anything of it; Ondaatje gives to Garrett a brilliantly sinister account of watching Billy subconsciously doing finger-exercises with his left hand. As already remarked, Ondaatje's subtitle, 'Left Handed Poems' derives from Penn's film *The Left Handed Gun*.

The film image is a further way in which Ondaatje transforms the historical Billy into a legendary image. The sub-title casts the image of Penn's film across the whole book, and also recalls Penn's later masterpiece, *Bonnie and Clyde*, in which the outlaw figures are subjected to a mythologizing process within the film itself. (As when, on their first meeting, Clyde asks Bonnie, 'Are you a movie star?') Penn also is fascinated by photography: in both *The Left Handed Gun* and *Bonnie and Clyde* important scenes are devoted to the outlaws getting their pictures taken, and the image recurs in all

Penn's films. Ondaatje uses comedy in much the same way as Penn: grotesque images of violence become almost simultaneously comic and horrible. Compare the poem about Gregory's death and the chicken with the scene in *The Left Handed Gun* where Billy's shotgun blast lifts Ollinger right out of his boots and leaves them standing, empty, on the street; a little girl starts laughing at the empty boots, until her mother's horrified slap stops her. In these scenes the humour works to intensify the image of violence; Ondaatje even succeeds in introducing a note of humour at the absolute climax of his story, as Garret is about to shoot Billy. A similar combination of violence and humour may be found in other of Ondaatje's favourite films, such as the Italian Westerns of Sergio Leone, or John Boorman's *Point Blank*. *Point Blank* also uses a fragmented time-scheme, with the same repeated, slow-motion, dreamlike exposures of violence as in Ondaatje's book. Further, *Point Blank*'s female lead is Angie Dickinson, and who should appear as Billy's sweetheart but 'Miss Angela Dickinson of Tucson' —a name entirely of Ondaatje's own invention, not present in Burns nor in any 'authentic' biography? The historical reality of the Old West and its Hollywood myth representation meet each other in the brief story Ondaatje inserts of Frank James tearing tickets at a Los Angeles movie theatre. Finally, closely akin to the movie image is the comic-book legend which forms Billy's apotheosis. (Ondaatje's own film on bp Nichol, *Sons of Captain Poetry*, celebrates Nichol's fascination with old comics.) This is the final transformation of Billy in pop culture into the upright clean-living hero, as in a delightfully absurd film, which I saw several years ago and which Ondaatje told me he had also seen, *Billy the Kid vs. Dracula.*

But although Ondaatje's image of Billy the Kid may be influenced by the images of comic-books and the movies, these references are merely the context in which Ondaatje sets his own central image of Billy: and, as with Nichol, it is the book's title which points to the nature of that image.

Immediately after the quotation from Huffman, Ondaatje gives a list of 'the killed'. To Billy he ascribes 20 victims (curiously, for the usual legendary number is 21), most of whom, including the 'blacksmith when I was twelve, with a knife', are totally unsubstantiated historically. Then he gives Garrett's victims, ending

. . . and Pat Garret

sliced off my head.
Blood a necklace on me all my life.

The strange, violent beauty of the image, together with the use of the first person, point towards the concept behind the title *The Collected Works of Billy the Kid*. Ondaatje's legendary context for Billy is poetry; the transformation will be carried out mainly through the poetic image; the book will present Billy himself as an artist. Of course, 'works' is ambiguous: it can also refer to Billy's actions, the killings. But Ondaatje is clearly working within the Romantic tradition of the artist as outsider, just as Samuel R. Delany in his novels is obsessed with the identity of the artist and the outlaw. Nichol's Billy 'was not fast with words so he became fast with a gun', but for Ondaatje Billy's status as outlaw is intimately connected with the nature of his perception. He is placed outside society not only by what he does, but by the very way in which he sees the world:

> The others, I know, did not see the wounds appearing in the sky, in the air. Sometimes a normal forehead in front of me leaked brain gasses. Once a nose clogged right before me, a lock of skin formed over the nostrils, and the shocked face had to start breathing through the mouth, but then the mustache bound itself in the lower teeth and he began to gasp loud the hah! hah! going strong —churned onto the floor, collapsed out, seeming in the end to be breathing out of his eye —tiny needle jets of air reaching into the throat. I told no one. If Angela D. had been with me then, not even her; not Sallie, John, Charlie, or Pat. In the end the only thing that never changed, never became deformed, were animals.

Of course, Billy's poetic personality is not entirely distinct from Michael Ondaatje's. The concern with animals—apparent throughout the book—is familiar to any reader of Ondaatje's poetry. What results from the title '*The Collected Works of Billy the Kid* by Michael Ondaatje' is in fact a composite figure: Billy the Kid, outlaw as artist, and Michael Ondaatje, artist as outlaw, meeting in one persona, which is part history, part legend, part aesthetic image, part creator of images. It is in terms of this complex persona that the book approaches its material.

That material may be seen as a narrative with two main strands: the conflict between Billy and Pat Garrett, culminating in the manhunt and the deaths of Tom O'Folliard, Charlie Bowdre, and

Billy himself; and the opposite of conflict, the scenes of peace and companionship, centering on Miss Angela D. and the Chisum ranch. Underlying these two narrative strands is the central theme of violence, as it erupts in both outlaw and artist.

But fully as important as what *is* in the book is what is missed out. Ondaatje has exercised great selectivity in his presentation of Billy, and what he deliberately omits or suppresses from his sources is of great interest. One thing that should be noted about the narrative structure outlined above is that it ignores, almost completely, what is for all the biographers, however 'true' or 'authentic', the most important event of Billy's life: the Lincoln County War. (Burns devotes over half of his book to it.) Ondaatje's one reference to it is in connection with the question of motivation:

> A motive? some reasoning we can give to explain all this violence. Was there a source for all this? yup—

There follows Burns' account of Tunstall's murder, which he says Billy witnessed 'from a distant hillside' having luckily been off 'hunting wild turkeys'. (In fact, it appears more probable that Billy was with Tunstall, and ran away.) Most apologists for Billy make this the central point of their exposition: Billy's career begins as an understandable search for vengeance on the murderers of his idealistic and honest friend. 'Others fought for hire,' Burns claims; 'Billy the Kid's inspiration was the loyalty of friendship.' (Again, in fact it is certain that Tunstall was neither idealistic nor honest, and highly doubtful that he was especially friendly with Billy.) But the casual tone of Ondaatje's 'yup' suggests that he does not take this idea too seriously, and there is no further mention of this stage of Billy's career. It is possible that this passage is introduced only to make fun of simplistic psychological 'explanations' of the sources of Billy's violence. Ondaatje has more serious things to say on that subject.

Similarly, Nichol introduces an 'explanation' of Billy's violence as a joke, but a joke with more serious implications. The central conceit of Nichol's book is the reversal of 'Kid' to 'Dick'. Indeed, reversal of the normal image is Nichol's central tactic. So Nichol presents the extended joke that all Billy's activities were due to his having a small penis. At one level, this a light-hearted version of the too easily oversimplified theory that guns are used as compensation by males with fears of sexual inadequacy. Nichol recognizes that this can be used too simplistically, and also makes fun of psychological determinist attitudes by revealing that 'the sherrif had a short dick too, which was why he was sherrif & not out robbing banks. these things affect people differently.' But behind these jokes is a serious awareness, present also in Ondaatje's book, of the tremendous force of the connection between violence and sexuality, and the centrality of these two aspects in contemporary American life. Make love not war—if you can. And it is surely no accident that Nichol twice points out that Billy's short dick is 'short for richard'. Richard, that is, as in Nixon. The Lincoln County War has been represented as a clash between the 'good guys', Tunstall and McSween, idealistic supporters of the small farmers, and the 'bad guys', the oppressive monopoly of Murphy, Dolan, and Riley; in fact, it appears to have been a fairly cynical gang war for economic control of the territory, in which neither side shows to advantage. Most of the victims in the 'war' were shot in the back or from ambush. Parallels to the Vietnam war may be drawn at each reader's personal political discretion; but it does seem clear that Nichol is fully conscious of political applications, in his use of 'richard', and again, later, in his cynical comment on one of Nixon's favourite slogans:

> billy ran around shooting his mouth off, & the dicks off everybody else, & the sherrif stood on the sidelines cheering. this is how law & order came to the old west.

Nichol's jokes on Billy's motivation also touch lightly on a subject which is absolutely central to his own poetry: the power of language, the almost magical efficacy of words.

> could they have called him instead billy the man or bloody bonney? would he have bothered having a faster gun? who can tell.

Again, the joke can be taken absolutely seriously. Names make you what you are; you become what you are called. The historical Billy went through several changes of name. He started life as William H. Bonney; when his father died, his mother reverted to her maiden name and he became Henry McCarty; she remarried, he became Henry Antrim; when he first began to run foul of the law he acquired the name The Kid; by his own choice he reverted to William H. Bonney; but to history and legend he is only Billy the Kid. The naming is all-important: it fixes the image, it creates the personality. In Nichol's study of Billy's motivation, that non-committal 'who can tell' is the most loaded phrase of all.

Having rejected any 'historical' explanation in terms of the Lincoln County War, and omitting also such legendary accretions as Billy's youthful murder of a loafer who had insulted his mother, Ondaatje presents Billy's violence in terms of the poetic image of energy: the energy necessary to both outlaw and artist. The central text for this is the poem on page 41:

> I have seen pictures of great stars,
> drawings which show them straining to the centre
> that would explode their white
> if temperature and the speed they moved at
> shifted one degree.
>
> Or in the East have seen
> the dark grey yards where trains are fitted
> and the clean speed of machines
> that make machines, their
> red golden pouring which when cooled
> mists out to rust or grey.
>
> The beautiful machines pivoting on themselves
> sealing and fusing to others
> and men throwing levers like coins at them.
> And there is the same stress as with stars,
> the one altered move that will make them maniac.

Energy tightly controlled by form is one definition of a work of art; and in art the 'one altered move' will result in the dissipation of energy, a bad poem. Or, when the energy of the work of art is directly expressive of violence, and when it is transmitted in a context where such artistic controls as irony are severely compromised, then the 'one altered move' can be physically destructive beyond the aesthetic bounds, as in the case of the murder by the Hell's Angels during the Rolling Stones concert at Altamont. Ondaatje's book depicts the shattering of the precarious control over the energy of Billy's violence, and the violence he evokes in those around him; the events then drive inexorably towards his death. There is a close relationship here to the previously mentioned two strands of narrative: the scenes of control are (mainly, but not exclusively) associated with the Chisums and Angela D.; the 'one altered move' is (mainly, but not exclusively) Pat Garrett. And, despite Billy's statement that 'the only thing that never changed, never became deformed, were animals', both the harmony and the maniac destruction are most clearly seen in the animal references.

The first of Ondaatje's images of harmony, of what might be called the 'pastoral interludes' in the book, comes in the description of Billy's weeklong stay in a deserted barn. Here, attracted by 'the colour and the light', he stays to get rid of a fever. 'It became a calm week' in which Billy and the animals are able to live together in harmony.

> There were animals who did not move out and accepted me as a larger breed. I ate the old grain with them, drank from a constant puddle about twenty yards away, ate his disease and kept it in him. When I walked I avoided the cobwebs squat the best way when shitting, used leaves for wiping, never ate flesh or touched another animal's flesh, never entered his boundary. We were all aware and allowed each other. The fly who sat on my arm, after his inquiry, just went away, ate his disease and kept it in him. When I walked I avoided the cobwebs, who had places to grow to, who had stories to finish. The flies caught in those acrobat nets were the only murder I saw.

But if this image of harmony is presented in terms of animals, it is also in terms of animals that the 'one altered move' breaks in and destroys this scene: rats eat grain fermented by rain and become maniac, killing a chipmunk, eating each other, until Billy, with 'the noise breaking out the seal of silence in my ears', exhausts his bullet supply in shooting them. At the end 'no other animal of any kind remained in that room', except the human with his gun. This brief scene is a paradigm for what is to come later, at the Chisum ranch.

If a writer's intentions can be most clearly seen in the places where he most drastically alters his source material, then Ondaatje's metamorphosis of the Chisums must be the very centre of his work. The impression that Ondaatje's book gives is that the Chisum ranch is a fairly small place, out in the desert miles from anywhere, inhabited only by Sallie and John, who is seen as a gentle, peace-loving man with little interest or influence in the world beyond his ranch. In fact, John Chisum was one of the largest and most influential landowners and cattlemen in the territory; and Burns describes the ranch thus:

> Chisum abandoned Bosque Grande as his headquarters in 1873, and moving down the Pecos forty miles, established South Spring Ranch, which remained his home to the end of his life. Where the South Spring River gushes from the earth in a never-failing giant spring of crystal water, he built a home fit for a cattle-king and made it one of the show places of the Southwest. Cottonwood trees brought from Las Vegas by mule pack-train he planted about his dwelling and in two winding rows that formed a noble avenue a quarter of a mile long leading from road to residence. He sowed eight hundred acres to alfalfa. He brought fruit trees from Arkansas and set out a vast acreage in orchards of apple, pear, peach, and plum. He imported roses from Texas to make a hedge about the house, and scarlet tanagers and bob-white quail from Tennessee—birds unknown to New Mexico—and set them at liberty in the oasis of beauty he had created.
>
> Here, with royal hand, Chisum dispensed frontier hospitality. His great, rambling, one-storey adobe house, with verandas at front and rear, stood on the highway between Texas and New Mexico, and the stranger was as free as the invited guest to bed and board for as long as he wanted to stay, and no money or questions asked. Every day at breakfast, dinner, and supper, the table in the dining hall was set for twenty-six guests, twelve on each side and one at each end, and hardly a meal was served in ten years at which every chair was not occupied.

Ondaatje has not merely 'edited, rephrased, and slightly reworked the originals'; he has made a complete, vivid, and detailed creation in absolute opposition to his original.

Ondaatje's suppression of the Lincoln County War also involves his omitting the facts that Chisum was the chief (though silent) force behind the Tunstall-McSween faction, and that after the war there was considerable conflict between Chisum and Billy, who claimed that Chisum owed him money for his part in the fighting. Burns quotes Sallie Chisum as attempting to discount this conflict, but there are persistent stories of Billy rustling Chisum's cattle, and, in some more imaginative versions, killing Chisum's cowboys. In a letter to Governor Lew Wallace, December 12th, 1880, Billy blamed accusations against him on 'the impression put out by Chisum and his tools'. Steckmesser speculates that Joe Grant, one of Billy's victims, 'may well have been hired by Chisum or another cattleman to remove the troublesome Kid'. Even Burns, who downplays the whole conflict, admits that Chisum was responsible, along with other local cattle barons, for hiring Pat Garrett to get rid of Billy, and that their motives for this were primarily commercial. All this is totally changed or omitted in Ondaatje's version. It may also be noted that Garrett's own account never mentions his meeting Billy at the Chisum ranch, either for the first or any other time. (Garrett is, of course, understandably reticent about his early friendship with Billy.)

The image presented in Ondaatje's book is, then, largely his own invention; and the pains he has taken to alter his source material indicate the importance he attaches to it. The Chisum ranch is the 'still centre' of Billy's world. It is a place of peace, of affection, of comradeship. None of the apologists for Billy as a poor misunderstood child driven against his will to violence have ever provided him with such a beautiful and fully realized context for his 'true nature': but Ondaatje succeeds in doing this without in the least sentimentalizing Billy.

The first presentation occurs in Billy's mind as he and Angela D. ride towards the house 'Forty miles ahead of us'. As they approach, Billy remembers in a wealth of loving details the small, everyday details of the life of John and Sallie Chisum: the remains of breakfast, their wordless 'dialogue of noise', the shutters which made the house 'silent and dark blue with sunless quiet', and Sallie herself, in her bare feet,

> like a ghost across the room moving in white dresses, her hair knotted as always at the neck and continuing down until it splayed and withered like eternal smoke half way between the shoulder blades and the base of cobble spine.
>
> Yes. In white long dresses in the dark house, the large bones somehow taking on the quietness of the house. Yes I remember.

These ethereal images of peace and beauty are reinforced by the solid human friendship, the recollections of long evenings on the porch when 'we have talked slowly through nights expecting the long silences and we have taken our time thinking the replies.' Even throwing up after a long night's drinking becomes a kind of act of community; and it is significant that Garrett is specifically excluded from it, just as he falls asleep during the conversation on the porch. Again, this is a detail specifically altered from Burns' book, where Sallie Chisum describes Garrett as often being 'the life of the company that used to sit on the porch of an evening'.

Angela D. fits into this world: Billy brings her to it. (Garrett arrives on his own, by accident, and is 'deaf' when he arrives.) The most graphic of the sexual scenes between Billy and Angela D. takes place at the Chisum ranch, and Billy wakes there to the vision of 'Beautiful ladies in white rooms in the morning'.

But, as in the Pastoral tradition, *et in Arcadia ego*, elements of disruption are present even in this perfectly achieved harmony, balance, control of energy. Indeed, the indications of the 'one altered move' are introduced, typically, at the very centre of the harmony, Sallie Chisum's love of animals. The first description of the Chisum ranch ends with an account of Sallie's strange collection of pet animals: 'the tame, the half born, the wild, the wounded'. John Chisum takes Billy out to the cages in darkness: 'You could peer into a cage and see nothing till a rattle of claws hit the grid an inch from your face and their churning feathers seemed to hiss.' There is the bizarre image of the one-eyed owls, the intense realization of the animals' presence and awareness, which 'continued like that all night while we slept'. Despite the love which Sallie obviously bears for these animals, the atmosphere of the scene is sinister, filled with impending violence. Billy feels himself to be standing on 'the edge of the dark' and concludes 'The night, the dark air, made it all mad.' The madness and violence break out immediately in a poem in which mad rats fight in Billy's head, horses foam white with madness, and a deadly barracuda floats in his brain.

Another extended episode at the Chisum ranch is John's horrifying story of the man who systematically breeds a group of dogs into madness until they turn on him and rip him to pieces. The story is shatteringly out of place in the calm and beautiful atmosphere of the ranch; Sallie comments, to her dog, 'Aint that a nasty story Henry, aint it? Aint it nasty.' Henry, like Ondaatje's own dog, is a bassett; Henry is also what the H. stands for in William H. Bonney.

Garrett's presence at the Chisums' is another signal of disruption, and it is Garrett who narrates the story of Billy killing Sallie's snake-bitten cat. The imagery is closely tied together: it is this event which, according to Garrett, terrifies Angela D.; the account of Angela's shot arm immediately precedes the narrative of the night of slow talking and drinking from which Garrett is so pointedly excluded; and the beauty of the morning after is brought to an end when Billy sees that 'On the nail above the bed the black holster and gun is coiled like a snake'. Another careful juxtaposition is that between Billy's shooting the cat and the first flashforward to the final shooting; and this flashforward begins:

> Down the street was a dog. Some mut spaniel, black and white. One dog, Garrett and two friends, stud looking, came down the street to the house, to me.

As a final touch to this continual association of animals and violence, Ondaatje tells us, right at the end of the book, just before the climactic description of Billy's death, that Garrett also liked animals: but not live ones, like Sallie Chisum. Pat Garrett stuffed dead birds.

But Garrett is an essential part of Billy's legend. Many reasons can be given for the longevity of that legend—Billy's youth; the attractiveness, admitted even by his enemies, of his personality; the possibility of seeing him as fighting on the 'right' side of the Lincoln County War; the fact that most of his victims in one sense or another deserved what they got; the exotic Mexican background—but one of the strongest motifs is that of Betrayal. Kent Ladd Steckmesser says of this point:

> The theme of 'betrayal' has been carefully pointed up by Bonney's biographers and has gripped the folk imagination. Time and again we are told that the Kid would have settled down and become a law-abiding citizen if only the man hunters had given him half a chance. But Governor Wallace 'double-crossed' the Kid by reneging on a promise of an amnesty. Garrett was a Judas who tracked down his friend for a few silver dollars. The story unfolds like a classical Greek drama, with the tragic hero moving inexorably toward death by treachery.

Just as Robin Hood had his Sheriff of Nottingham and Jesse James had Robert Ford, Billy the Kid had Pat Garrett. As has already been remarked, their fates are linked in legend as in life. So long as Billy was regarded as an extravagantly evil villain, Garrett was a hero, saviour of law and order, etc.; but as the view of Billy changes, Garrett becomes the betrayer, the manhunter, the assassin. (In 1908, Garrett was himself assassinated, in circumstances which have never been fully explained.) This is, essentially, the approach which Ondaatje takes; but Nichol, characteristically, takes the whole idea and stands it on its head.

Nichol's version of Pat Garrett is 'the sherrif' (sic), and

> the true eventual story is billy & the sherrif were friends. if they had been more aware they would have been lovers. they were not more aware.

Nichol's sherrif does not betray Billy: Billy is betrayed by history, by legend, by god, and ultimately by himself, but not by the sherrif. Indeed, the sherrif occupies in Nichol's book much the place that Angela D. occupies in Ondaatje's. Nichol takes the idea of the symbiosis which binds together hero and villain, hunter and hunted, assassin and victim, and turns it into an identity of interests directed against the outside world. The sherrif shares Billy's predicament, but, as already noted, 'these things affect people differently'. The sherrif simply 'stood on the sidelines cheering'. This can of course be read as a cynical comment on the collusion between lawmen and criminals; but it seems more important as Nichol's only expression of community, of a harmonious relationship between two people. The two outsiders, losers of society, join together; their friendship is beautiful, the fact that they 'were not more aware' is tragic, the farewell they take of each other is touching in its simplicity. Again, Nichol's surface tone is one of light-hearted joking, but the words he puts down can be taken perfectly seriously. And the sherrif does not destroy Billy: Billy in the end destroys himself, as his own violence catches up with him in a furiously self-destructive joke:

> the true eventual story is that billy the kid shot it out with himself. there was no-one faster. he snuck up on himself & shot himself from behind the grocery store.

Nichol's Billy is in fact a much more violent character than

Ondaatje's: but he is not betrayed. Whatever God, history, or legend say, rumour and the sherrif remain true to him. They deny the impositions of history and legend, presenting instead, clearly and strongly, a reversed image. The subtitle 'Left Handed Poems' could well be applied more accurately to Nichol's book than to Ondaatje's. In the reversed photo image, William H. Bonney becomes The Left Handed Gun; and Pat Garrett, strangely but not without beauty, becomes a sherrif not quite aware enough to be a lover.

Ondaatje's view of Garrett is more conventional; and here it should be noted that Ondaatje's highly selective presentation of Billy's history involves a very strong bias against Garrett. As already noted, Ondaatje omits any account of Billy's early activities, such as his murders in the Lincoln County War, and presents him mainly in two contexts: the peace and beauty of the Chisum ranch, and the final chase and manhunt. In other words, Billy is seen almost entirely as victim. There are three extended accounts of killings in the book—those of Tom O'Folliard, Charlie Bowdre, and Billy himself—and in every case the killer is Garrett. We never get any similar account of a killing by Billy. Even in the strange and bizarre account of the killing of Gregory (whoever he is supposed to be), Ondaatje is careful to have Billy say that:

> I'd shot him well and careful
> made it explode under his heart
> so it wouldn't last long

In other words, Billy is a humane murderer; the gruesome images which follow can be blamed on the chicken, not Billy. There is a detailed narrative of the chase and of the tortures Billy suffers in captivity, but only the sketchiest idea is given of Billy's escape from jail, and his murder of Bell and Ollinger. Ondaatje concentrates instead on the depiction of Ollinger as a sadistic villain: a device, largely invented by Burns, which has no historical basis whatever. In short, Ondaatje stacks his deck. If the reader reacts in horror or disgust from the violence in the book, he is reacting mainly *against* Garrett. Although Ondaatje's Billy is far from a blameless character, there is a definite implication that the violence exists around him rather than in him; Nichol's farcical conclusion gives a far greater sense of a character destroyed from within by his own violence. The interconnectedness of Garrett and Billy works inexorably: if Nichol makes Garrett a friend, then the violence has to shift back to Billy, while the more Ondaatje presents Pat Garrett as the assassin, the man-hunter, the more he whitewashes his Billy.

Garrett is presented as 'that rare thing—a sane assassin'. Ondaatje's account of his early life gives a plausible background of psychological motivation for Garrett's suppression of emotion; but it stresses that even before Juanita's death Garrett was capable of efforts of will such as his learning French and learning to drink. Garrett 'comes to chaos neutral': but his neutrality cuts him off from any contact with humanity, so that his violence becomes cold and inhuman. Twice we have the picture of his victims (Tom O'Folliard and Charlie Bowdre) staggering towards him in death; in each case he stands unmoved, waiting for them to die. Even his reaction to Billy's death is reported in a totally unemotional manner. Garrett, more than any other single factor in the book, *is* that 'one altered move' that makes everything around him 'maniac'. The word itself is echoed in the description of Billy's arm breaking through the window after the shooting:

> Guitterrez goes to hold the arm but it is manic, breaks her second finger. His veins that controlled triggers—now tearing all they touch.

Nichol's Billy destroys himself; but Ondaatje's is destroyed by something outside himself, something that itself remains calm and indestructible: and therefore, all the more terrifying. Garrett's character thus presents an interesting paradox: he is himself an embodiment of order, control; yet in contact with Billy he becomes the 'altered move' which produces chaos.

Or is it chaos? It is violence, certainly, and death; but there is a kind of direction to it. Within the terms of the legend, it is an inexorable progress, and what it ends in is not Billy's death but Billy's apotheosis into legend: the creation, that is, of an aesthetic image. If Billy is one image of the artist, then surely Pat Garrett, even if his material is dead bodies, like his birds, is another? *The Collected Works of Billy the Kid* is, after all, a tightly controlled book: Ondaatje is a careful artist, and the images of violence are never allowed to get out of hand in the book. The book is not chaos, the book is not manic. It is an attempt to comprehend the legend of Billy the Kid, to see him as one of the exemplary figures of modern consciousness, outlaw as artist, artist as outlaw. He is involved with violence, but the violence results from the conflict between himself and his society, it is a product of his symbiotic relationship with Pat Garrett. Ondaatje's final image of Billy sees him waking up after a bad night: the smell of smoke, the stain of violence, is still with him—but only in his shirt, which can be changed. We turn the page and find a photograph of a small boy smiling in a cowboy outfit: Billy's costume of violence turned into an image, a toy. That small boy is Michael Ondaatje, poet.

Ondaatje's Billy does not have the substantiality of history; his history is changed and fashioned into something else: legend, the aesthetic image in all its depth and detail, its vividness and force. Nichol's Billy is, in its way, a much more radical image of the outsider's consciousness, for it rejects any notion of substance whatever. His Billy is rumour, and essentially short-lived, like the smoke which Ondaatje's Billy sees on his ceiling, ready to blow away whenever a window is opened. His energy dissipates itself, sneaks up behind and shoots itself. Yet Nichol's is also a carefully crafted and constructed book. The surface seems superficial and whimsical, yet the words will always yield a serious meaning if you give them a chance. Perhaps rumour is that way too. The truth lies only in what the words can say, and what they say is never fixed. It is a process, an event, a becoming; the truth is always eventual.

Such as, for example, the 'truth' that on July 14th, 1881, in Pete Maxwell's dark bedroom, Pat Garrett shot Billy the Kid just above the heart, and the next day, 'neatly and properly dressed' (according to Garrett), he was buried in the military cemetery at Old Fort Sumner, in the state of New Mexico.

[No. 54, 1972]

---

[1] In a letter to the author, bp Nichol states, 'my version of Billy predates michaels I told michael in 68 when he let slip at a party at his house that he was working on a billy the kid poem that id written it & he refused to read it coz he didn't want to be influenced by it in 69 we swapped manuscripts.' Incidentally, Nichol also notes that the total amount he and Ondaatje received as Governor-General's Awards—$5000—is the same as the original reward offered for Billy the Kid.

NOTE:
The primary texts are:
Nichol, bp. *The True Eventual Story of Billy the Kid*. Toronto, Weed / Flower Press, 1970.
Ondaatje, Michael. *The Collected Works of Billy the Kid*. Toronto, Anansi, 1970.

For a great deal of my information about Billy the Kid in both history and legend, I am deeply indebted to:

Steckmesser, Kent Ladd. *The Western Hero in History and Legend.* University of Oklahoma Press, 1965.

I have also consulted the book which Ondaatje acknowledges as his main source:
Burns, Walter Noble. *The Saga of Billy the Kid.* New York, Doubleday & Company, 1926.

Finally, I have made reference to:
Garrett, Pat F. *The Authentic Life of Billy the Kid.* With an Introduction by J. C. Dykes. University of Oklahoma Press, 1954.